MY LIFE
ON THE SWINGSET

ADVENTURES IN SWINGING & POLYAMORY

COOPER S. BECKETT

HUMP &
CIRCUM
STANCE

Published Internationally by Hump and Circumstance

ISBN: 978-1-946876-06-5

3 5 7 9 10 8 6 4 2 1

Third Edition

"A straight line may be the shortest distance between two points, but it is by no means the most interesting."

- The Doctor

CONTENTS

PART III
SPACKLING OVER ENTROPY

FOREWORD

BY GINGER BENTHAM

As Prof and I return from paradise and hosting the Swingsetters for another week of bliss, it seems crazy that this whole adventure blossomed from a connection in the vacuum that was advice for the ethically non-monogamous. Our research led us to a fun, swank website that still had that new car smell: LifeOnTheSwingset.com.

I still remember clicking and reading Coop's Manifesto in its first iteration. Who was this guy? Outspoken, well-spoken, and using impeccable grammar? Color me impressed. But then I kept reading. I was compelled by the way that this human, yet unknown to me, was pouring himself into these electronic words. He was forthright, vulnerable, and insightful with an intelligent sense of humor.

After reading for a few more minutes, I did something for the first time in my life: I wrote a fangirl letter, email-style.

Soon after, I had a reply from Cooper Beckett himself. He said, "Thanks for the very kind words. I've seen your site before, and actually spent some longer time there today. You guys do good work as well. We the non-monogamous need to stick together, maybe even form a web ring... hmmm..." That was in 2010.

As we began to get acquainted, Coop eventually asked if I had listened to the podcast. Nope. Couldn't say that I had. He invited me to have a listen, because in the midst of our get-to-know-you exchange this intrepid man invited me to climb on up onto *The Swingset*. I had no idea how grateful I would become that there was a swing available just for me.

Having no idea what was in store, I did know one thing: *The Swingset* was a much-needed resource for all of us ethical non-monogamers seeking knowledge and community. Cooper and Dylan created an honest, approachable, and sexy source for exploring the light and the heavy issues we all contend with living the *Swingset* life.

As I continued to explore the site and the podcast, getting to know Coop was a flirty foray into sapiosexual deli-ciousness that lead me to a podcast threesome I'll always remember. Coop and Dylan were gentle, gracious, and made me come back for more.

And that I did. Week after week, Prof and I connected over our learning and I brought it to the podcast. All the while, *The Swingset* gained momentum while Cooper continued to be Cooper: sincere, sometimes strident, always willing to give us all the gift of his raw vulnerability in learning.

Joining *The Swingset*, I felt I had stumbled upon kindred spirits. Later I would learn that is an understatement, as since then the Crew have become fellow revolutionaries in reinventing relationships. And without question, Cooper has become my mind-melded partner beyond charac-teri-zation. He is simply My Cooper.

Since then *The Swingset* community has become a force in the sex-positive world: Offering new ways to think about sex, proselytizing pegging, cultivating bisexual acceptance, taking on barriers between the ethically non-monogamous communities, encouraging risk aware sex, and even bringing Swingsetters together in-person to know that there is indeed a real welcoming hand to guide you into this life we call the Swingset. And that warm hand is that of Cooper Beckett.

INTRODUCTION

In the last six years of my life, I've gone from mono-gamous to swinger to polyamorous to a rider on the nebulous frontier that is non-specific non-monogamy. I've been married and divorced, in multiple open relationships, began dating and broken up. I've had one night stands, long term sexual playmates, orgies, gang bangs, risk aware sex, explored my sexuality edges as a Dom and a sub, played with men and women (both cisgender and transgender), and redefined sexuality from merely referring to PIV and PIA (Penis in Vagina and Penis in Anus) to a host of new definitions with a spectrum of options ranging from exceptional kissing right down to anal fisting.

"Well," as Emperor Joseph II would say, "there it is."

The above explanabrag aside, though it might seem as if I had no time for anything else, I've also run *Life on the Swingset*—a website and podcast by and for the sexually open (as we used to say at the beginning). And this all started with a crackpot and egotistical idea that I ought to write *Swinging For Dummies*.

After all, I'd been in the lifestyle for a grand total of eleven months at that point, and clearly had learned everything there is to know about a strange, unique, and complex alternative to monogamy. I knew one thing for sure, though: there wasn't enough of a presence for swingers online beyond the swinger dating sites, and most of those sites are, frankly, little more than excuses to use cocks and tits as profile pictures. The rest were forums and sites that acted aloof and better than me. Yes, I may have had an inferiority complex toward some websites back in 2009.

Swinging is such a tremendously foreign idea to someone unfamiliar with it. I consumed every bit of material I could get my physical and digital hands on. But even with as much information as I could collect, the only website that offered anything like the comfort level of "it's okay" I so desperately wanted, was the (unfortunately now defunct) *Sex Is Fun* podcast. Their funny and relaxed discussions of all things sexual, freely and without judgment, made me realize that there were people in the world who wanted to explore open sexually, whatever that meant…people unafraid to feel good about what their amazing bodies could do, and even better about what they could do when multiplied by more than two.

So, I thought I should do the one thing that made sense: take my total lack of objective experience and fake it. With co-host Dylan Thomas, *Swinging For Dummies* became a podcast. A website was birthed from that to be the open-handed welcome that this fabulously diverse and fascinating lifestyle deserved. Men have been drawn and quartered for less hubris than that. We wanted to provide a safe haven in a sea of repressed attitudes, to show others that it's okay, comfort those who are nervous, applaud those who are bold, thank those who provide support, and strike forward into a future where open sexuality may become more and more acceptable.

On February 7, 2010, *Life on the Swingset*'s first post went live, a review of Tristan Taormino's fabulous non-monogamy bible *Opening Up*. If you haven't read it, stop reading this book right now and go pick it up. We'll be here when you get back. Since that first post I have written some 120,000 words of content in blogs, essays, reviews, advice columns, and (my specialty) ill-advised ranting. That's a number that floored me when I first compiled all the text three months ago. It seemed such a staggering sum to be birthed by my weird habit of saying, "Huh, that thing I want doesn't exist. Well, guess I'll make it."

So, what's all *this* then?

My Life on the Swingset represents my first five years of writing about non-monogamy. In the following pages, you'll find much of what I've written on the site, some new content, some adjusted content (both out of respect to my ex-wife Marilyn and because I thought of something funnier, or truer, or better, or corrected the typos), and—

I'm sure—hundreds and hundreds of parenthetical asides.

You may ask, "Why should I buy this book when I can read the content for free at LifeOnTheSwingset.com? Are you trying to scam me? To make me out to be the fool?"

That's an excellent question, belligerent guy who often interrupts my writing. Did I mention there's new stuff?

You should buy this book because if you find what's carefully hidden within the pages, through painstaking code-breaking techniques, coordinating with the titles and page numbers, collating the first letters of each paragraph, and assembling these things into a grid, you can find a word search that will tell you the exact location of Curly's gold. And not even Billy Crystal could find that. Or was the gold a metaphor? I don't know if I saw that movie twice.

You should read this book because it represents my journey. From starry-eyed newbie swinger, through my dealing with jealousy and conflict, through the triumphs of orgies and play parties, through the devastation of breaking up, through exploring polyamory, through divorce, through major life changes, through depression, through success and failure, through the rise and fall of new relationships... through it *all*. It was a very different Cooper Beckett who first pressed "publish" on Wordpress on that fateful day in February than the one who sits before the keyboard at this moment.

I've done my best not to "adjust" my opinions to reflect my evolution throughout my time on *The Swingset*. I have adjusted things which plainly didn't make sense, and others that betray my habit of simply producing a first draft stream-of-consciousness ramble and then hitting the publish button.

I can promise you honesty, and genuine appreciation for this lifestyle called swing, poly, or non-mono. You'll see an awful lot of my growth in here, and how I developed over time. My failures, my stresses, my successes, my orgasms (seriously, the prostate orgasm story, I'm still impressed), my major mistakes—I made them so you don't have to.

I have created a mix tape of my life for you here. As with any mix tape, sometimes it's fun to listen straight through, sometimes it's fun to fast forward and rewind. While the following essays were written in chronological order (i.e. I wrote them as I moved forward along the stream of time) they are not meant to be read in any specific order.

So as Ginger always says, climb on up, there's always a swing available. Welcome to *My Life on the Swingset*.

- Cooper Beckett
December 13, 2014

ON THE NOTION OF LEXICONS

So, yeah…lexicons, glossaries, these are big things, right?

I mean, if you have no idea about the lifestyle and its lingo (like the use of the phrase "the lifestyle" for example), you might be quite lost on the following pages. Thus I'm compelled to do a legit(ish) glossary and give you all that stuff right here, right up front.

Okay, so, **The Lifestyle** can refer to a number of things. Not so helpful, that. For our purposes in this book, The Lifestyle refers to the Swinging lifestyle. So every time you see The Lifestyle just add the word Swinging right into it. Unless there's some other modifier there already, of course.

Swinging is the practice of having sex with people who are not your partner, with the partner's full knowledge. This and **Polyamory** (forming loving relationships with multiple partners, with everybody's full knowledge) make up the two most common shades of **Ethical Non-Monogamy.** Non-monogamy is the opposite of **Monogamy,** which is having one partner satisfy all your needs emotionally and physically. A lot of people claim they're doing that monogamy thing when they're really cheating behind their partners' backs and engaging in decidedly **Unethical Non-Monogamy.** The ethical part is our tip, our purview. It's the part that includes the repeated "with the partner's full knowledge" phrase above. Everybody being aware of everything going on (except for details they don't want to know, this isn't **Forced Ethical Non-Monogamy** after all [not really a thing]) is the most important part.

    Open Relationship is a sort of umbrella term that can fit all different types of non-monogamy under it, but it generally refers to the ethical kind. Sometimes people use open relationship as a way to describe a **DADT Relationship** (I've never heard it referred to specifically like that, but this is a lexicon, so there's some lex for you) which is a "don't ask, don't tell" situation; meaning you can do whatever you want to do with whomever you'd like, but I don't want to hear about it. So, don't assume what people mean when they say open relationship.

    Really, don't assume what anyone means when they say anything. Because you know what happens when you assume, don't you?

    What's **Vanilla** besides a flavor? Well, it's a contextually derogatory term used by many facets of sexually open people to describe those with no kinks, or sometimes those whose kinks are not their kinks. Enjoy missionary with your wife with the lights off and nothing else? You might be vanilla.

    Okay, moving on. You all know what **Jealousy** is, so I won't explain that to you. You may be jealous right now that this book knows more groovy words than you. But hey, you shouldn't be, because it's gonna dump all that knowledge down your head hole.

    Ahem.

    So, yes…jealousy. Well, do the opposite of jealousy (i.e., be excited by the fact that your partner is happy, or having fun, or having sex, or coming hard) and that's called **Compersion**. This one's fun because it doesn't show up in the dictionaries, and was coined in the free-love '60s in San Francisco.

Moving down the line. **Gay** and **Straight** I'm not going to define for you. But I will tell you that I personally believe gay and straight are the outliers (maybe 10% on each side) and the 80% in the middle is some shade of **Bisexual,** meaning "interested in both same sex and the opposite in some way." **Bi-curious** means curious about same sex contact. Before I descend too much into the **Gender Binary** here (the idea that there are only two genders) I'll throw a caveat down: That shades of bisexual thing I'm talking about above also encompasses the wide variety of gender expression.

Along those lines, two common terms for sexual attraction without boundaries are **Pansexual** and **Omnisexual**, both meaning generally the same thing: I don't care what your naughty bits look like, if I'm attracted to you then game on! **Sapiosexual** is a term that is possibly younger than *The Swingset*, meaning being attracted to intelligence and intelligent people. Like a guy who can write a whole lexicon. Text me!

Let's wrap back to the beginning and dissect swinging 'cuz there's a bunch of terms that you'll hear all the fuck over in this book. **Full Swap** and **Soft Swap** are identifiers for the type of swinger you are. These refer to how you play, and generally mean anything from kissing and touching up through oral sex with someone other than your partner counts as soft swap, anything beyond that (i.e. penetrative sex) would be full swap. And I know, I know, oral sex *is* penetrative sex when it comes to fellatio (don't know that one? Blowjob. I'm uninterested in being clearer than that as you may not be ready for this book if you've never heard of one of those) but let's not beat ourselves to death with semantics here.

I recommend you consider **Sex** to be anything you do of a sexual nature (full swap, soft swap, no swap, jacking it, etc.) but that's more of a philosophy than a definition, so I'll move on.

One of the coolest things about non-monogamy is the fact that it instantly unlocks (as in *Super Smash Bros.*) a host of new sexual things you can do. A **Threesome** is also a **Ménage à trois** which, I'm sure you don't need me to tell you, is sex with three people. Three people involved, I mean, not three in a row. And not you having sex with three people, because that'd actually be a **Foursome** which doesn't get a fancy French name. Add another, as I'm sure you've figured out the pattern by now, gets you to a **Fivesome.**

We here at *Life on the Swingset* put more than five into **Orgy** category, though there's always room for discussion (and field testing) about what actually constitutes an orgy. For our purposes here, an orgy is many people, mostly engaging sexually with as many of the others as possible. Not to be confused with a **Gang Bang,** which involves one person being fucked by many at once.

One of my favorite sex acts is the one named by Dan Savage's *Savage Love* readers: **Pegging.** This is where a man receives anal sex from a **Strap-On** dildo (harness based dildo suspension system) worn by a woman. Why so specific for this act? Because a girl using a strap-on on another girl isn't pegging, and a man receiving anal from another man isn't pegging. It's a unique act with unique circumstances, and I suppose the only things that really matter are anuses and strap-ons. For this act, not in life. Try to just relax.

STIs used to be called **STDs** and are Sexually Transmitted Infections. **Safe Sex** became **Safer Sex** because there's no such thing as 100% safe sex, and then our good friend Dr. Antoinette Izzo recommended **Risk Aware Sex** because you can have sex regardless of STI status as long as you know your protection methods and determine what level of risk you are okay with. Because knowing is half the battle. Go Joe!

Cis or **Cisgender** means you identify as the gender you were assigned at birth. If the doctor said "Congrats, it's a boy!" and you identify as a man, you're cis.

Modicum, Myriad, and **Simulacrum** are big words that Cooper uses to feel good about himself and reel in those sapiosexuals. Sometimes it works.

Rim Jobs are **Analingus** which is oral-anal interaction. **DP** is double penetration, which involves two penises or simulacra (see what I did there?) penetrating one person. This can be anal and vaginal, oral and vaginal, oral and anal. It can also include two penises (or…you get the picture) in a single orifice, but that gets us to **DVP** and **DAP**. Both **Double Vaginal Penetration** and **Double Anal Penetration** fall under the DP umbrella. These are varsity moves. Speaking of varsity, adding another cock to the mix can lead to **Airtight**—oral, anal, and vaginal filling.

Cum is two things, both when we orgasm, and the expulsion of fluid that shoots out. Unfortunately, decorum and publishing conventions require me to call and spell it **Come**. I debated rebelling, but I don't care that much. **Spunk** and **Jizz** are also synonyms for the stuff. **Ejaculate** is a word that makes me grimace. Like **Moist**.

BDSM. Can I really do it justice in this glib lexicon? Let's try. BDSM is an acronym standing for a whole lotta kink. BD stands for **Bondage** (tying up or restraining) and **Discipline** (teachers, rulers, bad boy!). DS stands for **Dominance/submission,** the roles of being in charge or being told what to do. SM stands for **Sadomasochism**, and of course, **Sadism** comes from our good friend the Marquis de Sade and the wonderful/horrible pain he used to inflict (or perhaps just write about) on people for pleasure and **Masochism** is about pleasure from receiving pain. How clever of BDSM to overlap their acronym.

We're trying to launch our own acronym in the style of **LGBTQA** (Lesbian - Gay - Bisexual - Trans - Queer -

Asexual). **SOP** for Swinger - Open - Poly, an acknow-ledg-ment that the ethical non-monogamy community all share the same umbrella.

Speaking of acronyms, some of us in the safer sex community have become literally so cool we don't have time to say penis-in-vagina or penis-in-anus when we're talking about that type of sex, so instead we say **PIV** and **PIA**. Don't you feel cooler already knowing that?

Do you feel all informed? Have you memorized your vocabulary words? You should print them out on flashcards and leave them around your house or apartment. It can be a little game you play with your parents.

Anyway.

Now that you know a myriad of lifestyle related words, let's have a modicum of seriousness and get to the real content of this book.

Bonus points for finding my go-to phrases (also known as writing crutches). They are legion.

PART I

LOOKING THROUGH
NEW EYES

1

BE COOL

I am very positively, very certainly, *not* cool.

I've alternately been a nerd and a geek as long as I can remember. You know, the kind of person who discovers something cool like swinging and rather than bask in the light of it and suck the marrow from its bones, builds a website and podcast to talk about it. That kind of uncool. Oh, yes.

So, would it surprise you, faithful reader, to know that I was also tremendously uncool in high school? In college? Only once did I get to hang out with the cooler kids, and it was because our school froze one day. Literally. Gotta love the Midwest. That day I somehow got invited along with a bunch of others to one of the cheerleaders' houses. I spent my time watching these cool kids. Thinking about how nice it must be to have their friends and their fun and their relationships and their (I was very sure then, mildly sure now) kinky sex.

Whereas, I lost my virginity the summer *after* high school…in a long term monogamous relationship to boot.

So why dredge all this up?

Well, I sorta realized something. While I still would *never* consider myself cool, these days I'm doing the things cool people do. Exploring sexuality and experimenting, going to *very* interesting parties, enjoying friends from all walks of life, and most definitely having sex with people outside my relationship with my partner's full permission and partici-pation. In fact, I'd like to jaunt this thought one step further. I'm reasonably certain (because how certain can you be?) that the football team captain I vaguely wanted to be in high school (mostly because he slept with *both* the girls I confided in him that I liked) has had fewer sexual partners than I have. I'm *far* more confident that he hasn't participated in a sixteen person orgy.

In fact, this can be said about the vast majority of the folks that I wanted to be in times gone by. I wanted to be them because they were having all of the cake, as it were. They were living glamorous lives, and doing glamorous things, and having glamorous stories.

In high school.

Now, as I am friends on Facebook with quite a few of these folk, I know *exactly* what they're doing and who they are. Most of them are popping out their second or third kid, talking about which Mega Church they cult off to every week (like jacking off, but with "God"), and other-wise living the preposterously mundane life that, well, I used to live in high school.

The cool kids always seemed exceptional to me, like they'd managed to tap a vein of gold that was making them emotionally, sexually, and physically rich beyond their wildest dreams. Sure, many of them would argue with me that they had problems too, and it's not easy being popular, and that not everything was as it looked, and that...oh my, I just fell asleep boring myself with their woes. And now, the vein seems to have dried up.

I'm confident that many of them are quite happy with their lives, and more power to them. But as news trickles in through the grapevine of troubles all around, I observe that a lot of them peaked early. That they had their days of fun and those days are behind them. It's time to be grown-ups now.

Which is, I think, why we "play." By "we", I mean swingers.

They've all grown up to their grown-up jobs and their grown-up responsibilities and their grown-up hobbies (like fly fishing) and their grown-up lawn mowing and dog walking and carpooling and minivanning; all looking back on what The Boss called *Glory Days*. Days that can't be recaptured. Days that are long gone. As though they've forgotten where the fun is and have replaced it with simulacrum.

But still, we play.

We haven't forgotten how to play. From the youngest playmate I've had in their twenties to the oldest in their fifties, we remember to enjoy…to suck the aforementioned marrow out of life (as well as other stuff out of other things) and seize us some *diem*.

I'm tempted to reach out to some of them and remind them that they can still have fun being grown-ups. Others it just makes me snigger that I've finally found something cool that I get to do and they don't. 'Cuz even if I can't fathom that I might be considered cool, I'm doing something that not many people get to do in their lives, and something that might cause others, even that high school jock, to envy me.

Holy shit, that's odd.

2

OUR FIRST DATE AS SWINGERS

Our first date with swingers lasted four and a half hours, in a booth in a low traffic area of TGI Fridays. I remember the build-up to it far more than the date itself. We both changed several times, trying to figure out what to wear. *How do swingers dress?* Trying desperately to remember how to go on a first date.

Marilyn and I assured each other that we were, in fact, looking good. We repeated what was rapidly becoming a mantra: "We can do this." Deep breaths all around. Here came the deep end, yawning in front of us. No matter how many times we held hands on the drive over and repeated our words, they masked an alternate set in our minds: *This is insane!*

"Well, there's always swinging," had come out of my mouth only a week prior to this terrifying prospect of meeting people, of going on a date, of going on a date with really-for-real swingers. So casual. An off-hand remark meant as almost a joke response to the stress of our rising mutual wanderlust. We'd discussed those four words for an hour over dinner, considering what they meant. "Well, there's always swinging." Those words seemed weighty, as though they could change things. That they *would* change *everything*.

But even when we took it from off-hand into reality that night, after discovering the wonderfully silly short film *The Lifestyle and You*, we didn't expect that we'd be on our first swing date in the space of a week. Yet here we were, telling ourselves, "We can do this," as we stood in the vestibule waiting for our semi-blind date to arrive.

We'd only seen vague photos of them, the kind that are all style and no substance. The kind of photos you show to people before you know who they really are. The kind you show to those "not certified as real" folks on the swinger dating website. We were waiting for the first couple we really seemed to have something in common with. They only had a few years on us, age-wise, and were willing to take it at our speed. We'd flirted and exchanged these basic hesitant photos. We thought, "Yeah, this could be fun, we should get together sometime."

So when they asked whether we could meet that coming weekend, and sometime became this time, we, flustered, couldn't think on our feet quick enough to come up with an excuse not to go and wound up *actually making a date*. Actually making a date with swingers. Real swingers. Been doing this for years and all. So we stood, waiting for our nebulous dates to arrive at Hooters.

"Now *wait* a minute," you say, "Cooper, you can't even keep your damned venues straight. At the top of this post you said Fridays, and now you've changed it to Hooters. Well, which is it?"

I'll tell you, ornery reader. We made our date for Hooters, but found it unnaturally busy at 9pm on a Sunday night and once our dates arrived we had to change venues. Now, will you just let me tell the story my damned way? Thank you!

She arrived first, beautiful, long curly hair, huge smile on her face. She must have known us from the "deer in headlights, could bolt at any moment" look in our eyes. She said he was parking the car and gave us both a warm and gentle hug followed by a light kiss on the lips. This is a moment that stands out for me. We knew her name, we'd seen her body, but this was the first time we'd seen her face, and this beautiful girl kissed us. As shy and nervous as we looked, her kiss to each of us was gentle, non-threatening. It was the first touch of lips other than Marilyn's in quite a while for me. For Marilyn herself, well, it was the first time her lips touched another woman's.

As I said before, the date itself sits without form in my memory. I know the facts: we moved the date over to Fridays after it became immediately apparent that we wouldn't be able to really *talk* at Hooters. It lasted four and a half hours. We ordered drinks and a Jack Daniels chicken appetizer. We sat across that table being flirted with, an experience that we'd almost forgotten.

Early on, perhaps sensing our unease, he leaned us in and said something that would stick with us as the perfect thing to say to scared newbies. A phrase I've used myself since, in fact. "Let's make this a little easier on you both. We want to be your friends regardless of where else this goes." With that, all the desperation to impress, to prove to them that we were indeed that free form idea of "cool" that we aspired to be on this date, just flittered away.

Marilyn had been, once upon a time, before our adventures began, a very quiet girl. This didn't change significantly during this first date, but there was a spark there, one that I noticed. One that showed me that while this decision we were making wasn't traditional and would probably be frowned upon by many, maybe, just maybe, we needed this.

As we left the restaurant that night, we walked out together. There was a goodnight kiss for both of us from her, a kiss for Marilyn from him, a solid handshake for me.

"See, not so scary," he told me. "You let us know."

"We will," I replied.

"This lifestyle can change your life," she told us, taking our hands a last time.

"Promise?" we asked.

3

CHARGED BATTERIES

L eaving the restaurant that night, we were like teenagers again…giggling the whole way home. There was a "What the hell are we doing?" sense in the air, despite the fact that we'd not done anything other than talk to really-for-real swingers. That talking had been enough, though, to remind us about how fun life could be. We'd been married for a good long time, together for just about ten years at that point. As often happens, we just sorta forgot what fun was. We forgot to enjoy sex. We forgot to be like young lovers. Neither of us had stopped wanting, desiring or needing these things, we just forgot.

Then, on the ride home, my hand kept drifting between her legs and her hand onto my lap. Something happened that night, something *very* simple. We were validated. It's so easy to forget that your partner's opinion matters when they say, "You look sexy, you look beautiful, I love you." 'Cuz you start to feel like, well, they *have* to say that. But these new friends didn't have to say it, and they still talked about us being attractive, made it clear beyond a shadow of a doubt that they were interested in us. Let me repeat that last part, because even having been in this life-style for around two years, I sometimes forget the amazingness of this sentence. *They* were interested in *us*. I think we all tend to feel these things about ourselves, that we're less exciting, less attractive, less interesting than we'd like to be. So to have someone else give us that validation, well, that's like a very special kind of drug right there.

When we got home, we found that we'd been "certified real" by them on our swinger dating website, which meant we could finally look at more than just the general public photos. Now we got to see all the fun and exciting pictures that He and She had posted on their profile. This is the section where the really dirty pics hang out. This is also where the face pics live, because you don't want just *anyone* browsing the site to see who you *really* are.

With this access at our disposal, this whole section of the site opened up, we thought that we ought to get some pictures up there ourselves. So we took some, and we fucked. We texted our new friends, and we fucked. We took more pictures, and we fucked. We exchanged photo requests, and we fucked. This may sound like an exag-gera-tion, but I think in that week between meeting the swingers for the first time and getting around to our first sexual contact with them a week later, we'd had more sex than in the six months leading up to it.

We knew that this was special, even before the first real physical contact with an outsider (i.e., not in our imme-diate marriage, 'cuz there were only two people there). Something major had changed inside us. We saw potential, we saw personal growth, we saw warm and fuzzies in the future. This amazed me because I would've never thought it possible to discover a completely new side of myself after 30. But the *real* changes happened in my wife.

She'd been a quiet girl the whole time I'd known her, always letting me dominate the conversation and sort of hanging in the background. She didn't dress to be sexy. She didn't feel comfortable asking for sex, or using the small (and rather crappy) collection of toys we owned. But in this week, it was as though she'd shed an old body, metamorphosed into something…someone…*completely* different. There was confidence where there hadn't been before, along with determination, excitement and enthusiasm. I realized that she'd been repressing all of this for her entire life, and now she'd set it free.

As time has gone on, I've found it hard to explain to our swing friends how different she used to be. So evident was the change that friends and family noticed her newfound confidence very quickly. This, of course, is one of the reasons we decided to tell our friends about us. We didn't want them to assume she was simply cheating. The change was *so* evident that even our first couple noticed it when they met us for drinks a week later.

That second date with them, the one where we actually became swingers, where we did the soft swap tango, that was really amazing; because this lifestyle can enact dramatic emotional change, the recharging of the sexual batteries that people so often neglect. For us it was enlightening, and amazing. I think the reward was so high because we took such a big risk. The excitement of doing something different, something you're not supposed to do, worked *really* well for us.

Remember NRE, new relationship energy? Those awesome first days of a relationship where everything is about promise and possibility? Sometimes it can even last months, while you're getting to know them, while you're still amazed they like you as much as you like them. That's what the lifestyle brought to us…the possibility of that excitement without jettisoning the support and security of our real long term relationship…the possibility of orgasmic delight.

4

WANDERLUST

LET'S ALL GO EXPLORING

I t's in all of us, even in those of you who say you can't imagine sex with anyone but your significant other. While that may be true, there are still those lustful thoughts that creep in while watching television or your favorite movie. Maybe that actor or celebrity that makes you tingle in that oh so delightful way. Your thoughts may in fact linger on those imagined moments later, while in the bath, or in a private second away from the family, while you do those things that the Holy Church warned you you'd go to hell for doing.

You might say, "That's just fantasy, nothing wrong with fantasy."

I agree with that, it *is* just fantasy and there *isn't* anything wrong with it. You may really only have these thoughts for fleeting moments. I'd wager, though, if you're one of the people saying you can't imagine sex with anyone but your significant other, you're also not telling your significant other about these debauched thoughts you're having.

In fact, I have a theory that it's the people who constantly tell you they couldn't imagine, or they never fantasize, who would put even us swingers to shame with the depth and breadth of what they're thinking about and considering in the dark corners of their minds when no one else can see.

I'm not judging you in the least! We're all entitled to our fantasies. It's not lying to keep these little fleeting lusts from your partner. You're not doing anything wrong. That said, you *are* deluding yourself if you don't believe you have some inherent wanderlust inside of you. Maybe just a teensy bit, but it's certainly there.

When we find out about celebrities cheating on each other, we're perplexed. Like when Brad cheated on Jen with Angelina, we can't believe that with someone like Jennifer Aniston at home, Brad would be compelled to cheat. We look at them with amazement, in fact. Or, for those of us who would vastly prefer Angelina, we wonder how he lasted so long. There's this overwhelming opinion that when you have something amazing you should be happy. You know, like Prince Charles. He had a real life Disney princess in Diana, and threw that away for Camilla. Why?

When I talked the talk and walked the walk of a mainstream vanilla husband (I did this for far too long, mind you) I couldn't, for the life of me, understand it. Charlie Sheen was fucking Denise Richards and (allegedly) all of Heidi Fleiss' girls on the side! Mystifying. If we, the common folk, are supposed to be happy for the rest of our lives with our, let's face it, less than perfect bodies, and our only modest monetary worth, how could we possibly hope to do that when the folks who have everything cannot get it together? Because we're trying to hold fast to the great tradition, that age-old idea that you can find that perfect person and be happy for the rest of your lives.

Yet we have wanderlust.

We try so hard to quash it, but it keeps bubbling up and over, like that pot of mac and cheese that you can't seem to keep from boiling right over the sides and onto the burner. This wanderlust manifests itself very simply sometimes, just a glance at someone in a restaurant and that momentary sinful thought. I say sinful not because I believe it is in any way, but because that's why most of us try so desperately to hold it back. We feel the thoughts themselves might be wrong, evil, disgusting, awful, the kind of thing our parents and family and friends would be horrified to find out we were thinking. But they'd only be posturing horror while trying to keep from you their own thoughts of wanderlust.

As vanillas we all seem to have this idea that we're alone in the world, that we alone shoulder this burden. When we look at these celebrities, experiencing their own imper-fections, and their own very public wanderlust, we gather the stones and start throwing.

"How dare he?"

"She's gorgeous, I never would..."

And so on and so on, *ad nausem*. This is the same phenom-enon that creates the politician who hates gays so very vocally while taking a male escort on vacation, and why family values purveyors are constantly getting divorced.

We hate so very much anything that reminds us of this horrible little thing inside us.

Now, if only we could believe it wasn't horrible. If only we could recognize the fact that not only is it not horrible, but it's in all of us. It's perhaps one of very few things that bind us together through race and creed. We all are fasci-nated by what other people have, what other things feel like...the "grass is greener" bullshit.

It's not greener, it's just different. But different is good.

If we can accept the wanderlust in ourselves, and in those around us, we're less liable to condemn those who feel it, which makes us less liable to create rules, statutes, and sins that condemn it. Yes, I said "create sins," don't pretend that all concepts of sin aren't creations of man.

Without them we'd all be allowed to explore safely, to sate our wanderlust, to share of ourselves.

5

BI THE WAY

MALE BISEXUALITY AND SWINGING

Future Cooper Note: This post was written when I was very unsure whether or not to come out as bisexual on Life on the Swingset. *It was a difficult position to be in as I saw how poorly bisexual males were treated. I thought I could work the system from the inside by raising awareness.*

THERE IS A HUGE DOUBLE STANDARD IN THE SWINGING lifestyle when it comes to acceptance of bisexual males. We all know this, it's endemic. As swingers we seem perfectly happy that our women are bisexual. We encourage, and expect them to be, so often. Some more than others, but by and large, definitely bisexual. Now don't jump down my throat here, I'm well aware that straight swinging females exist, and probably in a decent sized number, but wouldn't we all agree that the *vast* majority of females in the lifestyle are bi?

This fact isn't really shocking, as even the mainstream vanilla world has embraced girl-on-girl action in the past ten to fifteen years. So when a lifestyle such as swinging presents itself as an option, affording them the opportunity to play with girls, well, there ya go. That's where the bi girl inside comes out. Many of the swing couples I've met said that this was one of the prominent reasons they got into this lifestyle in the first place: so Mrs. could play with another woman.

You raise the call for bisexual males, however, and tumble-weeds blow by. Invisible because it's been made very clear in club and party rules and pricing that a man who wants to play with another man is an unwelcome addition to the scene.

This doesn't make sense.

Let's check out the Kinsey scale. Most of us have heard of it, but I'd wager few actually know it beyond the name. This is the Kinsey Scale.

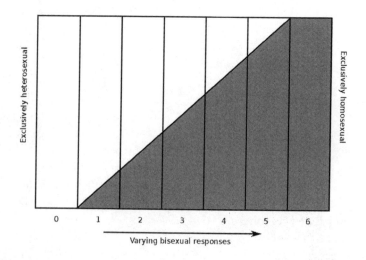

Back when Kinsey did his extensive sexuality research in the 1950s, he found that 11.6% of white males between the ages of 20 and 35 identified themselves as a 3, which as you can see sits right smack in the middle on the scale. This identification means roughly equal amounts of sexual contact with the same sex as sexual contact with the opposite sex for the period of time the study covered, with pretty much the same percentage for females.

Interesting.

There are a number of conclusions we can draw from this. First, that the results could be flawed because it was so bad to admit to any homosexual feelings back then, so gays could be sliding further towards 0 than they otherwise would. But even with a bit of a skew, roughly one in ten men and one in ten women identified themselves as bisexual during Kinsey's research. And that was back when men were manly, right?

With society opening up a bit ('cuz it has) and men being allowed to shrug off the shackles of the old school ideal of *Man*, it stands to reason that the number would be at least the same, but more likely higher. If the number of bisexuals isn't increasing, surely the number of people who feel they can admit it must be.

Now here's where it gets more interesting to me. The statistic I choose to repeat, even though I'm sure it's woefully inaccurate, is that 1 in 70 people are swingers. We're going to do some fun math here, with actual statistics drawn from other websites without citing my sources. So, take or leave the accuracy, this is just food for thought. It's also been a long time since I did any math with desired accuracy. If my figuring is wrong, well, I'm not claiming to be a scholar.

There are 309,699,000 people in the US as of this moment according to Google. 75% of them are over the age of 20, giving us 232,274,250 adults. By Kinsey's numbers (numbers that are over 60 years old) there are 26,943,813 bisexuals out there. So, now if 1 in 70 people are swingers, that assumes 4,424,271 swingers in the US, with at least 442,427 of them being bisexuals. With the ratio of bisexual women being sky high in the lifestyle, wouldn't it follow that that number seems quite low for bisexual or at least bi-curious males?

Now, a characteristic I would give many swingers is their willingness to be open to new ideas sexually. Generally speaking, the people who're going to cad around and just fuck, and that's what it's all about for them, just go ahead and commit adultery and leave the hassle of swinging out of it. So let's say that half of the swingers, just over two and a quarter-*million* people, are this more enlightened and open-minded group that I speak of. Wouldn't it follow that those would be more likely to allow for the possibility of a bisexual experience? To try it?

I'll try anything once, twice in case I did it wrong the first time. It's a good motto, and it's one espoused on many swinger profiles.

On the very first swinger profile I listed myself as bi-curious because I figured, "why on Earth would I want to limit myself when presented with the unlimited bounty of sexual possibility." The Mr. of our first couple suggested I change my answer or suffer the desert of responses and the slings and arrows of the swinger community.

So I did. Male: Straight.

Why the bias? Many think it's because bi males still fall under the unfortunate stigma of homosexuality in the 80s, and the fact that it was quite common to see AIDS as a gay disease back then.

Some assholes still think it is exclusively a gay disease, and they're ignorant assholes.

Truth be told, anal sex *is* more likely to spread STIs than most other sexual activities. But, with a condom, that "more likely" is almost completely negated.

Then is it just paranoia about STIs? Doubtful. I think it's predominantly fear of what your peer group would say. It's amusing to me the profiles that say "MY HUBBY AIN'T BI, SO WE DON'T WANT THAT!" The dialect is due to the fact that it is a direct quote, capitalized yelling and all. It seems so close to the general homophobia amongst men that say, "I just don't like the idea of him looking at me." Despite many lifestyle nights not including any bisexual female activity (even when both females are bisexual) a not insignificant number assume that the moment there's a bisexual male in the mix, it means he's gonna want to put his dick in you. The proverbial "you." You know, the homophobic male "you."

I've spoken to a LOT of bi male swingers, and all but one are listed as straight on their profile. When speaking to couples, they generally realize pretty quickly that I'm 100% open to any kink. Nothing fazes me. I may not understand or be interested, but it doesn't matter to me if it's your groove.

Except those foolish non-exclusive bareback couples. Yeah, I'm talking to you! *You're part of the STI problem!*

All it takes is the realization that I am not going to judge them for their interest. So what this suggests is that there are a lot of bisexual males in the lifestyle who'd love to come out of the bisexual closet if only they could be guaranteed that they wouldn't be judged.

So I'll leave you by trashing an idea that I've heard all around the lifestyle: the idea that bi male activity makes one gay.

Does that mean your wives and girlfriends are gay now? Because from where I sit they've been eating a lot of pussy and still come back for the cock.

Interesting.

6

HER HAND ABOVE MY KNEE

I'm frequently asked, by people who have never explored open relationships, why I do this, the swinging thing. I mean, the main reasons are obvious. I'm not so much into the whole monogamy thing. But the secondary reasons are pretty interesting as well. Friends. Connections. Social group expansion.

My circle of friends is very different than it was before opening up.

But for me, one of the best parts of this wild ride is very simple moments of contact. Perhaps it's because I'm a tactile person, and touch means so very much to me. There are these little moments strewn throughout our lives where we touch others. As vanillas, you touch your family, you touch the innermost circle of friends, and there it stops. There's so much that could be misinterpreted, taken out of context. Your hand on someone's arm or back when you talk to them, for instance. The wrong person sees that and suddenly there's rumors flying and feelings are hurt.

God, I don't miss that at all.

I've always been close with my female friends. I've always been a hugger, and with select few, a kisser. It's who I am. I'll admit that it has likely always been indicative of that deeper personality (you know, the swinger) trying to claw his way out. Instead of exploring "touch as swinger," for this instance I'll simply go with open. Being open allows for so much more of that touch in a world that finds itself deprived.

As a man watching women with their friends, it's easy to feel that we somehow got the short end of the stick. Women touch, and kiss and hug so often, and with little regard for looks or murmurs, because society doesn't disapprove. But a man gives the same type of greeting or farewell to a woman and people start wondering what he's really after. And men that hug? Usually they have to do that thing where they shake hands and pull it in and slap like crazy on each other's backs so as to say, "I may be hugging you, but I'm sure as hell hitting you too!"

Upon opening up, I found that there's so much opportunity for that wonderful bit of contact.

One of my favorite moments, of the entire time I've been open, was at my first house party. I was having a glass of wine and talking to Hannah, a playmate I'd met up with, and we were joined by Kay. She and Hannah had known each other for a long time, but hadn't seen each other recently, so they began to catch up. Kay was telling a story about her eldest son who'd announced, "I know you're lying to us about what you do at night." In the middle of this story that had both Hannah and I laughing, Kay put her hand on my leg, just above the knee.

This was the first moment where someone had done something like that to me outside of a play date. No preconceptions, no planned "first we will have small talk, then we will have touching, and then we will have the sex." It was such an innocuous thing, the hand on the leg as she talked, the slight lean in, but that small gesture had a profound effect, because it was so alien in the vanilla world.

Which is a damned shame, really.

Because having intimate touch in our lives is something

that so many of us crave, even though we don't realize it… someone's hand on your shoulder, or brushing some hair out of your eyes. These are little things that we can't do because of the privacy bubble. Even if we asked, we'd get a crazy reaction like, "Why would you think you'd be allowed to do that?" I'm not talking about "capital I" *Intimate* touch here, just slightly more intimate touch than we're allowed in polite society. Nothing scary, I promise!

I've had some great sex in this lifestyle, with amazing people, and done many things I never thought I'd do and wouldn't trade for the world. At the same time, when I look back at year one, that moment with her hand above my knee stands out as the far favorite.

For the first time in my adult life, the pieces seemed to fit. For the first time I felt like I'd found home.

7

THE SAFE ZONE

GIVING YOURSELF PERMISSION TO SCREW UP

A while back I found myself flirting with some Canadian friends, newbies to swing. We talked about the possibility of a play date somewhere mid-way between us ('round middle of Michigan). They were understandably nervous, as it would be their first time doing anything, and I stumbled across an idea of how to look at the possibility of sex activity on our weekend: The Safe Zone. In The Safe Zone, they can try things they're nervous about trying without repercussions afterward.

If you designate a day or a place as an anomaly in your life, it allows you the freedom to explore those taboos and things that make you nervous. If you wind up not enjoying yourself, or feeling jealousy, or having an issue, you can write it off as a self-contained package. That happened in The Safe Zone and it doesn't need to happen again.

My Canadian friends were worried about what might happen if they tried something they wound up not liking and left discouraged or angry or jealous or regretting the weekend. These are all valid concerns, and things that could very well happen as you dip your first tentative toes into the waters of any variant in the non-monogamous lifestyle spectrum. My Safe Zone idea is about giving yourself per-mission to make those mistakes and fuck up, because it's those potential mistakes, those things that *could* backfire so greatly, that wind up being the absolute *best* things about the lifestyle.

I suggested that they look at this weekend trip across the border into Michigan as stepping outside their lives together. Whatever happens in Michigan can stay in Michigan if they want. If something bad happens, like jealousy or anger, they can give themselves permission to "leave it in Michigan." Going forward in life they can look at it as a minor aberration, something that need not be repeated, something that they did "in Michigan."

I think this can easily apply to most of the things we do at the beginning of the lifestyle.

If you're planning a date with a couple for the first time you can designate that date as The Safe Zone. Once you give yourself permission to take the risk, to really hold your breath and jump, it is like the waters of freedom rushing in. Plus, with true freedom and openness comes the likelihood that you won't create lasting scars.

There is an essential component to this, however: the agreement that whatever issues crop up in The Safe Zone do, in fact, stay there. This is indeed a hard one. If you see your spouse or significant other doing something surprising and it raises deep new feelings and jealousies that you didn't expect, it sure as hell can feel impossible to leave those issues at the door.

But I think that part of the price of admission to this lifestyle is pushing yourself to leave some of these things behind. Not all of us will get through our first experiences without feeling conflicted and jealous. In some cases that'll be the end of the experiment. But these feelings of conflict and jealousy needn't mean that this lifestyle shouldn't be for us, or isn't for us. They just mean we're processing feelings differently than expected.

Like the removal of The End Game (the idea that any breach would be cause to immediately shut down your relationship), this is something that you have to implant inside you. This is a completely external concept, that I simply won't hold this or that against my partner if things go badly. Even if I so desperately want to. Even if things go so unbelievably bad, this is the risk of the leap.

I believe that even our worst anger, our worst jealousy, the most angry and selfish thoughts we have towards our partner are optional, even if they don't feel that way at the time. We can decide that yes, I feel this way, but I'm going to own and stop it. That I'm going to change the dialog. That I'm going to decide to be alright.

Because if we can do that, if we can decide that The Safe Zone exists in its own little bubble in time and space that may be a swing date, or a swingers club, or somewhere in the middle of Michigan's wine country, and no lasting relationship damage can come from anything we try there, we're giving ourselves permission to be who we truly are; which can only teach us and our partners more.

Experimentation and pushing boundaries are the bread and butter of a happy life. The mantra that "I'll try anything twice (in case I did it wrong the first time)" is so very important because that's how you learn who you really are.

You know what? It's fucking okay if you try something you don't like. That moment is not a failure. That's a moment you learned something new about yourself. If you never try these things for fear that you may not like them, you cut yourself off from the possibility of discovering something exciting. Something you never thought you'd like. And you might really like it.

The Safe Zone is about allowing yourself to fuck it all up, to destroy it and rebuild it, without fear of retribution on the outside. It's within that freedom that catharsis can happen, and it's within catharsis that true learning lives.

'Cuz sometimes you learn, in a little hotel in Michigan, that girls are soft, and smell good, and taste good, and you're only able to learn that because you felt safe.

8

WE WERE ALL NEWBIES ONCE

"So..." we begin in as roundabout a way as we can, realizing that this question will change the direction of the conversation, which thus far has been about things that most people talk about. And by most people, we mean vanillas. At that moment we straddle two worlds, the vanilla world that would be shocked at what we're here to do, and the world beyond, the world of openness, of non-monogamy, of swinging. "How does this work?"

We asked it on our first swing date.

Since that first date we've been on dates with three newbie couples, just dipping their toes in, just seeing how the water feels over here, unsure if they're ready to buy some white rocks for the front yard, all asking that same question. Because we like plans, don't we? This is what separates our experimentation with that of the wild college years that are sort of a hazy testing ground for the new and different, where it's societally acceptable for girls to have trysts with their female roommates when drunk/high/otherwise out of their gourds.

"How does this work?"

What we really wanted to know is: *does* this work? Can

you look us in the eye right now and actually confirm to us that you're happy, that you enjoy this thoroughly, that swinging is a boon for your relationship, a positive addition to your lives? "How does this work?" is also a question that asks, "Is this okay?" It's a process question. We want to know the process of swinging. What happens now? What happens next? When do we kiss, get naked, start fucking? We want to know all of that, but we also want to know how on Earth this wild thing that spits in the face of thousands of years of marital tradition *works*. How could it possibly?

It's with a certain bit of desperation that we ask the question, "How does this work?"

We want so desperately for it to work. We have this idea in our heads that's pushing out the fears of jealousy and finding another lover, the idea of true happy swinging with all the supposed perks, the communication boost, the redirection of wanderlust. Some of us just want to do it like rock stars.

The answer to "How does this work?" is different for everybody. For some this date stage is skipped entirely, and even the newbies walk into sex clubs and get right down to business, sometimes with nary a name exchanged. Just a thanks afterward, perhaps a pat on the ass, and a fare-thee-well. For others the discussion process is almost interminable, endlessly running scenarios and plotting next moves the way a grand master plays chess.

In my mind, the best path has always been fairly middle-of-the-road between those. I won't jump into bed without names or chat, but I won't make potential playmates fill out a complete sexual history either. For me, the answer to "How does this work?" was letting fantasy guide me, especially at the beginning.

We'd met our first couple, asked them how it worked, and they told us how it worked for them. In the week between our first date and our (far more adventurous what with all the soft swapping) second, we fantasized together;

which is something we'd never really done before. We asked each other, while in the throes of ecstasy, what we wanted to do, what we wanted to see, how we wanted to act, where we wanted to go, and how we wanted them to fit into our lives.

This prep work helped ensure that the jealousy monster could be held down at least, maybe with tape over his filthy lying mouth. So when we did get together with them the next time, we were able to almost articulate where we might want things to go, or at least were far more willing to be led.

Now, "How does this work?" is often left up to our friends.

I've gotten to a point in this lifestyle where there's really very little that makes me uncomfortable or take pause. Same room or separate rooms play, full swap or soft swap, girl/girl, guy/guy, all in the bed in a pile. Because of that, it's a very easy for me to cede the lead to the newbies asking the question. Of course, I'm perfectly willing to nudge them a bit on their way as well, but let them dictate the level of play, knowing full well that we'll be able to have enough control to redirect if anyone seems uncomfortable.

Our new friends we met Monday are just beginning their journey. It's just a twinkle in their eye right now, a fantasy in their sex life.

So, "How does this work?"

Well, we shall see.

Or, put another way, "How does this work? It works great!"

9

WHY WE SWING

I 'm not going to spend a whole lot of time going into philosophical reasons for swinging, or even anthropological ones (though there are many for both) in this forum, because what I've found is that people tend to invent the philosophical and anthropological reasoning as a way of validating their chosen lifestyle. Instead, I'm focused more on why *we* swing, the "we" being Marilyn and myself. We got into it for all the wrong reasons (according to most websites and books), because we got into the lifestyle to fix something in our marriage.

Whoa!

I know, right? Never become a swinger unless your relationship is perfect, because swinging will magnify all your problems and something, and buzzing, and a high pitched sound. There is a lot of validity to that, I'm sure of it. Swinging has magnified problems, but again as this is a *Why We Swing* story and not a *Why They Swing*, or *Why One Swings*. I can assure you that for us, swinging was the answer to a question that had been nagging us since the beginning of our lives together some 10 years before. Why do we want to fuck other people?

From the looks of our friends and loved ones, we were

not alone in this thought. Look at sitcoms on TV if you need more proof. I don't think there's a "fat guy/cute wife" sitcom out there that hasn't done the "Why did you look at that other girl? Does she have something I don't?" plot-line at some point in its run. We're dishonest though, as a society, because we want so desperately for this to make him "the bad guy." But don't worry, 'cuz they laugh and love their way through it, mostly giving a resounding assurance that "I love you and don't need anyone else, honey."

Awww.

It may be true, that's the thing. It may definitely be true that he doesn't need anyone beside his partner, ever in his life, *but we all look*. That bothered me for many years. I agonized over why my "I want to fuck that girl" drive would so quickly kick in when I'd meet a new female friend. Or why I never seemed to have any female friends I didn't want to fuck. These are things we're not supposed to be thinking, right? Right?! So we hide from ourselves and our partners. At least I did. For ten years. I pretended to not think of anyone but her.

Then it all fell apart. Because as we know, entropy ensures that the center will not hold, and our feebly constructed fantasies will all come tumbling down around us in the end. Or sometimes well before the end. So one night I spilled my guts. It bothered me that I'd only been with one woman besides her, and that we got married too early, and that sex was more of a chore sometimes than it should be. I piled it on, and unfairly so, because I left Marilyn dazed and almost unable to respond. This is why you should most assuredly talk early, and talk often.

She was glad I told her. She was hurt I didn't tell her earlier. She asked questions, was patient, and for the next month tried very hard to hide her certainty that I was going to leave her. But then, through a lot of soul searching, she realized a very similar fact about herself. She was also bothered by the fact that she'd only been with me her entire life, that we got married too early, that sex was a chore, and for the first time since our first anniversary, mentioned a vague concern she had sometimes that she might be gay.

Rock bottom was there. We felt like roommates who loved each other and very occasionally had sex…friends more than lovers. It was rough. Despite our friends saying, "You guys have the friendship, many marriages don't have that," we even got around to discussing the big D word. But that didn't last too long. A few days later we both came to each other saying, "I don't want to get divorced, I want to fix this." We looked over our issues and came to the conclusion that the rotting core of our problems was this desire to fuck other people. And we *both* wanted the same thing!

We began to discuss our options. There weren't many. Taking a break, opening up our marriage so we can see other people, both of these came with the same rather glaring fault, the words, "Yeah, I'm married, but it's cool, really!" To this day I'm still not sure how that works. But then came the off-hand comment, almost a joke in fact. "Well, there's always swinging…"

But the next day, that comment came back. How would that work? I didn't know, exactly. My only notion of swingers was hardly modern day, as it consisted of the key party from Ang Lee's *The Ice Storm* (and that didn't exactly go well). So we did a Google search, and discovered the brilliant site CoupleDoingIt.com and their 50s style video about becoming a swinger. It was all so cute, and fun, and…friendly. Suddenly this scary word "swinging" looked like something people like us did.

If people like us could do it, so could we. We pulled the trigger, joined a site, went on a date and officially became swingers; almost a year and a half ago.

So, the crux now is why we swing.

In the time since those first tentative kisses and gropes, those nights where we needed the ice breaking games to get naked, the days terrified about what might happen if our friends found out, Marilyn and I have grown closer than ever. We talk about anything on our minds these days. I mean, nothing's really as bad as that initial conversation. It's no longer scary to discuss sexual needs and wants, to say things like "I want you to peg me," and "I'd like to be whipped." We've gone from the "We don't want to be that couple who only has sex weekly" to the couple who has sex multiple times with each other and multiple times with our other friends on a weekly basis.

Why we swing? Must you really ask? Because we've gotten to meet some of the most genuine and open people we've ever met. We've surrounded ourselves with a brand new crowd that, for the first time, doesn't have to be held back by society's decorum and the sexual tension that accompanies wanting to fuck your friend's wife. We're on even keel, for the first time in our lives. And now even the problems seem minor.

Do we fight? Sure! Who doesn't? Has swinging caused issues? Absolutely! The way any new life focus can cause issues that simply couldn't have been there before without it. Is it worth it? With every fiber of my being, I say "yes."

Why do we swing? Because we *love* it. Because we can't imagine not doing it anymore. It has opened up our lives in so many wonderful ways that we can't offer enough thanks to those who guided us through those first shaky steps. We went in looking for a simple fix, something that might ignite a flame that really was never in either of us. We found a blowtorch.

Now we try to help others understand why they might or might not be a good match for this lifestyle. It's not for everybody. The risks are catastrophic. The issues too. Jealousy is a bitch if you don't know how to manage it. And it's true, if you have a bad relationship, it very well may implode. Perhaps we're just the lucky ones.

We swing because it allows us to see the best in each other, to see why other people find us attractive, to wrap ourselves in the warm embrace of people who understand, to quell the questioning inside that asks if we're normal, to feel the unbelievable highs of new relationships, and to over and over, experience the joys of unique orgasmic delight.

We swing because we can't *not* do it.

10

IS MONOGAMY SAFETY?

L ast night a thought occurred to me (as thoughts often do while I'm trying very hard to sleep because I have to be up frightfully early), that monogamy itself may be an attempt to defend against our nature to compare and rank. I'm not speaking anthropologically, as I'm not qualified to do that, nor do I care to bother myself with such things as research. Also, I would never live up to *Sex at Dawn*. This was just a concept that hadn't struck me before and I felt the need to chase it down since I had to be up in less than four hours.

We already have the compare and contrast problem in life with previous lovers. We look at our current lover, and our previous, and compare their strengths and weaknesses. The dichotomy of the previous is interesting though, because I think we often rail very hard against them, due to a mediocre denouement or exceptionally bad breakup. This colors things, usually long enough to entrench ourselves in our next relationship which is, of course, so much better than our previous.

Sometimes the opposite happens and we tint the entire past relationship rosy so that our current always has to live in the shadow of the past. Perhaps because we were younger then, and more excited…or less afraid. I myself have never had this happen to me, but I'm told it does. I'm damned lucky to be rid of most of my previous lovers. There are a few I look back on fondly, though not longingly.

What happens then when you introduce concurrent lovers? When we casually date we often employ a variant of non-monogamy, whether conscious or not. Lovers overlap, with two or three people on the possibility train at any given time. While they're not actively competing, you're ranking and adjusting for the curve. Until one wins out. The "marriage lottery," as it were. That one obviously was... better?

New Relationship Energy kicks all emotion up a notch. With all the excitement and energy, the new relationship is often standing below a flashing neon light that says "better" indeed. This is what makes the external relationship so appealing in an affair. It's new, it's exciting, it's…different. Sometimes, especially after a long period in one relationship, different is all you need to make the leap to better.

The relationships compete.

Which makes me wonder this: do we align ourselves with monogamy (as a species, not "we" meaning "me", because I do not) because it takes away the opportunity to rank and contrast? Because with one, it can only be The Best (though also the worst, but that's a thought for another day) without confusing us, without making us think too terribly hard.

We do often wonder what else might be out there. We mourn the end of possibility with wakes called bachelor and bachelorette parties. Though, if you want to see where people do bachelorette parties CRAZY, just look on over to Europe. And if anyone can explain to me those gigantic room parties with all the sex and blow jobs and that endless loop of *It's Raining Men*, I'd really appreciate it. But we take comfort and safety in the fact that, at least until we have children, we are the best thing in our partner's life.

Non-monogamy introduces a variable we're often not prepared to deal with, doesn't it? The possibility that someone else could be more exciting, more attractive, more fun, more engaging, more adventurous, more "more" than our partner.

Monogamy gives us a bit of a defense against this, by making it forbidden. This is not to say that it works, though. With some staggering estimates of infidelity frequency, one would suggest this defense works very little, but it creates a system and mechanic that simply reinforces "partner = good."

Safety. Security.

But it's an illusion.

11

NERVOUS NEWBIES

I like playing with new swingers.

A lot of people don't. Mostly because newbies often don't have their issues worked out yet, especially if it's their first fleeting experimentation with the lifestyle. There could be all manner of hideous buried conflicts that could tumble on out like the nameless creatures beyond description in an HP Lovecraft novel, all wringing of hands and gnashing of teeth.

So, why do I like playing with newbies?

It's really the adventure of it, I'd say. There's this strange extra newness that comes with it, the extra apprehension of what's going to happen, if anything. Let's face it, most swingers are a sure thing if there's a connection. Newbies make you work for it.

I realize what I'm saying may not sound the most appealing. The main reason I like newbies is because early on in our swinging lifestyle, Marilyn and I were lucky enough to meet great people who were patient, answered our questions, and took things at our pace. We hear so often about bad first experiences ruining things, or sending people out of the swinging lifestyle altogether. I like being there to offer a welcoming hand for the newbies, to show them that they needn't be afraid.

That's the whole reason I started *Life on the Swingset*, in fact, to be able to help newbies through the rough and scary spots. To reassure veterans that it's okay to evolve with your swinging lifestyle, and extend that hand to those considering climbing on the swingset.

Alice and Mark, our newbies, were very nervous. When it became apparent that they would be unable to come out our way, they took a deep breath and asked us into the city, even though Alice's sister was staying with them. "She works late," they told us, and reinforced, "and were not sure we're ready to do anything."

I restated our mantra, "We want to be your friends regardless of where this goes." They thanked us again for our support and understanding.

We arrived at their place, had a lovely dinner that they cooked for us, had some wine, some great conversation, really hitting it off. We were answering their questions as they came up, getting a good vibe, making good progress. The night was all about reinforcing that we're nice and normal, and that the lifestyle can be as well.

Then Becky, Alice's sister, came home early.

There was a lot of surprise and some "What're you doing home so early?" Then we settled in for more wine with this newfound fivesome. With the already minimal prospect of play moving to zero, Marilyn and I allowed more and more wine in our glasses, enjoying ourselves thoroughly. Shortly after Becky arrived, I realized I couldn't openly flirt with Alice in front of her, but Alice had accidentally mentioned in passing that Marilyn and I were swingers, so I knew I could flirt with Becky, and proceeded to direct all my flirtatious energy in her direction.

More glasses of wine than I care to admit later...

We'd moved the conversation and revelry to their back porch. Alice needed to check on their baby and invited

Marilyn in with her. They seemed a bit giggly when they came back out, but I didn't really process that. I went into the kitchen to procure another bottle of wine, when I'd found one I went to return to the porch and encountered Mark.

"I need to talk to you..."

Oh fuck, I thought, *I'm in trouble, shouldn't have flirted with the sister so much.*

"Do you have condoms?"

I didn't initially process the question. "What?"

"Alice wants to play."

My brain caught up to our conversation. Play with them was still a mystery. We were unsure if they were a girl/girl only couple or a soft swap couple. They had seemed pretty confident they weren't full swap at least, so condoms seemed patently unnecessary. I quickly checked with Marilyn, who confirmed that our auxiliary safer sex kit was fully stocked as always. Just in case.

Please keep in mind that we did *not* come prepared to play that night. Marilyn always keeps a kit in her purse with condoms for her partners, condoms for me. Prepared, maybe, but when we come to play we come with accessories! Toys, lube, Liberator Throe, these are all necessities. Sure, we might leave the more intimidating toys like dual dildos or the nJoy Pure Wand out for first timers, but due to my wife's squirting, the Liberator Throe is a necessity.

"You need to pretend to leave," Mark told me.

This struck me as absurdly funny as I pointed out that neither of us had done the below the belt cleanup date prep before because this wasn't supposed to be a date. He confirmed that they hadn't either, but when your previously uncertain wife says "swing," you ask, "How hard?"

So we pretended to leave, saying goodnight, gathering our things. Our pretend exit must have seemed rather abrupt to Becky because she gave us an "Oh, okay. Nice to meet you," and we headed off into the rain, to take the alley around to the back and be let back in, then quickly shuffled into their bedroom.

It was all I could do to not walk like a cartoon criminal trying to sneak in, all exaggerated steps and twirling an enormous invisible handlebar mustache.

Light playtime did happen, the kind of hazy surreal wine colored glasses playtime. Bits and pieces of that remain, enjoyable, sexy, exciting.

We went back home, hours later than expected, again sneaking past Becky, now passed out in front of the TV.

Gotta love newbies.

12

SHOULD YOU USE CONDOMS FOR BLOWJOBS?

The email read, "So, what are your thoughts on couples, or people in general for that matter, that abide by safe sex via proper use of condoms for PIV intercourse but then go ahead with bareback oral (fellatio or cunnilingus) and may even swallow with fellatio? This seems a very common paradigm yet seems so horribly hypocritical. Are people really just not thinking this through fully?" I leaped to answer it.

Okay, so first, confession time. Up until about two years ago, I was one of these swingers. 100% condom usage for penetrative sex (penis in vagina, penis in anus) but not for blow jobs (the *other* penetrative sex). Is this a big confession? Not really. Am I alone in this practice? I'd say the vast majority of the world (behold as Coop makes sweeping generalizations with his bare hands!) practices what they term "safe sex" this way.

Are they wrong? Hypocrites? Are they calling down the wrath of some Elder God to punish them for their misdeeds?

No.

'Cuz Cthulhu cares not for cunnilingus.

Anyway. So what happened? Why'd I change? Well,

used to be I'd wait around the week after playtime for the telltale signs of one or more STIs to start showing up. Often feeling those telltale signs because I'm a *major* hypochondriac and could feel absolutely anything *WebMD* said I might feel. This was with partners who were careful and tested, and I had no reason to believe that they might have anything. But I was certain I had caught something.

Eventually this feeling was so prevalent, I started to beg off of play dates.

I was asked very recently, "Doesn't oral sex suck with condoms and dental dams?"

To which I confidently replied, "A little."

"What? Coop! You're blowing the sex-positive cover here!" you say, assuring me that I should tow the company line that says it's not different at all.

But it is different. Without question. Does a blowjob while wearing a condom suck a little bit? Did ya like that turn of phrase?

To wit, there's a certain amount of awesome inherent in a blowjob. Does a condom reduce it? Yeah, a little. Doesn't wearing a condom reduce the awesome during penetrative (see above) sex? Yeah, a little. Does a dental dam detract from the glory that is pussy licking? Yeah, for both parties, a little.

Does it keep you from getting diseases that may *literally kill you*? Yeah, a lot.

And here's my obligatory disclaimer that condoms and dental dams only prevent skin-to-skin infections like HPV and HSV for the areas that are covered by them. But HSV and the vast majority of HPV won't even try to kill you. The rest of HPV is a sneaky little bastard. Get PAP smears regularly. The more you know!

Then I answered the above question (about oral sex sucking with condoms and dental dams) by laying down one of the massive Glyde dental dams (my personal favorite) atop her pussy and going to town. Having had my cock sucked while clad in a condom, I fully admit that it does cut down on the sensation slightly, but no more than it cuts down on the sensation during penetration.

And I know I don't have to say the words "Antibiotic Resistant Gonorrhea of the Throat" to remind you that a slight reduction in sensation can be a huge boost in survivability.

But maybe I'm just a wacko.

And my friend who experienced my tongue behind a barrier? She said, "It's distracting at first, and a little bizarre, but with the right combination of skill and enthusiasm you forget it's there."

Yes she did.

13

GETTING THROUGH AIRPORT
SECURITY WITH SEX TOYS

Almost every time I fly, my luggage gets one of those lovely TSA homeland security notifications. You know, the ones that say "Hey, we're friendly, no big, but we had to open your stuff to check things out. This is just a friendly notification. Had we found anything, you'd probably be in a windowless room right now. But we didn't. So, we good?"

I think it's because of the large metal toys I routinely pack. One of the downfalls to being someone with a great sex toy collection is that it's rather hard to leave anything behind. When your "anything" includes two nJoy Elevens, an nJoy Pure Wand, the custom made "Cooper" and many other uniquely shaped items, not only do suitcases get heavy, they get, shall we say, "far more interesting."

Especially in the run up to one of our yearly trips to Desire Resort and Spa, I'm asked almost weekly about getting through airport security with sex toys, or flying with sex toys. It's always asked with that elongated "Sooooo..." at the beginning.

The tl;dr answer? (Too late?) Airport security has already seen dildos far bigger than yours, far kinkier accoutrements than you're packin', bigger floggers, longer lengths of rope, more gallons of lube, etcetera. They've seen it. It's not surprising.

Really, the fact that my luggage gets opened is because some of my devices are oddly shaped (The Cooper) and could, I'll admit, be something else. So my luggage is inspected to verify that no, it's just a giant toy that he probably puts into his ass. We should put it back. Glad we're wearing gloves.

Put anything you want to play with in your checked luggage, leaving off those things that you're not allowed to fly with anyway. Carry on? Hmm, well…that's where your discretion comes in, I suppose.

I've heard tell that the nJoy Eleven may get taken away from you if you're attempting to carry it on. Homeland Security doesn't have it included in the "things you can't carry-on" diorama (the one that used to have a chainsaw in it), but let's be honest here. The Eleven is a club. A heavy metal club. And you could very easily brain someone with it. So should you be able to carry it on? Probably not. Check it.

Other items, especially those more obviously geared toward sex (had you never before seen an nJoy Eleven, would you peg it as a pleasure object? [see what I did there?]) will likely have little trouble getting through security. You may also encounter that grumpy TSA agent that wants to embarrass you a bit. But we're all sex-positive here, right? We all are confident in our toys. Odds are they'll be more embarrassed than you!

Confidence that what you're carrying is awesome can make the more otherwise awkward moments better too. Like on our way into Mexico, when the agent monitoring the x-ray called not one but two other agents over to point and whisper about what was in the toy suitcase. I gave her a wink when she made eye contact.

The real problem with bringing all of that awesome

along is, of course, suitcase weight restrictions. That, I can't help you with.

Because either you're willing to leave that bit of awesome behind or you're not.

I'm not.

14

NERVES AND DYSFUNCTION

Women have it easy.

That's right, I said it.

The prevailing notion is that a man can and will fuck anything presented to him, and to be fair, some men can and will. But in the lifestyle there are a few added stressors that can make that stereotype a bit less possible.

Uh oh, settle in. Cooper's talking Erectile Dysfunction.

Look at it from our perspective here for a moment. My partner, even if she's feeling a bit self-conscious or nervous, can, with some lube and a few well-timed moans, perform exactly as expected. Not that I'm suggesting she should fake it, I'm just saying that she *can*.

We can't, really.

And for a lot of us, especially those new to the group sex experience, especially those who have been monogamous for a long time, well…things don't always function as well as we'd like. After all, there's another guy there with another cock, and this is often a *very* new experience indeed. Then assume that guy is performing the way you wish you could be. And then assume (perhaps the biggest hurdle of all) he's doing this with your partner while you sit on the other side of the bed with a gorgeous woman you desperately *want* to please, with an unimpressive flaccid shorty hanging between your legs.

You know, hypothetically, of course.

I've been told by several women in the lifestyle, and believe them when they say, that as long as the man (and his tongue and fingers) are willing to overcome this minor inconvenience they're pleased as punch.

But I don't think women quite understand the psychological feedback loop we can find ourselves in. It happens once, then next time we worry if it'll happen again, which of course makes it that much more likely, then after another time or two the doomsday scenario appears where we begin to wonder if we'll *ever* get it hard with a playmate again. Not tonight, for the rest of our lives!

The first thing we have to acknowledge as men in the lifestyle is that our cocks will fail us. It's a fact of life. Could be this time, next time, or in five years, regardless of health or masturbatory regimen. It may fail us in the erection (aka, classic failure) or it may decide fuck all you want, no orgasm for you! (aka, new and surprising insanity.)

These things can be medical, to be sure. If they're happening in all situations, not just lifestyle ones, you should definitely schedule a visit with your doctor to be poked and prodded. For many of us, though, it's a situation where I'm fine with my partner as well as when I take matters into my own hands, but when you add others, or add condoms…

The condom conundrum (dibs on that band name) is very common. Many men, pre-swinging, haven't used condoms in years, and when one goes on the erection flees from its latex containment system. This one can be worked at. Immediately start using condoms with your partner, and when you masturbate. Get used to them. They're a part of your awesome new life. Learn to love them. We're all in this together.

My message to the guys dealing with the cycling ED is

simple: know that it happens, and not only to you. Know that worrying only reinforces that feedback loop, and as hard as it may be (phrasing!), relaxing is often the cure. Also, know that it will probably just pass on its own.

I've got a tip or two for the ladies, too (I'm on a roll!). When dealing with this situation, we're probably going to apologize. We feel as though we've let you down (and you know how emotionally fragile men can be). Just make sure we know you're having fun regardless, and perhaps direct our face between your legs. Often, while we're working on something else and aren't thinking about our neurosis, it resolves itself.

We know that most of you have far more orgasms through oral sex than penetrative sex, but that societal definition that has turned "sex" into only cocks going into holes (I say holes so as not to exclude the bis and gays. Hi, guys!) has made us really second-guess our urges. While for you, the main course may well be us licking your lap.

Now, onto the topic of assistance. Prescription pills like Viagra and Cialis, as well as those herbal supplements like you find in the toy shop, can and do help. Though, if you're going the toy shop route ask the girl at the counter (overcome this fear) which ones she's heard people say good things about. One of these can be great for breaking the feedback loop and popping that boner when you really need a "win." But if you don't need them, you want to be careful you don't set yourself up for dependency by taking them every time, because that's a whole other feedback loop that you don't want.

Last, a word to those of you who complain about men who can't always get it up, and put on your profiles that you're looking for men who can get and maintain an erection: go fuck yourself!

You're part of the problem.

THE AGONY AND
THE ECSTASY OF PORN

As sex-positive people, it's tempting to champion porn as an absolute good, to extol its merits and talk about broadening horizons and spreading the idea that sex is good (a sentiment that we're also often amazed still comes up for debate). The trouble is, for every open-minded person who longs to create something of value in porn (and of course make money as they do it, I don't believe that we have porn messiahs riding into town to selflessly produce porn for humanity) there are plenty of people who don't actually care at all about furthering human sexuality and growth. So it begs the question, "is porn bad or good?" And the answer, as you all know, is: Eh...?

As a porn consumer, and a consumer of all levels and classes of porn while I'm at it, I can definitely tell the cynical porn from the quality. Quality need not be a term that defines production value, or performance, or even "writing" (like the quotes there?) but instead could just be determined by whether or not I can get something out of it aside from a quick wank and squirt.

Note to self: *Wank & Squirt*, great musical duo, cop show, or soda name.

I'm hesitant, though, to condemn those videos. After all, who among us hasn't played the roulette game that is *YouPorn*, *XTube*, *PornoTube*, or *XHamster* (Yeah, I don't know about that last one's name, either) to watch a bit of the old in-out in-out and rub one out before bed.

What does it matter, then? If all levels of porn have some semblance of value, what could possibly be the harm?

It's interesting to me, with all the debate about legislating the use of condoms in porn in California, that the producers are coming out with a hard-line. People don't want to see that. They don't fantasize about putting a condom on (hell, some might) so therefore they don't want to have the fantasy that is porn broken by safer sex in this fantasy world. This is a very legitimate argument, and I've absolutely sought out bareback porn in the past. Because it's hot. I've also watched ATM porn (ass to mouth, for the uninitiated) and ATP (ass to pussy) - both almost guaranteed to bring along a little bit of bacteria and infection with it. Because it's hot.

So, we wonder, can that very thing, "because it's hot," be a good enough excuse for the breadth and sometimes shocking depths of "perversion" we can find. Dan Savage has said that if somebody is fantasizing about it, there's porn of it. Go ahead, think of any fetish, no matter how off the wall, type it in Google and throw the word porn after it and check out your results. Though if you plan to click on some of these back alley links, you might want to update your computer condom. I use Microsoft Security Essentials.

The ultimate great value of porn, and what makes it actually a locomotive of advancement for society, is the fact that it gives us ideas. Ideas are tremendously powerful. An aside here, porn also has been partially responsible for giving us the VCR, DVD, and Blu-ray, and helping create the online payment infrastructure that birthed commerce on the Internet. Oh porn, is there anything you *can't* do?

Now if we want to flip-side that, the ultimate bad that porn drags behind it is that it gives us ideas. Ideas can make us do unsafe, unwelcome, and profoundly stupid things.

Porn shouldn't be blamed for human stupidity. Just as violent movies don't cause violence, porn doesn't cause people to make bad decisions in their sex life. But it can influence, both good and bad.

There is a wealth of quality educational porn (much by our dear friend Tristan Taormino) produced with a mind to teach you about yourselves, and to go step by step on some of the advanced techniques we may have seen in mainstream porn and are desperate to try ourselves. Educational porn is also not shy about telling us we may not be ready, i.e. don't jump right into anal fisting.

There are waves of ethically produced porn coming out, featuring performers doing things they like and want to do, allowing these performers to help shape the course of the production, rather than being introduced to their fuck partner and told the scene. Some of the best ethically produced porn comes from new markets, and ranges from the amazing queer porn of *Crash Pad Series*, to the gorgeously photographed oral sex that Camille Crimson provides at *The Art of Blowjob*, to 24x7 live cams run and operated by the porn stars themselves. These are all produced with the performers' best interests, desires, proclivities and wants in mind, and should be celebrated.

I have gathered many ideas from porn. I have explored my sexuality as well as potential fetishes and kinks, safely from the comfort of my home, through porn. For this I owe porn a debt of gratitude, because without it I wouldn't be half the sex-positive person I am today.

But…

I've experienced tremendous body shame from porn. I've felt my decently large cock was too small. Thanks, porn. I've wondered why the woman I'm eating out doesn't have her eyes roll back and make that face they do in porn.

Why can't we do that position? Why don't *they* have to lube up before anal? Why doesn't any service person that comes to the door want to fuck me? Porn has lied to us in many ways, some obviously more destructive than others.

We, the consumers, have a role here. If you feel the porn is of quality, or up to a standard that you can get behind, purchase it. Because until people stop buying the porn that is degrading to women, men, and sex in general (not porn about being degraded, because often everybody involved in that shoot is loving every minute of it) the producers are going to keep making it. When we vote with our wallets, though, and tell people like Jiz Lee, Dylan Ryan, Buck Angel, Danny Wylde, and James Darling, that we dig what they're providing, and we want to reward them for it, then the quality of the industry improves.

And as that goes, so go our sex lives.

16

GET BACK ON TOP

Swinging is like anything else. Unless you're very lucky, you won't do it right the first time. Unlike most other things you try in life, in relationships, in marriage, swinging can be like disarming a bomb, if you don't get it right, and quickly, it can explode and leave relationship shrapnel everywhere. Though, in fairness to this mediocre analogy, good communication does not help when the timer reaches 000, but it can save your relationship.

"But," you say, "I thought swinging was a safe and harmless diversion to your workaday life."

What? Who told you that?

I have been extremely lucky in swinging. I'm not bragging, I'm just stating facts. The pendulum could've just as easily swung the other way and exposed me to relationship horrors that would've melted my face faster than Toht looking at the Ark. It's all about who you meet. The same way an early relationship can color your outlook on future relationships in "real life," in swinging it's far magnified. Because we just don't have all the media in the world telling us how to navigate this thing. We're already scared going in, walking into that first bar, for those first tentative drinks with our first swinger couple. We're scared shitless.

Excited, sure…very…but still asking ourselves those big questions. Can we do this? Should we do this? Is this even legal? What if they don't like us? What if we don't like them? Good lord, what if we're not attracted to them, or they're not attracted to us; this is all about fucking, isn't it?

Let me be quick to tell you to get a grip. It isn't all about fucking. It's just almost all about fucking. The rest is about awesome friendship.

There is a vast sea of one-time wannabe swingers who never got past their first furtive glances over the fence at the neighbor's swing set. Whose first dates in the lifestyle went badly, or at the very least not great. On behalf of our lifestyle, (even on behalf of those who I'm sure would rather not be represented by your old friend Cooper S. Beckett) I want to apologize to them.

I want to apologize for the pricks, the ones who take advantage, the fakers (*Adult Friend Finder*, I'm looking in your smutty direction), the cheaters, the liars, the bare-backing-pressure-giving folk. I'll admit that last one wasn't as well said. To all those I mentioned: you're what's wrong with swinging. You're the ones that make people hate us. Because you all ignore the fundamental central conceit of our lifestyle.

Open and honest communication.

Though some of you may just be pricks.

Seriously, that's all there is. Open and honest commun-ication is the secret. At all times. That's what elevates those who practice it. That's what makes this lifestyle possible. Because rather than cheat on our partners, we choose to acknowledge and be honest about the urges that lie (per-haps not so) deep inside us.

These poor folk who open themselves up to other couples, and get stomped and fucked over, will have a very different opinion of the exact same community I'm so tremendously fond of; all because of that bad apple that's trying very hard to spoil the bushel. But it can't unless we let it.

We swingers who have the positive experiences need to demonstrate what our lifestyle and community is all about. That we can be honest and genuine, and that we seek the goal of fun and enjoyment for both ourselves and those around us.

Now I've been taken to task in the past for generalizing that swingers are open minded and positive and honest and genuine. Call me naive all you'd like, but I know what my little corner of this world looks like, and it is full of awesome, sexy, smart, interesting, funny, genuine, and honest people. We can't be the anomalies. These swingers are everywhere, and they represent the ideal. What we all should be striving for.

I implore those who got thrown off the horse the first time, by a less than ideal first swinging situation, to give it another go. There's a good chance that if you give it a solid second try you'll find someone who'll treat you the way you want to be treated.

Don't give up and get discouraged.

And when you find that community, the good people, the honest and awesome swingers, feel free to tell us *all* about the liars and pricks.

Because it's high time our community started to take out its trash.

17

LIKE A COUPLE OF TEENAGERS

THE JOY OF MAKING OUT

I'll admit that I haven't really spent a whole lot of time making out since, say, college. I remember the first time I made out with a girl, in high school, in the basement, while my parents had guests over upstairs. Guests who were well aware that me and my new girlfriend were going downstairs to make out and who made a point to talk loudly every time they passed the basement stairs, loudly pondering whether they might come down, giving us that jump to separate sides of the couch moment. That night we "watched" two movies, but made out until our lips were sore in the dim flickering light of a 20 inch CRT television.

When we grow up, we get distracted, don't we? Especially as swingers, we tend to make out for a few minutes, but then hands are here and there, and before long tongues are in anuses. Or is that just me? Maybe I skipped a few steps in there, but I think my theory is sound. When you're very likely to fuck on the first date you tend not to devote a lot of time to the simpler niceties that really should be given more focus and attention.

Because making out is a fucking blast.

I've had a few swing partners who have really loved

kissing, and since I love it too, I'll spend more time making out with them than others, but still nothing compared to what awaited me upon exploring polyamory and relationships. When I first started looking around for poly girls to date I went out one night with a former swing playmate but on what I thought was likely a poly date.

"You'll know it's a poly date if you don't have sex," was the thought that came to me from my poly guru, Shira B. Katz.

I'll admit it'd been roughly twelve years since I last had dates that didn't have expectations of sex, or at the very least Dirty Sanchezes. I kid, of course, nobody likes the Dirty Sanchez.

Because of this long hiatus, and because of a pretty successful couple years of swinging, I'd really forgotten how non-sex-dates go. I'd forgotten how to do the build-up, forgotten how to adjust the barometer of relationship that doesn't stampede down the sexual brick road.

All that being said, it's not like I'm immediately thrusting my cock inside my dates. I'm skilled at long and detailed foreplay. The dates just rarely involved extended making out without...other stimulation.

On multiple poly dates I was reminded of the simple pleasures that come before the foreplay. For the first time in twelve years I made out until my lips hurt. What a glorious thing, to spend the hours kissing and mingling tongues. To return to those moments of fevered groping outside the clothes, to experience that fleeting connection through two layers of jeans. We forget about this, and it's a shame.

So I'm trying to relish it across the board; with my partner again, with my swing playmates who enjoy the art of the kiss, and with my poly relationships, who will kiss for hours, before grabbing me by the dick and pulling me down the hall to the bedroom.

I encourage you to slow things down for a night, be high-schoolers again, to make out and have some heavy petting and dry humping. It's a glorious experience that connects us to our youth, to ourselves, to our partners, and to a point in our life where we weren't all jaded cynics who don't even blink at the words "anal fisting."

Yep. Anal fisting.

Enjoy it.

18

GREETINGS FROM THE DEEP END

Swinging, as a lifestyle, affords moments unlike any other.

Watching a gorgeous, sexy girl wielding a nine inch silicone cock, putting it to another gorgeous, sexy girl who happens to be your partner, is one of those moments that is almost indescribable. Unique in every sense of the word. One of those moments where you lean back, and after thinking "It's good to be me," and "This is amazing," you begin to think "This is the deep end! How the hell did this happen? How did I get here? One minute I'm swimming around in the three foot shallows and the next there's strap-ons and fisting."

I'd always been jealous of the glamorous people, those people we see on television and in movies, the rock stars, the celebrities. Then I realized that so many of them seem to have poor monogamous relationships. Even nice guy/role model Tiger Woods: great at golf, bad at marriage. Bad at communicating. Bad at "figuring it out." They have regular monogamous relationships; at least until they fuck them up by cheating, by lying. Don't get me wrong, plenty of swingers cheat and lie as well, but by and large these people, the beautiful people, the elite, the key players in our nation, they don't have what I have: open-ness, honesty, and sexual freedom.

And damn wouldn't they be jealous of me for having it?

It's a fascinating idea when put that way, because we, the open, are the elite in this case. The (approximately) one in seventy people who identify as swingers. We are the ones who can make them jealous, because we've figured it out. We've learned how to play this game, to do this unique and coveted dance out on the raggedy edge of sexuality. One where we can be ourselves, where we can be honest about what and who we want, and where we can, by and large, find likeminded friendly people who want nothing more than to pleasure us and themselves in all manner of filthy ways that'll bring us to the office the next day with a smile we cannot explain because we still can't believe it happened to us and not in some letter to Penthouse. *[Deep breath!]*

"Dear Penthouse, I never thought this would happen to me..."

I've known that I lean toward some idea of open for about the last ten years. For nine of those I sat idly by and said nothing, did nothing. For the very reason that I'd wager more people don't experiment. Simple words, a simple phrase, heard all around the world: "My husband / wife / partner would never go for that." A phrase often accom-panied by a deep sigh. These words are spoken to us and swingers like us, when we regale friends with stories of exploits the likes of which they didn't know even existed outside of Cinemax After Dark.

That's what interests me most about that statement: that "they" would never go for it. "They" being the prim and proper, the good girls and good boys, the friendly, the Christian, the upstanding citizens, the husband, the wife, the partner, the *they*. But all of us are "they" to another. I know for a fact that people have thought this about me, that I would never go for it. We think, beyond a shadow of a doubt, that the answer to "what about swinging?" would be "what about you get the fuck out." There's no way that my partner would be interested in threesomes, or group sex, certainly not double penetration with a tall blond in the back and her husband in the front. No Siree, not a chance!

That's why the key to it all is communication. When you ask a long time swinger what keeps it going (besides the sex with others, that's a given) it's that they talk to their partner, and each understands where the other actually is. It's not about this perceived reality of their partner, a perceived reality where, like the Madonna/Whore complex, I could never smack her ass or call her a bitch and pull her hair till it hurts the way she likes it (because she wouldn't tell me she likes it). I could never tell her I want to eat her cunt, nice girls don't have cunts, they barely even have pussies, they have vulvas that must be treated with respect. Right? Right?!

If my partner is the Madonna and I'm presented with a potential mistress that is the whore, that's a Relationship Extinction Level Event there, isn't it? Mistress here can be anything you like, from an actual in the flesh affair, to phone sex, to cybersex and sexting, to even looking at porn on your computer while you pull your own cock or diddle your own clit. Those fantasies in your head can get pretty dark and scary sometimes if you're not willing to open yourself up to your real sexuality, to look it right in the face and admit to yourself, "I'm looking for *this*."

Admitting these wants and needs to yourself isn't the most important step, unfortunately. The most important is that rough patch, the admitting it to your partner, the one who would never go for it, whatever it is. The sweet and innocent, or the angry and jealous.

So many things can go down when that admission happens, where you specifically tell your partner that you're having trouble because you've been wanting to see what it'd be like to fuck other people. You flinch and wait in that interminable silence, regretting what you've said, wanting to take it back so desperately. To go back to the way things were, to the quiet internal thoughts. You'd even be willing to go back to the self-loathing.

But sometimes they say "I've been thinking about that, too."

What is it then, that separates us from the glamorous people jumping from bed to bed and collapsing seemingly every relationship that they start?

I can't state enough how important real communication is. Not just talking and honesty, but being up-front about what you really think/feel/want. It may feel pretty shitty to tell your partner you've been thinking about other people, but it's far shittier to just go fuck the others.

Look at me, proselytizing, spreading the good word of communication all over this land of ours. Of course, I'm not saying that everyone who talks about swinging with their partners can become swingers. In fact, you'd better be prepared for that conversation to blow up in your face. I'm more speaking about knocking down those perceived walls between you...the "I don't want to upset" wall, the "They're not dirty enough to be into that" wall...all these things which may not actually exist outside the confines your mind.

'Cuz it was communication that brought me here. The deep breath, the let-it-go, the say-what-you-want. That's what led to nine inch dildos and DP. That's what led to many of the greatest friendships I've ever had. That's what led to, for the first time in my life, the feeling that I was where I was supposed to be, body, mind, spirit. I finally figured it out.

And all I had to do was *get over myself*, take a deep breath, and jump into the deep end.

After all, you can't get wetter than wet.

PART II

THANKS FOR SWINGING BY

1

ZEN AND THE ART OF SWINGING

OR HOW I ACHIEVED EQUILIBRIUM

That title makes it sound like I'm going to explain something to you, or take you step by step through a process, doesn't it? I'm not sure I could do that.

I am going to tell you that I feel enlightened. I feel calm and comfortable. I feel like, for the first time maybe ever, I understand a great mystery about male and female interaction that I never quite grasped before. But before you ask, I don't think I could put it into words at the moment.

"Real nice, Coop," you say. "So you called us all here to say nothing?"

Not "nothing." This is gonna be a bit of a stroll for me as I sort of center around a concept. It's well known that I have a problem with expectations, the want for something to happen that almost becomes a need, but it wasn't until recently that I realized how powerful that drive within me is. How strongly my brain pushes its expectations.

I was having dinner with a friend in the lifestyle, ostensibly to help him with his own troubles, and he wound up giving me a great bit of insight into myself.

Forever, at swinger gatherings, I was playing some sort of a Bizarro version of *Beat the Clock*. Early on I was at a swinger party that quickly paired up, my partner found

some action, and somehow I got left holding the metaphorical purse. Ever since then it's been a race against time to
partner up so as not to be the "last picked" or last man
standing. If I didn't find connection or fuck or whatever, I
felt as though I'd "lost the night."

And, as any lifestyle man will tell you, we all lose the
night, except when we win.

So my friend, over some scotch, told me of a trip to
Vegas with an evening involving a several club bar crawl
where he did very well with the ladies without even trying.
Fascinated, I asked for more.

"Because we were going to these other clubs, I wasn't
worried about making any big moves all night. I was able
to just talk to women, flirt a little, and they came to me."

It was the removal of the "end game goal" because
there was always a "next club." The concept of removing
end game entirely fascinated me. And when I said goodbye
for the night, he went home to think about the things I'd
said, and I thought deeply about those comments.

I'd been given the key to a lock I hadn't even realized
was there before, and the next night was the first swinger
party I'd been a guest at since that fateful night that almost
destroyed the entire swinging experiment in one fell swoop.

I committed to myself that I would go in without end
game in mind. That I was arriving at 8pm to a party that
generally goes till 4am. There's no need for quick plays, for
pushing, there's really not even any need to hook up. We're
there with friends, and my partner promised not to leave
me holding the purse.

"I've got your back," she said.

"I love you," I said, "Let's go sexin'."

It's entirely possible I didn't say that and instead it's just
a quote from a John Waters movie I happen to really enjoy,
but that's neither here nor there.

Once inside, I found that for the first time I didn't feel
nervous. I didn't have the pressure cooker going. I was able
to say hello to people, and have some wine, and mingle

and talk with friends, and introduce myself to people I didn't know. To tell women they're beautiful, glad hand, talk websites, talk movies, talk sexy, really get to know people.

And somewhere along the line I was fucking a girl doggy style on the kitchen floor with people enjoying the view, thinking "How the *fuck* did I do this?"

I didn't.

That was the key. That was the piece of the puzzle that'd been eluding me and it makes sense and looks really fucking obvious looking back now because it's not a new insight. My interest was ambiguous. Not obvious, not needy, and because of that, I was alluring. Me! Cooper Beckett! Being told, "I want you to fuck me right here!"

I know, I know, the readers of this website seem to have a misguided belief that I'm some sort of überswingen. But no, no, I wrestle with myriad insecurities that hamper that status on a day to day basis. But this, this was a breakthrough. Later in the evening, it happened again, with another girl I'd flirted and chatted with, gave a momentary kiss to, now on the bed, panties down, asking me to fuck her.

I marveled that the seeming secret to having control of yourself in this lifestyle (perhaps in any) is to allow yourself to relinquish control. As soon as I stopped trying to hook up it suddenly became easier than I ever imagined.

Taking my newfound realization a bit further, on a play date with a close friend I was having difficulty reaching orgasm from a blowjob. After a while I had difficulty maintaining the erection. I could sense this happening for a number of reasons including the amount of wine I drank at dinner, the very full meal, the very long day. In the past these moments of what I'd considered failure were terror inducing. I'd close my eyes and try to talk some sense into the cock. As nothing I told it made a difference, I only would become more and more panicked, and more and more stressed.

In this moment I told her "I don't think it's going to happen, and it's okay, I'm not worried about it. This feels amazing, and I'd love if you continued."

I don't even know where the words came from. It was as though I was telling myself this very thing at the same time I was relaying it to her. It's true that even in the past when I've had trouble, the sensation from the handjob or blowjob or whatever was happening at the time was always wonderful. I was just spending too much time stressing about things to notice. But here I was completely extracting the perceived end game from the proceedings. And you know what? Even though I didn't come, I had a wonderful time as always, just this time with none of the stress of wondering "Why can't I come?" or "Why am I not hard?"

So what am I saying? Sometimes the greatest insights are the ones that seem bleeding obvious to you after that moment of ostensible enlightenment.

Maybe I'm trying to tell you that you can do this too. 'Cuz I'm a fucking neurotic and a paranoid. My brain doesn't know how to turn off to just enjoy. It sits there and evaluates and reevaluates over and over until I can't focus on anything except the questions in my head.

But I did it. I hit Zen.

I turned the questions off and enjoyed the ride.

Now go and do likewise.

2

ON SWINGER EVANGELISM

I grew up Catholic. I feel that this experience is the direct through-line to who I am today: someone who's rebelled against the inherent nature of Catholicism, but mostly against the associated guilt. When my Catholic school, in fifth grade's laughable sex ed curriculum, said, "If you masturbate, you go to hell," they lost a follower. 'Cuz I'd just discovered this awesome thing that my body could do.

Telling me that I'm going to hell for that? Fuck 'em.

Over two decades later, I'm confident that if a Catholic hell does happen to exist I'll be there to dine with you all. Because let me tell you, I've done my fair share of coveting my neighbor's wife. Of course, I've also fucked my neighbor's wife, so I guess there's a special level of hell reserved for me. I mean, Dante told us that the mastur-bators get turned into trees and eaten by Harpies, so…that's weird.

But that's all miscellany. This is the curious case of Cooper Beckett, who seems to not employ the shame about his lifestyle that a lot of swingers feel. He sees the potential for emotional growth that a lot of swingers don't.

"Shame?" you ask. "The swingers? Do tell."

It's not shame at what we're doing. It's knowledge that

they wouldn't understand. Substitute pretty much anything you'd like for *they*. Your employers. Your family. Your friends. Your school board. So these swingers, living with the shame, hide their true nature. This is a lifestyle that is pretty much still entrenched in the closet, wedged somewhere in the back behind the garment bags.

For me it's a little different. For whatever reason, my shame quotient is far lower than most I talk to. I decided as soon as Marilyn and I realized we weren't just dabbling, we were changing our lifestyle, that coming clean to our friends was a good idea. That way they wouldn't find out from other people. That way they'd understand why we weren't around as much. Then they wouldn't feel like we were keeping dark and dirty secrets from them.

Most of them gave us, "Well, we're happy this is making you happy. Now let's never speak of it again," and left it at that. Which was fine.

A few friends drifted away, which is certainly sad. But for the first time in my life I felt like a whole person, like I wasn't hiding anymore. I'd been hiding from myself, the world, from religion, from oppression. I knew who I was for the first time, a new sexual being in the universe, discovering what hedonism has to offer. And I liked it.

I soon came to realize that a lot of people don't know that swinging still exists. For the public at large swinging conjures the 1970s, key parties, wife swapping, days before AIDS. The bygone artifacts of what the love generation of the '60s became when they grew up. And who's to blame them? What indications do they really have that swinging is alive and well? The only non-monogamy ever talked about in mainstream media is the ubiquitous threesome that all guys want and all sitcom women like to tempt their men with so they can laugh about it over cosmos later. There's only one mainstream media example, *Swingtown*, set in the '70s. A nineteen episode series cut down because CBS wasn't ready to be HBO. (And I highly recommend picking that one up)

So, you have a general population where an estimated 1 in 70 are swingers. That statistic that you've heard from me before was pulled out of my ass after reading a bunch of books on swingers. I believe it came from *The Lifestyle: A Look at the Erotic Rites of Swingers* by Terry Gould. That said, since so many swingers deal with the shame, it follows that most statistics involving them are meaningless. I guess that means I could just invent numbers. Like a bajillion. Within that population you have a small, small chunk who knows about those swingers. Then you have those who're shocked and appalled and implore you to please think of the children! But you have a majority of the population who're blissfully unaware.

Those are the interesting folk to me. While a portion of them would slide into the shocked category, some would ask, "Really?" I'd want to answer that question with a strong "Yes," and a smile. A wink. A comforting squeeze on the shoulder. Something to reassure them that we do exist, that these thoughts they've been having about that couple they have over for drinks every once in a while aren't evil. That there is possibility of extramarital fun without cheating.

I'm sure, should swinging be suddenly thrust into national consciousness, there'd be all sorts of bible thumping, wringing of hands and gnashing of teeth, talking about the sanctity of marriage. Movie stars can live crazy hedonistic lifestyles and we find it glamorous, but if the couple down the street does, well, that's just a dirty shame. So, they'd go on and on about how what we're doing violates the sanctity of marriage while they're off lying and cheating to fuck people outside their relationships.

I can't help but think that I am better than them.

I acknowledge my imperfections, my lusts, and I share that with my partners. A study revealed that, promised they'd never get caught, 74% of men and 68% of women would have an affair. I actually have a citation on this one: InfidelityFacts.com. Though in fairness, *they* don't have a citation. That should be shocking to anyone who still thinks we're meant to be monogamous.

So I spread the good word. I am evangelical. Part of the bonus of being open with your social circle is that people will come to you and ask how it works and if it might work for them. You can give them honest, open, and reasoned advice about it. The beautiful thing is when you're no longer afraid to talk about sex, people will go out of their way to ask you about it. Because they often have no one else.

What people want to hear more than anything else are the words, "Don't worry. It's okay. You're not bad."

3

NSE: NEW SWINGER ENERGY

We often hear about NRE, New Relationship Energy. Even if we don't know the term, we know the feeling. It's that battery super-charge you feel when you meet someone new. It happens to all of us. You want to see them as much as possible, you relish every advancement in physicality and emotion. It's the thing we're chasing when we're single in the vanilla world. And when we're not so single anymore and the NRE has faded into background noise, it's the thing we often miss most. For me it was the first kiss that I missed most; that uncertainty, that buildup, the moment where the first kiss would not be held back anymore and faces drifted together. I treasured that. In my monogamous life it was what I yearned for most because I knew it could never happen again in monogamy.

One of the most exciting things about becoming a swinger isn't even really the sex.

"Hey now, Coop, don't be sayin' things you can't take back!" you say.

But I grow weary of having imaginary conversations with imaginary readers in the middle of essays so I give you the cold shoulder and continue my point. Of course the sex is exciting. The sex also brings along with it the allure of new, different, unique. But by default, for me, the most exciting thing about swinging is being able to live in almost a perpetual state of New Relationship Energy. Keeping everything from growing stagnant and dull, keeping excitement up and reinvigorating you. I've cultivated a wonderful group of playmates that I see regularly. But as schedules fill up and jobs/family/etc take up lots of time for friends, I always keep eyes open for the new and different. This is something we're specifically not allowed to do as monogamous folk.

I've noticed that there's another level to it, beyond simply meeting new couples and developing new relationships. There is the New Relationship Energy that you feel with new couples, new playmates, wanting to spend time with them, exploring their likes and dislikes, their turn-ons and offs, their kinks and quirks. There's also something else that has the potential to crop up with each new relationship.

New Swinger Energy. (You may not have heard of this one 'cuz I made it up.)

After you've been swinging for a long time, it's tempting to get a little jaded. Well, it's not so much tempting as just happens. The lifestyle isn't all shiny and new anymore. You're no longer feeling that "Oh my god, we're doing something really unique!" feeling because you've been living it, breathing it. Just like a regular vanilla relationship, your relationship with swinging is settling into its own sort of routine.

I don't want anyone to misunderstand here. Swinging has never felt dull to me. It has never been what would be considered routine in the vanilla world. Even routine swinging is far more exciting than anything I ever did as a vanilla boy. But it is very easy to settle into whatever your routine is. If you go to clubs every Saturday night, that's your thing, it's expected, it's done. Same as having a swing date every Friday. You probably have some amazing hot sex on those nights, but it may lose some of the pizazz.

The pizazz is the shakeup.

It's why people in long term monogamous relationships tend to chase younger, faster, more exciting people to have affairs with. They shake up the status quo. They introduce a little new, a little exciting, a little strange into the mix.

Every once in a while you'll meet a playmate or couple that you connect with in such a way that it not only activates your NRE switch but also flips the far more elusive New Swinger Energy switch. They put in a fresh set of batteries and remind you what it was like to be young, naive, newborn swingers—eyes wide and mouth agape at the world you stumbled upon, where your hedonistic delights were suddenly of utmost importance. After their first date with an awesome couple, we swingers often start fucking our partners like teenagers again, as though a light had been shown into the very core of this lifestyle, and reignited that flame at the center.

This is the difference between New Relationship Energy and New Swinger Energy. With New Relationship Energy you wind up creating an intense connection with your new playmates, and you want to spend all the time getting to know them. New Swinger Energy actually does something very unique. It turns the process back in on itself like a hall of mirrors. Your relationship between you and your primary experiences the spark and the pizazz is back. You find yourself taking new sexy pictures, updating your web profile, fucking like bunnies again. The very same spark most of us felt that first week we were officially considering ourselves swingers.

We all know that the lifestyle has its ebbs and flows and that your personal lives and relationship with your primary will also have peaks and valleys, but those who make the suggestion that New Relationship Energy is superficial are missing the point. It doesn't matter if it's superficial or even that it is artificial because your brain has just turned on the happy juice in your body. It's what gives you a very real high, the glimpse of euphoria that we so rarely get to see in life.

When swinging is at its best, it's not what you do with the other couples that matters nearly as much as what you're doing with each other. Is it new, is it exciting? Are you experimenting? Are you using these relationships with others to reconnect in your primary relationship, which sits at the heart of your swinging lifestyle?

Every time you can flip that NSE switch and remind yourself of the exciting realities that what we're doing is amazing and that our lives aren't like other people's, you solidify the foundation on which you're building.

4

SAFER SEX WITH COOPER'S KIT

My name is Cooper Becket and I am a germophobe and a hypochondriac.

These two things have combined to make me very paranoid about sexual encounters in the past. Previous sexual encounters, that is. I'm not talking time travel. I was never paranoid enough to take precautions beyond condoms, mind you, but paranoid enough certainly to panic and worry for days after new encounters to see if I'd develop symptoms.

I'm reasonably certain that this was not a healthy thought process.

There is the acknowledgment as swingers that we are taking on a level of acceptable risk in this lifestyle. This activity we're doing carries with it a modicum of risk. But then we can line this activity up with other activities we wouldn't freak out about doing that also have risk. Like, oh, say, driving. Smoking. Drinking. Boating. Skydiving. Level of risk may have elevated there, but you catch my drift, I'm sure.

When I went to my first non-monogamy conference there was the promise and potential of a lot of sexy fun time. I confronted my anxiety, my hypochondria, and my germophobia, head on. After all, is an activity really worth doing if you're going to experience extreme anxiety afterward? All of these other risks that we choose to take (like skydiving) tend to have a finite risk period. Once you get back out of the car, your odds of being killed driving that car are far lower than when you're actually driving it. Some might say they're beyond low. Those people would be right. Math rules! With sexuality and non-monogamy, the risk may not continue after you've been with someone new, but the chance of something new showing up in the days, weeks, and months out, well they're much higher.

This thing we do carries risk. Most of the risk is rather benign, and most of it easily curable or simply mildly irritating. After all, you say The Clap (does anyone really still call it that?) and people go "Huh? What?" But you say "Antibiotic resistant gonorrhea of the throat," and we've got a panic on our hands at the Fourth of July.

It's possible I just slipped into some *Jaws* geekery. Let me wade back out. See what I did there? Wade. Water. *Jaws*. Never mind. For a neurotic like me, antibiotic resistant gonorrhea of the throat was the last straw.

So I put together a crack squad of safer sex aids that come with me to every single event that has even the most remote potential to descend into sex. Come along with me, won't you? Let's explore Cooper Beckett's Safer Sex Kit! (-it -it -it -it. [that's my echo.])

1. CONDOMS

Duh. I mean really, if you're not traveling with condoms you're doing this wrong. I'm firmly in the camp that everybody who enjoys the company of penises, either their own or those belonging to others, should always be traveling with condoms. If all involved have condoms with them, the phrase "man, I don't have a condom, are you okay going bareback?" will never need to be uttered. I use Trojan Magnums, and that's not me telling you for the sake of bragging (though it *is* a bonus), it's me telling you to remember the fact that not all condoms work for all people. This is why my safer sex kit contains several specifically for me as well as some standard sized and slim condoms, some lubed and unlubed, some flavored, and some polyisoprene for those who are allergic to latex. The unlubed and flavored are great for blowjobs. You know, 'cuz of *Antibiotic Resistant Gonorrhea of the Throat*. That fucker.

2. DENTAL DAMS

Yep, I've got several different brands and types of dental dams, some flavored, all latex. I've used these. I don't mind them much, they're good in a pinch. I've just found the latex often feels quite thick and distancing, which is interesting considering how thin condoms have gotten. (It's worth noting here that a condom can be slit up the side and laid flat to be used as a dental dam.) My preference for oral barriers is Saran Wrap. Let me put a huge honking disclaimer on this. The FDA has *not* approved Saran Wrap for preventing the spread of STIs. Because, why would they? It's fucking Saran Wrap. I cannot promise you that this is safe sex, 'cuz I'm not a doctor or a researcher. What I can do is tell you that I've had several very prominent members of the community tell me they use Saran Wrap, as well as some very smart people pointing out that Saran Wrap can keep liquids and scent from passing through it, therefore it stands to reason that it can prevent viruses and bacteria and fluids from passing through. All of the above said, I take comfort in using Saran Wrap, because it's thin, it's clear, you can have a massive sheet of it (which allows you to poke and prod it around, as well as lick both the front and back erogenous zones) and, well, no one can deny that it's much safer than non-barriered oral sex, which is what I was doing. Having licked my fair share of pussies and assholes through Saran

Wrap now, I can tell you that while I miss the taste, cleanup is certainly easier, and there's far less anxiety. And I do as many things as I can do to cause myself less anxiety.

3. LUBE

Is lube really a safer sex thing? Well, yes. Lube prevents friction which can compromise the integrity of the barriers you're using. Lube inside a condom before a barriered blowjob. Lube on the pussy or anus side of an oral barrier. Good stuff. Some of the better lubes also come in packets. It's nice.

4. GLOVES

I love gloves for sex play. Perhaps it's because I go into scientist mode when I snap them on. My kit contains both nitrile and latex gloves in three different sizes. Gloves can be wonderful for any and all levels of insertion, as well as for creating a smooth hand for a massage, as well as simply keeping lube off your hands. As much as I like lube for sex play, I hate applying it with my uncovered hand, because then I never know what to do with that hand, still lubed up. And sometimes it winds up on the wall. I wonder what the hoteliers thought of that hand-print. As a fan of anal play, the gloves also help remove some of that squick factor.

MY CHOICE IS TO USE ORAL BARRIERS, AS WELL AS condoms for penetration, as well as in-depth discussions of testing and histories. This is what I need in non-monogamy to feel safe. To be risk-aware. This is not to imply in any way that if you're not going to the same lengths as I am you're somehow lesser. We all should be free to follow whatever level of safety we are comfortable with. But we also must have that conversation, and absolutely must disclose if there are things to disclose. Because we need to take up the fight together for our safety as a community. Acceptable risk is acceptable risk, and this type of lifestyle is incredibly enjoyable and rewarding.

And you know what? Sometimes when you tell a girl you have a safer sex kit in your Go-Bag, it gets her all hot and bothered. Then you get to use it, and that's groovy.

5

PISS OFF, JEALOUSY!

At last the question: is it possible that jealousy is a choice?

I very rarely get jealous. When I do it's not for reasons that most of America gets jealous. I've watched my partners with others. Foreplay, flirting, conversation…these are the personal intimate moments that would drive most people crazy. But for me there's very little jealousy in that.

When my partner and I first started swinging, the first time I saw her with someone else, it struck me how *not* jealous I was. That concerned me for a tic. Why aren't I jealous? What's wrong with this situation? What's wrong with me? Luckily I didn't dwell on this long, as a certain beautiful curly haired girl was vying for my attention. It came back to me later, as I sat in the aftermath thinking about the evening, our first evening in a brave new world. This question: why wasn't I jealous, and what did that mean?

Why does it have to mean anything? My lack of jealousy was not a commentary on my relationship and the quality inherent in it (or lack thereof). It just was. Flashing forward to a play party where my partner got all sorts of attention and I got none. The jealousy came in waves.

Sweet blind rage jealousy. The "get your stuff, we're leaving" kind. The silent treatment in the car kind. Oh yes, jealousy, there you were. I wasn't broken. I did have feelings, I did care, clearly. But, aha, this jealousy wasn't about that. It was petty, childish. This was because Cooper didn't have any fun and he felt he should have if other people were going to.

I thought about that a good deal. I began to realize that trust is an antidote to jealousy, as long as it's real trust in your partner. The other antidote is confidence. As I began to become more confident in myself, my sexual abilities, my emotional availability, I began to be less and less concerned about these things that might "make one jealous."

Since then I really haven't felt the jealousy. An occasional pang here and there, perhaps, but I really have come to believe that jealousy can be moderated...muted.

It's not about repression either. I'm not suggesting that if you feel jealous you should bury that deep down inside, or grin and bear it. That would be like packing down the black powder. It may be more compact and less noticeable, but eventually a spark's gonna set it off.

That may not be a thing. Don't know anything about black powder 'cept what I've seen on *Mythbusters*.

What I think you can do, though, is when feeling that pang of jealousy, recognize that's what it is. Once you do that, you can analyze it. That's the hard part, of course: pulling the handbrake on that surge of emotion and saying, "What the fuck?" But that's where the solution really lies. It's the exercise burn. You gotta get there to move beyond.

Because once it's recognized, and you look deep down at it, you can see it for what it really is. For me, it was just leftover from high school and being left out.

And that's silly, isn't it? I mean it's a real emotion, and it's something I felt, but I didn't have to allow it. I didn't have to go with it. At the last minute, instead, I made a sharp left turn and used that moment as a springboard for a discussion of our rules as a couple, something that was patently necessary. But the best thing about this recognition moment, is that you can decide what to do with it.

I know! It's a rough suggestion. Jealousy is, like anger, an overwhelming emotion. It sets up shop in the center of your brain and says: "Fuck it, I'm in charge!" But just as most of us have learned to control our anger over the years, and haven't resorted to the option of anger management classes, jealousy can also be controlled. Like anger, jealousy is based in fear. The difference is that while our society helps teach us how to manage our anger (you know, take a breath, count to 10) we've been encouraged to nurture our jealousy.

It's what TV shows are about. It's what mainstream America wants us thinking about, building in our minds. Jealousy of gadgets, money, the sex we can't have with the people we're not with. Jealousy isn't just encouraged, it's *The Fucking American Way!* The tide can be turned, however. The change can be made. I've seen it.

Jealousy is like fire: the less oxygen it gets, the smaller and smaller it gets, until it's nothing more than a wick. Unlike those other emotions we've been taught to repress, killing the spark of jealousy won't make us dead inside. No, jealousy only becomes the flashing warning light that indicates you clearly should sit and think on this issue a bit, wait for calmer heads to prevail.

'Cuz maybe, just maybe, it isn't as bad as you thought. Maybe you were just being silly. Maybe after all is said and done, you trust your partner completely…that she won't run off with that guy she was flirting with at the bar, that he won't suddenly feel that sex with you isn't as good as sex with others. It's trust, it's confidence. It's the road to compersion.

6

HOW TO MAKE THE MOST OF
A SWINGER HOUSE PARTY

How do you make the most of a swinger house party?
Go in with no expectations. Next?

So, again I try to boil down an answer to a single sentence that turns out is true but not so simple as one might imagine.

Were you really imagining that it might be simple? I may as well just tell you that the answer to how to deal with jealousy is to not be jealous.

Luckily, I've evolved to know how to better deal with housebound play parties. So, step one, evolve. Hmm, perhaps not instructive. Or constructive. And rather dickish.

The evolution has taken quite a bit of time. I'm well into my sixth year of this thing called swing, and have attended quite a few house parties over the years. I've come a long way from the night I sat on a couch until 1am playing the long game that amounted to the saddest hand job in the world while my partner had the time of her life.

It's still terribly hard *not* to see a play party guest list as a menu and formulate a plan in your head about who you'd like to connect with that night. I'm not using that term as a euphemism, either. It's important to recognize that no matter what level of sexuality happens with any given party goer, you're connecting. From a "How was your week?" around the buffet table (the actual food buffet, not the dildo buffet) to having four fingers inside a lovely woman you met an hour ago, you're connecting.

So, step one, connect with people.

That "no expectations" part up top follows along with the connecting and checking the guest list. Expecting to fuck someone, regardless of the reason for the expectation (previous dates, verbal commitments, naked selfies) puts you in a precarious position if that doesn't pan out, and adds a whole lotta possible resentment. It also leaves you vulnerable to self-loathing if, for whatever reason (even your choice), you don't play with anyone at the party. I guess step one is don't expect to fuck anyone. Because then if you do, Yahtzee!

The bastard stepchild of the no expectations thing is "Try not to make plans." Making plans is just begging for things to fall apart. Worse, because plans usually involve someone else, you've got multiple people expecting something to happen. Disappointment can reign supreme if that falls apart. It's also tempting (and crass [and I've done it {many times}]) to make plans with many people. Especially if you only go to parties rarely, so only see these people rarely, and feel like you need to make the absolute most of this party by spending time and connecting with everybody you possibly can.

Which can be fun. It really can. But you're ultimately short changing them, and yourself.

"Fuck you, Coop!" you say, beginning to slur your words. "I can play with several girls at a party, get them all to orgasm, and come several times like the god amongst men that I am."

Let me set down my keyboard and give you a slow clap.

Slow and steady.

So yeah, sure, you *can* do that. Having once boasted on twitter about beating my previous party record of four women in one party by fucking five (this is not an explanabrag, btw, I'm actually mildly embarrassed by this tweet) I can tell you that it's pretty epic. But my for-real time-spent with these women was rather worthless and my cock was hard only because of the over the counter, surely dangerous, knockoff Viagra. Getting up moments after the pop shot to move along to the next person…fun? Yes. Fulfilling? If I'm auditioning for a Michael Fassbender role, sure.

Man he was great in that movie! And Carey Mulligan!

I really don't mean to harp on people who play that way. Good on you! Suck the marrow and so forth.

I just get a lot more out of parties now.

I realize that I sound an awful lot like an older man telling a teenager that he shouldn't just fuck around and should instead appreciate his girls, while said teenager is just pointing to his non-chemically-enhanced erection as he dials tonight's date on his cell. Hrm. Realizations suck.

But seriously, I do. Two things happened to get me there. Step one, forget your personal definition of sex if it only involves penetration. Step one, learn to enjoy not having sex.

Lots of step ones, eh? Well, it's all the most important part.

"Fuck you, Coop. You know you used to be a kick-ass sex writer! What happened?"

Let me be *very* clear, irate and belligerent reader (whom I understand is in my head). I very much enjoy that whole having sex with people at play parties thing. And I have had sex with someone at every play party I've ever been to. But enjoying *not* having sex is key to enjoying the entire party.

There's so much awesome at the best play parties. People in sexy outfits, great conversations, even some fun games. Seriously, when was the last time you played *Spin*

The Bottle? It's pretty awesome! Then there's watching people have sex, because voyeurism is participation. Then there's seeing what toys are in play for the evening. There's meeting new people who may go on to be the greatest sex partners you've ever known.

I know, I know, the best sex you have is with your partner (Coop makes jerk off motion).

There's meeting those people you've been flirting with online and finding out that they may be extremely hot, but when they talk it's just *fuck no*. So many wonderful things and times to be had between the sex at play parties.

And that part about letting sex be any sex act and not just penetrative? Just make that change. I promise you'll be happier, or your money back!

So really, how to make the most out of a swinger party? You ready? It's *really easy*.

Step one is to recognize that, like any other party you've ever attended, the party will be defined by many things: the location, the people who attend, your mood, your partner's mood, your paramour's mood (since it's non-mono), the traffic to and from, the booze supply, etc. But ultimately it's what you make of it.

And having no expectations. Because when was the last time you stormed out of a birthday party because they didn't make your favorite fucking kind of cake?

I didn't think so.

And if you did: asshole!

7

THE MYTH OF EQUALITY

E quality is a myth.

Or at the very least an unrealistic expectation, or goal, or whatever. Don't strive for it 'cuz you ain't gonna get it. And the quest will simply get you. You know, like the fountain of youth.

Maybe equality was within you, and the real quest was for yourself, and in the end—

"Cooper. Let it go," Sean Connery says.

Good call, I was losing track of my metaphor. But I stand by my first statement, that equality in swinging and polyamory, really any form of non-monogamy, is an almost unreachable goal. The most obvious reason it's so difficult to obtain true equality (i.e. I get this so she gets this) is the inability to really define or quantify what we're all getting out of this whole non-mono racket.

So many swingers have this if/then logic in them at the beginning. From the first soft swap experience, in fact. "Oh, my partner got her pussy eaten so I should be able to get my cock sucked. They're all kissing over there and I'm just sitting over here with a hard on looking grumpy." That trail often degenerates to a run of this on the way home:

"What's wrong?"
  "Nothing. I'm fine."
  "You don't sound fine."

Passive aggressiveness, resentment, and sometimes divorce follow. But perhaps I'm exaggerating.

As someone who has felt this in the past, though—my partner got to do something awesome, I wish I got to do something awesome, so clearly it's my partner's fault for not making sure I also got to do something awesome—I get it.

I don't *like* that I get it, but I do. I also don't like that this wasn't just a "once upon a time" thing. I've felt those feelings as recently as *Swingset Takes Desire 2013*. While I'd love to report I did the grown-up swinger thing and recognized them, processed them, then acted with compersion, I didn't. I had a freak out. And a snit. And other things that make me sound like a child.

It's all just us feeling left out.

This is why we feel the need for equality. Or strive for it. Or pretend it's actually something achievable, this myth that somehow things will be equal across the board and no one will ever feel left out.

I suppose that's the thing…the wakeup to reality moment…the fact that at some point, one of us will feel left out, and at another point the other will feel left out (and since this is non-mono, and so on and so on and so on). Because nothing will truly be equal, from that first moment of touching other people's naughty bits, all the way through the number of other people you fuck, to the number of dates you went on last month vs the number I went on.

Sometimes the numbers will be in my favor, sometimes in my partner's favor. What we have to strive to remember is to be happy when our partner is living it up and doing great, because we want our partner to be happy when the same thing is happening for us. If we can't do that, it all just descends quickly into chaos.

Compersion is the key, learning to be happy that your partner is experiencing pleasure of any kind, and trusting that at some point you will too.

As long as you go after it, that is. It's not your partner's fucking responsibility to bring you a sexy playmate and put them in your lap and reach down and insert bits into bits. You need to be the master of your own fate on that front, kiddo.

But it'll never be equal.

8

SWINGING WITH EYES WIDE SHUT

I have not attended a single swinger party that even remotely resembled the somber, moody, and frightening affair depicted in Stanley Kubrick's posthumously released 1999 film *Eyes Wide Shut*. It seems to be the not-so-secret desire of many a swinger to throw one, and it's often the case that when a swinger party or an openly sexual party is depicted in film and television it has a distinctly *Eyes Wide Shut* feel to it.

In the film, Dr. Bill Hartford (*Tom Cruise*) is thrown into a jealous snit (like how I belittled jealousy there?) after he and his wife Alice (*Nicole Kidman*) have a pot enhanced discussion about a man that Alice could've fucked (but didn't) on a vacation they had.

The very thought that she could've had sex with this man, and considered it, throws Dr. Bill's entire world into upheaval. He stumbles off into a very strange dreamlike version of New York City, finding an old friend who invites him to The Party. When people talk about *Eyes Wide Shut* they talk about almost nothing else, not the strangely amusing travels of Dr. Bill, who uses his medical license like a badge to get into places, who almost picks up a prostitute but then cannot, who accidentally breaks up what's either an underage pornography photo shoot, or a strange and creepy father selling his young daughter to associates.

No, what everybody wants to talk about is The Party.

The amusing thing is that even if you haven't seen *Eyes Wide Shut* you've seen this party in one form or another. It's the one with the people wearing Venetian masks, and the password *Fidelio* (ironically meaning faithful in Italian), the one with the strange Jocelyn Pook music, the blindfolded piano player, people in robes and hoods, digitally inserted silhouettes to block the fun. It's a party that quickly turns dangerous for our hero Dr. Bill, and not even flashing his medical license can get him out of the fact that he's an uninvited stranger in a strange land.

What's always fascinated me about the film is that there are really two parties with dangerous sexuality in them. The first is the party of Bill and Alice's friend Victor Ziegler (*Sydney Pollack*), a prim and proper party on the surface. Beautiful people having beautiful conversations about beautiful things. Not far beneath the surface a prostitute has OD'd, one that was the invited guest of the illustrious host. This party hides and pretends that there's nothing untoward going on. No overt sexuality, nothing wrong here. No, officer, I didn't see nothin'. Whereas party two, the masquerade, wears its sexuality up front at the expense of everything else. There are no faces, just bodies; no conversation, just fucking.

It's the two wild extremes and we swingers dance down the middle line between polite society on the one side, screwing around behind closed doors, doing incredibly debauched things and repenting on Sunday morning, flogging themselves for their sins. Then there are the unrepentant hedonists on the other, raising pleasure even above personal safety.

I watched series one of *Secret Diary of a Call Girl*. In the second episode Belle, played by the ultra-sexy Billie Piper, is hired to escort a man to an exclusive sex party, and this party instantly struck me as a mash-up between the two parties in the film. From the draperies of white twinkle lights and black-tie dress, very much reminiscent of Ziegler's party, to the plush and dimly lit rooms and rampant orgies of the Fidelio party. This is the party I want to have some day, when I have a space. A party where people can look their finest and still get down and dirty.

The best part about The Party is that it combines the elegance of the repressed and fighting-to-be-sexual vanilla world with just enough debauchery before it swings all the way around the horn and becomes dangerous. But that's the dream world swinger party, the masquerade...it's for the über rich. I'll just have to make do with sexy people doing sexy things and loving it.

I'll get by. Somehow.

But if anyone wanted to invite me to a party that maybe had a password like *fidelio*, I'd go. Just sayin'.

9

HAVING GREAT
GODDAMNED EXPECTATIONS

I t seems to me that there's a sort of swinger equilibrium, achievable after a few years, that I am only just now beginning to understand. That of managing expectations, and being able to say the words "no expectations" to potential play partners. For a long time this has been a struggle for me. I've found myself with intense desires revolving around potential playmates that lead to high level disappointment when these relationships don't progress, or turn out to be one-nighters, or if the others involved simply don't want the same level of involvement (emotional or physical) that I am offering.

It can become especially true when I feel a strong intellectual connection at our first meeting. When we've had a good talk, when we've flirted, when I think it's going really well, only to find, "Well, Coop, ya may have misunderstood that one." Rather than assume that the issue is something on their end that caused the dynamic change, I've turned it inward into a "what did I do wrong?" spiral. Even as I've done this, I've seen it's most definitely not the healthy way to go.

Case in point: I met some newbies at the local swinger

friendly bar on swinger night. We had a couple of drinks and some good conversation, established baseline mutual interests, and there was a reasonable assumption of attraction judging by the tongue she kept pushing down my throat. As we call it a night, they insist that we'll have to get together soon, mentioning reconnecting multiple times. So I go home and, high on the excitement of potential, drop them a line on *Lifestyle Lounge*.

Nothing.

I can see that they read my email, no response. I go over it all in my head, looking for the fissure, the thing that changed everything. But this was one of those cases that I couldn't pinpoint anything I could've done to take it from "We *definitely* have to get together, kiss me!" to no response. I was told by more experienced friends that I should chalk it up to newbies being newbies. They are, after all, notorious for flaking out/changing minds/being inconsiderate. Namely because it's sort of understood that newbies don't know any better. The advice was: "Don't let it get to you."

They were right. Let it go, it's not me, etcetera.

But I'd seen so much potential in that interaction. Close in age, had no kids, looking for the same things out of the lifestyle. They'd obviously been into it in the moment. So it was a bummer to say the very least when I finally did hear from them with a "We're new and didn't know how to respond to your interest in us. I don't think we're looking to meet up right now."

Why tell you this story?

Because, I could've just as easily not obsessed over any of it. Stuck with the "no expectations" mantra. I say just as easily when this idea is anything but easy, especially at the beginning. I still have the "rejection equals bad" mentality of the general dating scene where you're searching for a mate. Rejection is part of life as a swinger, part of the game. Show me a swinger who doesn't get rejected and I'll loudly tell you that *you've got nothing*! That's what the "no expectations" realization is all about. Looking at every potential meeting as "Cool people that we met one time" instead of "Really bitchin' people we want to be best friends with and fuck for the rest of our lives."

This was about six months ago now, and in the interim, I've been working hard to find that "no expectations" paradigm. It's elusive, to be sure, but when I make plans now, I don't assume sex any longer. The best "no expectations" suggestion that I've heard is when going out on a first date with other swingers, all you should expect is a great dinner-date with your partner. That way, even a full-fledged flake out and stand-up can't muck up your evening. If they show up and you don't click, you got to meet new people. If you click, new friends. If you click and play, you had a great night together.

This way, if you manage to make that elusive four way connection and take it all the way to Swingtown (population: you) with multiple dates and a (dare I say the R word?) relationship, it'll be the ice cream on top of that brownie sundae. I don't usually use food metaphors, guess I just want dessert.

This is, of course, far easier said than done...and seems to be a skill set that shows up after a couple has spent a good amount of time in the lifestyle. I think that this is due to some of the "wait, you mean we can really fuck other people?" novelty wearing off. Once you've really-for-real come to terms with this lifestyle, what it is, and the wonders it affords you, you'll find it opens itself up to you in many strange and interesting ways; from the ability to dramatically lower expectations (with the goal of eliminating them almost entirely) to the ability to partake in more advanced swing-play, like separate rooms and even solo dates.

There seems to be an overall mellowing mindset that settles in between one and five years as a swinger, allowing you to push your boundaries, explore your kinks and fetishes, stomp jealousy down into an ever smaller container, and all but eliminate expectations.

Because once we do that, *everything* is simply about having fun.

10

AGEISM IN SWINGING

L et's face it, we all have hangups. Regardless of the legitimacy of these hangups, we often will let them color our feelings, interests, and ideas.

When we're new swingers, we tend to have some very specific ideas of who and what it is we're interested in. What body types we like and don't like, what activities we like and don't, what age range we're okay with and find attractive.

I'm not saying that any of these ideas are bad, or that you shouldn't trust your gut, or that any of your thoughts about your attractions and interests are incorrect. But one of the things that I felt most strongly about at the beginning, and was most incorrect about, was my attraction age range.

My early vanilla dating was always within a couple years. Then when I became a swinger, I put a ten year range on my profile. I figured, as a 29 year old at the time, I'd stay in the legal range on the bottom, and 39 didn't seem nearly as scary an idea as 40.

The first two couples I interacted with were right in this age range, though both on the higher side. But the first woman I actually had penetrative sex with in the lifestyle was in her late forties. The experience was amazing, life changing, and quickly made me question my ideas about what I then considered "older people."

Through her and her husband I met many amazing people, most falling into the fifteen years above the high end of my intended range. (i.e. 40-55)

We have certain ideas of how older people act, what they believe, how they play, how they fuck. The bottom line is that the swing community is heavily weighted with people in their forties through sixties, and under twenty five. It's rather telling, in fact, that the generation that grew up hearing that sex could kill you (twenty-six to thirty-eight) is finding itself underrepresented in the non-monogamous community. The incredible range of ages in swinging, however, really exemplifies the idea of experimentation and new experiences.

The longer people do this thing called swing, the more they tend to relax their ideas of what they're into and allow themselves to explore. It's because we are often very myopic at the beginning. For many, opening up in non-monogamy represents their first steps into any type of non-traditional exploration.

The real lesson in all of this, though, isn't not to have a type, or a thing, or a desire. It's not to close yourself off to potential wonderful moments because of a temporary idea of beauty, of attraction. Our tastes evolve and change, especially as we encounter people that challenge those tastes.

Ageism is a very real issue in ethical non-monogamy. The issue is especially apparent in this lifestyle because of the relatively small size of the community. Profiles can get rejected out of hand because of ultimately inconsequential things like five extra years, or a little extra weight, or any of the many superficial things we think about when deciding to pull the yes or no lever on a potential playmate.

I can state that, without a doubt, if I had stuck to my initial range, or even an extra ten years up on that range, I wouldn't have had some of the most enjoyable and intense play sessions of my life. One of the best playmates I've ever been lucky enough to play with turned 56 yesterday.

And I'll rearrange life for a chance to play with her again.

11

THE SEND OFF

This is my least favorite part.

The "there's no spark" part. It can happen at many different times in a relationship with another couple, and it can be for many different reasons, but if you're on either side of a comment of that ilk, it's pretty sucky.

I've been on both sides, gotten the "We decided to just be friends" both before and after an intimate date. With one couple I was fine with "just friends," with another I wasn't. I suppose it's all about what you're after in the lifestyle. Many swingers will say "Who needs conversation, this isn't a relationship, it's fucking!" For them that might be very true. These are the ones who leave an open "booty call" advert on their favorite lifestyle site to see who might show up. These are the ones who are proud when they rack up over 100 notches on their bedposts in less than three months. Oh yes. They've bragged this.

But who am I to criticize how others want to spend their time in the lifestyle? That's their thing. A good percentage of self-described swingers probably could not imagine why I want to be close friends with my playmates, get to know them, have long term (oh god, there's the phrase) relationships with them. For me, it's a no-brainer, I couldn't imagine it any other way. The one frivolous one-night-stand of a night I had left me feeling a bit empty. The idea of doing this intimate and awesome thing with someone and then not seeing them again (except perhaps a nod and a smile at the bar) was really a bummer.

All this makes it so very hard to say those send-off words, whatever the reason. I'm invested at this point. I've usually spoken to the couple online a few times, and we've likely had dinner or drinks together. Or we've agreed to meet at our weekly swinger hangout bar and after ten, fifteen, twenty minutes of talking to them the realization hits.

No spark.

Which reminds me of a time in high school that I used that exact same phrase to brush off a girl I'd met online and didn't find attractive. I felt uncomfortable about it then, too, because I knew it was sort of a bullshit way of just saying no.

Because we can't usually just say "I'm not interested." And even though we may want people to say that to us, when we hear it, it's jarring, upsetting, personal. I definitely have an objective desire to have people be honest with me, and just say that they're not attracted to me, but it still hurts when it shows up.

So, we tap dance. "I'm just not feeling it. We're not looking for another couple right now. There's no spark."

We're trying to say that intangible thing, that general feeling we get when it's just not working. Often it's nobody's fault. One couple is no more responsible than the other. Many couples simply vanish. Why? Because it's easy. Cut off communication and eventually, the amputated couple will get the hint. It's the most painless way for the cutters, but those cut off are left to wonder what exactly they did wrong, even if it was nothing. "It's not you, it's me" may very well be the case.

What can we do? We all know that in this lifestyle (and

others, I suppose) your first inkling is going to be pure physical attraction...more so than other lifestyles since your goal is mainly sexual, if not entirely. I want to be friends with my playmates, but in swinging mode I surely do also want to have sex with them!

When you walk into that bar for a semi-blind date (photos rarely do justice, especially when they don't include faces or are out of date) and it's just not there, you share a drink, have a nice small talk based conversation, but then somebody has to grow a pair and say, "this was great, but I don't think we're quite compatible." Hopefully the other couple will understand, thank you for the meeting, and move along. Hopefully they won't ask, "Why?"

Even harder is when you've had those drinks, maybe fooled around a bit, spent some time, and then when all is said and done, just realized you have nothing to talk about. What we're attempting are relationships to be sure, but not romantic relationships. When the send-off happens, there isn't a deep emotional failure, you haven't got a crater inside you with some irreconcilable difference in it. It's a surface thing.

I've said goodbye to interesting people, I've said goodbye to sexy people, I've said goodbye to naughty people, and never has it been anything more than that nebulous "no spark" that I used to feel bullshitty about way back when. It's true, because no spark can mean a myriad of things. But when the chips are down it means the same thing: "I respect you enough to tell you to your face that I don't think this is going to work between us, but I'm not going to get into a discussion of fault or shortcomings because that would ultimately not make anybody happy."

Then you wish them well and send them back into the fray, where hopefully they already have another potential couple on the line, and in a month's time you'll just be another vague memory.

Maybe not even that.

12

CHANGING RELATIONSHIP DYNAMICS

One of the most difficult things to manage in non-monogamous relationships is the changing dynamic you can develop with your external relationships. How is this different from serial monogamy? Dynamics change there too, after all. Well, the primary difference is that you're often dealing with a number of different dynamic changes at the same time, and unlike in monogamy, these changes don't always lead to the termination of relationships.

The most fundamental difference is that one relationship doesn't end to make way for another. These relationship dynamic changes can change the nuance of a relationship without ending it entirely. This can be wonderful, and allow for a dramatic range of different relationships, energy, and connection in your life at a single time. The difficulty arises, however, when you feel a change in the dynamics (from sexual to non-sexual, from non-romantic to romantic) and your partner does not, or the others sharing that relationship with you do not.

I've encountered this issue most in a four-way swinging relationship with my partner and another couple. The four-way (couple on couple) relationship is by far the hardest dynamic to sustain, and the one that can most easily go awry. I have experienced a change in interest, where we begin a relationship with a couple all on the same page, but over time things begin to change, and one of us is no longer interested in a sexual relationship with the corresponding member of the other couple. This is hard as the person whose feelings have changed, as we know how it feels when someone who was interested in us, is no longer.

I know this has caused me a lot of anxiety, because so many factors go into that connection, that sexual dynamic, that emotional dynamic. I analyze like crazy, wondering if it's just a slight change in my mood, or a mediocre evening, or something independent of the relationship that's causing feelings to temporarily change.

When this happens, I try very hard to not be rash, to not make quick decisions that will affect others without a great deal of thought. On multiple occasions, a temporary shift in interest has changed back over time and all that was needed was a break. This isn't always the case, of course. Sometimes relationships just change.

The important thing is not to panic. Not to over analyze.

The beauty of non-monogamy is the ability to have all levels of these relationships at the same time. You can have romantic relationships and sexual relationships and intimate relationships and regular friends. This flexibility is why you shouldn't make snap judgments, why you shouldn't rush to end a relationship simply because your feelings have changed today.

It may be hard to discuss that change, to tell the people your feelings are different. It is especially hard in swinging to take a sexual relationship back to a friends-only relationship. This is a conversation that very easily can feel like a breakup.

If your feelings do begin to change for a couple, or a single person, from whatever variation on a relationship you have to something altogether different, then you need to give it that time to recognize if it truly is a permanent change in your feelings or one of those fleeting things that occasionally come up.

When the feelings are permanent, and you know you're not going to be sliding back into that old dynamic, then you must have the conversation. Don't just avoid the other person, especially if this dynamic shift is part of a four-way connection, because this can cause damage to your partner's relationship with them as well. However, if you are a couple who only plays together it's far more complex, because ending your physical relationship will in effect end your partner's physical relationship as well.

I'm not saying that you should continue in a sexual relationship or romantic relationship that you aren't feeling simply to allow for your partner. One of the biggest rules I have is to never take one for the team. I would recommend using their relationship as an added bit of information for you to consider and weigh when deciding how you are going to react, how you are going to adjust your relationship.

A friend of mine has felt at times that he needs to make broad sweeping moves when relationship dynamics change, or aren't fully realized. I've cautioned him against expecting too much from his relationships, against looking at them as needing to be something that they simply are not.

The facet of non-monogamy that is most intriguing to me is that it provides for relationships that don't need to be everything at all times, like a monogamous relationship is "supposed" to be. Without the requirement that your partners and playmates need to fulfill all your relationship needs, be they sexual or romantic or supporting, you can have relationships with smaller quantities of these qualities. Sometimes all a relationship needs to offer is a shoulder to lean on and a quick occasional fuck.

When a relationship changes, we don't need to over

think it. We can move from weekly to monthly visits/fucks. We can add a little romance here and there. Revel in the variety that is offered to us under the umbrella of non-monogamy.

And again, don't panic.

13

HOW TO HIDE A SEX SWING

So, you've done it! You've purchased a sex swing! You've gone ahead and joined the ranks of...people with sex swings. It's safe to say you're not playing at the amateur level anymore. Congratulate yourself on your excitement, your perviness, and most importantly, your willingness to hang yourself (or others) from the ceiling. Most people don't give it much of a thought when purchasing the swing, but in order to make sure no one crashes to the ground and hurts themselves, you're going to want to put a big ole eye hook in a beam in your ceiling.

By doing this you are making a bold statement, and one that most people, even in the vanilla world, can figure out. Something big gets hooked there. Looking around your bedroom will likely yield nothing in the way of punching bags or other miscellany that might be hung from it.

But what're they doing in your bedroom anyway? Narrowing their eyes, clucking their tongues, and knowing exactly what you get up to in the wee small hours, that you get incredible kicks from things they'll never know. This is not their business. They have no right to form negative opinions based on this newly discovered information. We all make sometimes significant concessions to friends and family in what should be our private space. Or at the very least only open to those who wouldn't mind (or those who would immediately call "dibs on next!")

Humbly, I suggest you tell them to fuck off.

I'll assume, however, that since you are reading this essay, you'd like to know how to hide a sex swing. Throw it in the closet. Hidden.

[Cooper brushes his hands and walks off. Yes, now he's putting stage directions in his essays.]

Oh, the swing isn't really the problem, you say. It's that eye hook that you ran over to Home Depot to pick up. The massive one. The one that's going to gleam its stainless steel gleam from your ceiling, daring your guests to wonder what its nefarious purpose might be. And it's not like it's the seventies or eighties and you could just throw a macramé planter on that bitch.

So, what're we going to do?

Step 1: Buy a sex swing.

I'm going to just go ahead and assume you have this step covered. If not, why don't you go ahead and take care of that. I'll wait.

Step 2: Determine where to hang it.

This is important, because you want to have freedom of movement as well as floor space for partner two to stand to, um, put it in, fit it up, do one or two odd jobs. (Name the movie/play and win our prize: Cooper's voice on your home answering machine.) The other part of determining where to hang this swing is figuring out the support structure. So find a stud, then ask him to use a stud finder to find the stud in the ceiling. Drill your hole, screw that eye hook in and hang that swing up. Why? Because then you can do step 3.

STEP 3: FUCK IN THE SEX SWING.

Oh c'mon, you've been waiting long enough, don't you think? Parents aren't coming over now to inspect your bedroom ceiling after all. Hang the swing, throw your partner in it, and go to town! This is also a good opportunity to check your aforementioned freedom of movement. Because you want to make sure that this thing is in the right place for real. If not, sadly unscrew that bolt and add spackle to your next Home Depot shopping list. Then repeat Step 2.

Well, then, you're done! Congrats, you have a sex swing that you've fucked in. That's gotta be a sexual bucket list thing to check off, right?

Wait, what? Oh. You're not ready to tell your parents to fuck off? Or the niece that likes to lay on top of all the coats late at night on Thanksgiving? Gotcha, well, we can't all be as belligerent as I am. You're probably better at that whole "winning friends and influencing people" thing. Don't worry, we'll move onto phase two of this project.

HOW TO HIDE A SEX SWING EYE HOOK

STEP 4: BUY A SMOKE DETECTOR.

This one is easy. Remember that this thing won't actually be detecting smoke, so don't read the box to find out its features. The only burning it'll be detecting is the one in your loins in that soft-core-porny way. With that in mind, just head over to your local dollar emporium and pick yourself up the finest piece of shit smoke detector you've ever seen. Just make sure it's as deep as your eye hook's eye.

STEP 5. BREAK THAT SMOKE DETECTOR.

Open that bad boy up and take out its guts. You don't want to have to change the stupid battery on this thing after all, or spend an eternity trying to ignore its incessant chirp. Pull out as much of the electronics inside as you possibly can. Drill a hole in the center with that same drill bit that you used to start the hole in your ceiling.

STEP 6. ATTACH SMOKE DETECTOR TO THE CEILING.

Line up the holes (something you should be relatively good at, being non-monogamous [didja see what I did there?]) and screw that thing up. Something else you should be— oh, never mind. Odds are that eye hook in the center is going to be more than enough to hold the smoke alarm in place, but if not, go ahead and use the screws that came with it.

STEP 7. FUCK IN THE SEX SWING.

Do this again to celebrate. Also to make sure the shell of the former smoke alarm doesn't crash down upon you.

STEP 8. HIDE THAT SEX SWING!

Throw the sex swing in the closet (or possibly the laundry first, depending on how filthy you are, and how washable your swing is) and put the top of the smoke alarm onto the base, hiding the eye hook and creating a perfect camouflage. No one will be any the wiser. You know, except that firefighter guest who notices there's no red light to indicate that it is working. But then you could always show him its true purpose. And seduce him.

Just a suggestion.

14

I AM A BISEXUAL MALE SWINGER

This may qualify as old news. Or even as "duh," for most of our readership. For the past few months I've made no secret about my distaste for the double standard against bisexual males in the swinging life-style, where women are encouraged to be bisexual and men are discouraged from even hinting that they might be interested lest it lead to being (as Shakespeare would've pronounced it) banish*ed*.

What I haven't done, though, is go ahead and talk about my journey on this issue…mostly because it's ongoing. There are things I have not done, chiefly having anal sex with another man, but having had a couple of male/male experiences now, I think I can say that I'm a 2 on the Kinsey Scale, and that I enjoy playing with men and women alike.

This qualifies me as officially bisexual (cue confetti, and maybe Rip Taylor), though I don't have a romantic interest in men, nor much interest in kissing them, so I imagine there'll be some who will argue that I'm still in the bi-curious category.

I've long postulated two things. One, that many girls are turned on by two guys playing; and two, that more guys would be up for experimentation if they knew their girls would get turned on by it.

That theory was called into question by some friends last night. He is very curious, and bisexual play is something he wants to experience. His wife, on the other hand, has seen him kiss another man, wasn't impressed or turned on, and is concerned that she will find him less attractive if she sees him play with another man.

I was asked for my advice. My partner had been unsure how she'd feel about seeing me playing with another guy. The big sexual paradox: you often don't know how you'll feel about playing outside your comfort zone until you actually do it, and at that point the damage may have already been done.

The bisexual urge has been with me for a long time, drifting in and out of my consciousness for most of my adult sexual life. Sometimes it was something I was more interested in, sometimes less, sometimes not at all. It was usually disconcerting due to the same issue that plagues other bi-curious men: the questioning of my sexuality, which I thought I had a reasonable handle on.

When I first got into the lifestyle, I saw how the women in my social group embraced their fluid sexuality. How for many, playing with a girl was something of an epiphany; that they could actually do something they'd always wanted. Their bisexuality so often became an important part of their personas, a cornerstone of their sexuality, a defining characteristic. Naturally, I wondered if it might be the same for me. Would I take to bisexuality like a newfound piece of me that had so far been missing? Would I dislike it enough for the pendulum to swing entirely the other direction?

When a couple I met early on in the lifestyle revealed that the mister was in fact bi, it was decision making time. I was concerned that if I tried it and I didn't like it, or reacted badly, it would cause an issue between me and good friends. I decided that this was not the time or the situation.

Women I've spoken to who haven't seen guy/guy action are ambivalent, uncertain that they'd react favorably. I think that this is common, since male bisexuality is so rarely seen in any form of popular media.

Except for *Torchwood*. *Everybody* wants to fuck Captain Jack Harkness.

Once I made the decision that I wanted to try, to explore this further, I began to build up nervous energy. I reached a point where I just wanted to get my first experience over with so I didn't have to think about it anymore. I had, after all, gone from monogamously-and-heterosexually-married, yet closeted-and-repressed-curious, to now-open-swinger and curious.

My first real experience with another man was unplanned during a MFM threesome, a spontaneous evening that included oral and hand jobs between he and I. The erotic details of this night can be kept between us three as I tell you that what matters about this event is that it didn't hit me in a dramatic fashion, negative or positive. I left that night feeling that I'd just done something interesting and fun, happy I'd added something new to my repertoire.

But this was not a game-changing moment for me.

I've never had strong sexual attraction towards men. I can easily acknowledge that a man is in fact attractive, but never have I felt the "Oh man, she's hot!" feelings I get for women. When I was asked by a friend if the men I've played with were hot, the best I could muster was, "um, yeah?" I think this comes from the same place as not being interested in kissing men. I can understand why women want to kiss other women, it's the same reason men do, they're soft and they smell good and they usually taste very good too. I don't get it with men. If I was a woman, I don't think I'd be interested in kissing guys.

I think it comes down to this: I like an occasional cock

mixed in with the sea of pussy. It shakes things up, it's fun to play with, and it doesn't really have much at all to do with the person it's attached to. If they came attached to women, I'd want to play with those instead, yet shockingly the trans community isn't lining up to sate Cooper's bi-leaning interests.

What the realization of bisexuality has caused me to do is dramatically reevaluate my prejudices and come to a far more open place personally. The bisexual "communities" have venom coming at them from all sides. The vanilla/straights exploit bisexual girls for their enjoyment, the lesbians dislike bisexual girls for playing both sides and then finding the safe haven of marriage. Gay guys tend to disbelieve there's any such thing as a bi guy, that it's just a rest stop on the turnpike before Gaytown, and straight guys, well they don't want bis near 'em any more than they want gays near them.

I do realize that the last two sentences are wild generalizations, but you can't argue that there isn't a significant chunk of truth to them. Not to mention Dr. Ruth insisting, in a jaw-droppingly huge case of running off at the mouth, that bisexuals don't actually exist. She has since recanted this flagrantly foolish statement, but one gets the feeling she only recanted because of the overwhelming tidal wave of bi that crashed down upon her.

It's an uphill climb as the reviled bi male. But in my own little corner of the world, on my little swingset, maybe I can provide that safe haven. Affect the change. Give permission to want what you want. If nothing else, maybe I can promise that *Life on the Swingset* is a place where you can be bi. Because for a lifestyle that revels in the bisexuality of its female members, they can be awfully prickish about the opposite sex.

That needs to change. Bisexuality is, after all a shade of gray, and we all know that nothing is black or white.

15

KISSY FACES

The concept of tokenization is not lost on me.

I get that swingers, especially at the beginning, might want to hold something back; something unique to just their "marriage bed," something for their primary partner alone. It makes sense, I get it. I have friends who don't swing in their bed, to them the bed is as sacred (to use a word I hate due to its religious connotations) as the acts that happen in it. This makes sense to me.

See, I get it.

I don't get the "no kissing" thing, though. Browsing profiles on *Kasidie*, I'm inundated with people saying kissing is a must, what's the fun without kissing, kissing is the most important part to me, and on, and on, and on. Then a few profiles creep in, maybe 5-10%, saying kissing is fine, as long as it's not the opposite sex. Or kissing is fine, just no tongue. Or the only thing off the table is kissing.

I'll be the first to say that everybody has a right to have their rules that make them feel comfortable. Rules can allow us to do this thing that we do, this complete breaking of tradition. Rules are important, they're helpful, they make us bolder, happier, safer. But I just don't fucking get this one.

And I blame Julia Roberts.

Well, not really Julia's fault, aside from the fact that she was so damned good as Vivian in *Pretty Woman* that she caused all of America to completely forget the fact that she's a prostitute (not a profession generally embraced by mid-America. I, on the other hand, love sex workers) and accept everything about her. She only kisses for love. Fucking, yes. Lots and lots of fucking. But no kissing. Not on the mouth anyway. Neck, sure. Tits, bring it. The lips down below? Why not? But surely you can't kiss on the lips, 'cuz that's for...I dunno, Prince Charming? It was a Disney movie, after all.

Regardless of the tokenization theory, I don't believe that anyone would have this rule if they hadn't been told by someone (Julia Roberts, other swingers, etc) that kissing on the lips is somehow more intimate than, um, having a load blown across your cheeks. Or double vaginal penetration. Or, hmm, airtight.

Let me throw the thing that infuriates me right the hell out there. "It's fine as long as it's not the opposite sex." What the fuck? How do the women in the lifestyle not let themselves be offended by this one? This doesn't imply, this outright says, that the act of two women kissing is less important, less "real," less intimate than a man and a woman kissing.

Another I've encountered is "Kissing is fine, just no tongue." The sentiment didn't bother me because they were newbies and feeling their way (and she was really fucking hot) but once I got in there and tried to play this way... Have you ever tried this? Go on now, go find your partner, start some fucking, and kiss, but no tongue. Every kiss was like one of those creepy brief familial kisses. And these kisses have no business being in a play situation. It was actually far easier to do the whole no-kissing-at-all thing than this weird plan. Luckily, they felt weird too, so the next visit real kisses were perfectly acceptable.

Let me restate, for the record: whatever floats your boat.

You don't want to kiss play partners, don't kiss play partners. That's fine. But sit back for a moment and think about why you're really doing that. Remember, the same intimacy things have been said far more often about sex than kissing. And if I were to go up to a friend and kiss them it'd be far more acceptable (though likely still surprising) than if I went up to them and put my cock in their hands. Intimacy isn't about the acts. If it were, we'd all be hemorrhaging intimacy all over this swing lifestyle of ours.

Intimacy is the bond you share with your partner. The "she's coming home with me" feeling you can hold onto. The idea that the one thing none of these other playmates can or will do, is be your partner. This is your connection. You sure don't need to artificially construct it by hypothesizing that kissing is somehow more intimate than your cock in that very same throat.

Think about it.

16

TAKING ONE FOR THE TEAM

It has been quite some time since I've taken one for the team.

The short answer to your obvious question, "What does that mean?" is playing with someone you're not interested in because it will allow your partner to get laid. I suppose it could also extend to playing with someone you're not interested in because you feel sorry for them.

Now that's a bummer, isn't it? That whole previous paragraph. It's why the easy thing to say is, "Don't take one for the team. Ever." But that's quite a short essay. Wouldn't even reach 100 words. So let's go deeper.

I have taken one for the team, and I'm rather certain that at least one of my playmates took one for the team in regards to me as well. The situation is not good on either side, so why would this happen?

Well, if we've been swinging for any length of time really, we've experienced the uneven chemistry that often accompanies dates of two on two. Or two on one, in fact. I'm going to get all heteronormative up in this bitch for a second because it's easier to explain that way. I'm sitting next to a fine woman that I simply have no chemistry with.

Or worse, she seems to feel that there's something there and I'm just sort of smiling and nodding. While across the table my partner is sitting next to a gentleman and they're eye gazing and giggling and flirting and touching and all is going swimmingly.

Most of the times I've taken one for the team, it has been a product of significant issues related to self-worth. I see that my partner is having a good time and I don't want to be the one to fuck that up. I see this woman I'm with is having a good time and I don't want to fuck that up. I tumble down the rabbit hole of "Who am I to turn this woman down? It wasn't so long ago that women didn't talk to me," and so forth.

Later, after the fucking and the cuddling and the good-nights, and the basking in the afterglow drive home where I'm sitting in my own personal shadow, I just feel shitty. I haven't just solved a problem for my partner and created one for myself. I've likely created an ongoing problem for both of us. Because three out of the four people on that play date thought things were groovy, and the one who didn't hasn't opened his dumbass mouth about it.

Now I get to reveal to my partner that I had a shitty time, which'll likely cause her to feel bad about the good time she had. It'll make it hard for her situation to continue and it'll give me a person who wants to talk/flirt/"do this again sometime" when I so very much don't.

It's a whole lotta bullshit.

I think it's because we often look at swinging in that scarcity economy. "What if this is the last chance for us to enjoy ourselves?" Or "This is the last night at Desire." or "It's last call at the play party." They don't actually call "last call" at most play parties, but we all sort of know when it has happened. And we'd better get it together for ourselves, or our partners, or that poor person we're doing this for.

But as someone who has been on the other side, it's

even worse. We get to feel the emptiness, the feeling that something isn't being fully explained to us. The distance. The unavailability to chat. The "Yeah, we're just really busy right now."

Don't do it.

Not under any circumstances.

Don't take one for the team.

17

COMING OUT SWINGING

I'm sorta out about my lifestyle. In the sense that those important to me know not the details of what I do, but know that I am intimate with many different people. By those important to me I mean those whom I might have conversations about sex with, i.e. my friends. I've never said "no" when someone asked me point blank, "Are you a swinger?" and I hope to never have to.

The bottom line is my parents don't really need to know what I get up to in the bedroom, and it's just as unnecessary to tell them about it as it would be to tell them what position I used last night. I am out at work. My boss & coworkers know what sort of shenanigans my weekends often involve and have no issue with it, with the "Don't fuck anyone in the office" caveat, of course. I'm lucky I work somewhere that's...let's just say...strange.

Why did I come out to my friends, then? They also don't need to know about my experience with double penetration. Mainly it was so I didn't feel I needed to hide my new friends from my old friends, or be concerned that there might be cross bleed from the two sides of my world. As it stands now, I can be perfectly comfortable when one of my swinger friends shows up to a vanilla party. Though, understandably, it's harder to convince my vanilla friends to give the swinger parties a try.

The cork is certainly out of the bottle, and the smoke can never all be crammed back in, so I'm ostensibly out. It's a bit of a preemptive strike, too. I read an article earlier this year about a couple in my neck of the woods who were outed by a neighbor. This sad human sent an email to what seemed like their entire neighborhood; friends, family, PTA, local parents, staff at their children's school, etcetera, notifying them of the "swingers in their midst." This horrendous act isn't horrendous just because I agree with the harmed party, it's horrendous because it's an instance of someone in no way affected by something making it their business, and that's a little thing I call bullshit.

This left me thinking about something I've grappled with a lot since opening up. I'm out, but not all the way. I am hiding. In plain sight. With my friends, I'm open, wanting to talk about it, etcetera—but not with everybody. I'm not the model "Oh yeah, I know a swinger, he's pretty normal" guy. We must remember, in times where we feel we're not out enough, that the closet is not a binary. We don't have to be "in" or "out." We can straddle the line.

Coming out is a massive and complicated process. This is why I may still be inside the closet, but the door is open, and I'm shaking hands with everybody willing to shake mine. If swinging seems "normal" because we see swingers around us, then it's really hard to suggest that we're seriously awful people who are going to burn in a fiery pit, etcetera. It is our duty, as non-vanilla thinkers, to stand strong and admit to the world that we exist, that we like these things that we like, that we may be wearing a mask, but we're still here.

I can tell you that being out amongst my friends is wonderful. I can truly be myself without having to worry about someone getting the wrong idea. It has hiccuped my relationships with a few people, and lost me one or two friends as well. But fuck them if they don't respect something I'm doing that has literally changed my life and made me the happiest I've ever been. If you can't respect that enough to accept it, I don't want you in my life.

Am I telling you to come out? Maybe a little. Am I telling you to take care in doing so? Certainly. Am I as all-over-the-map as to be expected at 1:38 on a Monday morning? Probably close, but slightly more coherent. Did I use any brackets? Not this time, baby! One thing I can tell you about coming out is that it has allowed me to surround myself with people who support me, and there is no greater feeling in the world than having that community.

18

OUTSOURCING EMOTION
AND SEXUALITY

The term "outsourcing" certainly fits the idea of non-monogamy being a way to distribute emotion and sexuality outside a binary relationship. It could also be thought of as a rather cold or unfeeling term. Trivializing, even.

I am simultaneously cursed and blessed with the ability to step back and evaluate my emotions and life with a modicum of detachment. The curse of this is I'm often struck by the absurdity of emotion. The blessing is that this objectivity allows me to take a deep breath and change my perspective, sometimes mid-issue.

As a long time believer that we can't be everything to one person (the largest argument for non-monogamy) I also believe that what works on the macro level of full relationship, also works on the micro level. Within the elements of your primary relationship, you can't always be everything your partner needs emotionally, and you can't always be everything they need sexually.

Sexual openness especially benefits those with a wide range of sexual interests. A couple tends to limit themselves to the overlapping sexual interests Venn diagram that they share. Sometimes this yields a smorgasbord of sexuality, other times it yields mild exploration, with certain fetishes and fantasies left unfulfilled.

Interest in BDSM is one of the most common outsource-able sexual interests, because the range of practices within can be very divisive. Thus far much of BDSM play, especially being Dom, hasn't really appealed to me. I'm more than happy to indulge a partner and have some D/s play, bondage, or spanking every now and again, but it's only recently that I've started to find enjoyment beyond my partner's enjoyment. My partners have been very into BDSM, and this was something that I have been more than happy to outsource to friends. Why not? Everybody wins! I avoided feeling pressure to do any specific thing because my partner loved it, and I got plenty of time to figure out where my interests lie within the BDSM spectrum. For those interested, I'm starting to enjoy spanking and looking into ropes, and lean toward the sub side of the spectrum.

This idea is a bit different when applied to the realm of emotions, and a bit more of a touchy subject. Many swingers believe that the "not everything to everyone" concept is perfectly valid when it comes to sex but recoil at the suggestion that the same could be said about emotion.

An important distinction is that I am in no way advocating a wholesale transfer of both emotions and sexuality from your primary partner. They should be let in on everything. The benefit of emotional outsourcing is that you get to share ideas/feelings/issues with a wider variety of people who have a stake in your life and relationships.

We live in a society that still suggests you should keep things bottled up and you shouldn't share, except maybe with your priest or therapist. The wonderful benefit of close relationships is a unique perspective on important emotions and life issues. To share this close relationship with many people gives you a variety of perspectives and can offer comfort, thoughts, ideas, suggestions, and any other variation on emotional fulfillment you might need.

While one partner may react in a progressive way, leading a charge toward solving a problem, another may just sit back and let you vent, or be that shoulder to cry on.

In the monogamous world, we may have friends for this, but I can tell you hands-down that I was never as close to my friends as a monogamous fellow as I am with those in my non-monogamous community. I have this new ability to be unflinching with my non-monogamous friends. This is not to say that certain things won't come up that challenge even the most open-minded companion's ability to remain, well, open-minded. This will happen. It happened to me when I decided to explore the world of polyamory.

But I have found that those moments of "I don't approve" are not only few and far between, they tend to go away much quicker, and I am validated by support, love, and sex.

19

ACCIDENTAL POLYAMORY

FALLING IN LOVE AND BREAKING UP

I t's funny.

You never quite expect how close you're going to get to some people. And you really don't think at the beginning, when you're meeting someone for the first time, that in the future, way out there somewhere, you'll love her. Both of you. The way you loved girlfriends in the past, close to the way you love each other.

People's fears always seem to be "What if my partner falls in love with someone else? What would I do then?" I know it was a concern for Marilyn and I way back in the beginning. When we were young and nervous and new and everything seemed big. The world was different...changed.

Changed with a decision, in fact. But in practice it changed with a kiss.

'Cuz it was she who made us confident. She who made us comfortable. She who walked in effortlessly, her curls bouncing around her smiling face and assured us, without saying a word, that this swinging decision was going to be okay. That yes, we were on a date, a swinger date, with a couple we'd never met, but we could relax. We could be ourselves.

We could rediscover who "ourselves" were.

Details are beside the point. Suffice it to say she introduced us to the world. With a man we'd sooner forget, who disappears from our memory often when thinking on her. So much so that despite the issues and conflict with him that would follow, there was always her, a possibility that we'd never considered.

The unexpected possibility of love, because they say you shouldn't love as a swinger. That it's the purview of the poly folk. Because we're just here for the fucking, right?

Right?

Anyone?

Yeah, we all know that's bullshit. Because while you worry about the "What if?" that postulates the nightmare swinger scenario that I imagine is far rarer than all the worriers believe, of your partner falling in love with someone else, falling in love and leaving you, falling in love and leaving you alone, as you worry about that one, you don't really worry or wonder about what would happen if you both fell in love with the same person.

Time can do such interesting things, can't it? For resolve, for interests, for relationships. Time and time and time. And suddenly you find yourself having the discussion with your partner, that strange discussion that in its first tiptoes wonders what it might be like for the three of you to be a couple. Is that the only way we know how to define this? Might be the only way it'll make sense to us.

We three.

Alas.

Is that why it hurts so much more? Because it was nebulous? It never really set up, did it? It stayed an "almost," an apparition...on the edge of reality, on the edge of happening...so close, yet oh so very far.

Is it better then, somehow? That we didn't have it fully, that we didn't engage, become the triad, become a unit? With questions of what we would say at Thanksgiving if we brought her home to the families, is it better that we never left the launch pad?

Perhaps.

We knew that poly relationships, especially these triads, seem to have distinct shelf lives. That the primary may stay constant, but those in secondary positions often drift in and out. Or is that even the case? I really have no idea. Just that there was this girl, and she made us happy, she enriched our lives for good, whether she remains in them or not.

The events of late steal nothing from those that came before. The moments after that first kiss, through the two and a half years we explored this crazy idea in various capacities, sometimes not seeing her at all, other times when she was sad, other times when we were, times when we were happy, times that were sexy. These are all still with us, not diminished in the least.

They shine brighter, in fact, as indicators of happiness and love.

A love that we never expected, and will never regret. She brought more love into our lives, and into our marriage, and for that we thank her, and wish her luck.

We give her back to the world, and hope it treats her well.

PART III

SPACKLING OVER
ENTROPY

1

THE SWITCH

DOM AND SUB IN A SINGLE NIGHT

I am Dom and I am Sub. Two partners. Two scenes. One night.

Never went there before. Have considered, have tried. Never actually let go.

When I am Dom I know she wants to be humiliated, to be held down, to be called a whore and a cunt and fucked.

When I am Sub, I want to have choices taken from me, to be treated however my Mistress feels I deserve.

Both in a single evening. Both in a city far away and different enough to be a product of my imagination. Both without foresight, without my standard hemming and hawing.

When I am Dom I follow her into her hotel room and put my fingers inside her, my hand tight on her throat. We don't say much, though I leave the scene to ask, "Is this okay?" once or twice. Her moaning fuels the desire to continue, making me hard, making me realize why people like this, and scaring me a bit.

When I am Sub, Mistress tells me she wants to put me on a cross and beat me. These are not words I've been told before. They engender mild panic, out of my element and far from home. But that very distance, and the fact that I stand in front of a St. Andrew's cross when she tells me this, are what finally allow me to just let go.

I've long known I am a switch, if I am in fact anything at all on the spectrum, because I'm not overwhelmingly drawn in either direction. I can be Dom and I can be Sub. I feel I'm just a bit on the sub side of the line, but not far enough that I could never dominate.

That sub side is what holds me back, the "check in" can break the mood. Yet when I am Dom I still command my sub, in her hotel room, to remove her clothes and then mine, like the dirty whore she is. These words are interesting to me, difficult to say were it not for her clear enjoyment of hearing them. These habits that porn has taught us, holding her head against my cock until she chokes, spitting on her, making her feel like an object, these things I've pushed away from, never to do.

This is what my sub wants to feel, and I want to give it to her. Because to be a dom is to give, right?

To sub, for me, is to allow myself to relinquish control of the scene, because in life I'm in charge far too much... of projects, of *The Swingset*, of my life.

When I am Sub I don't even find myself topping from the bottom. I am blindfolded, gripping the St. Andrew's cross. I submit to Mistress SinD. I dwell in darkness, holding onto the rings at the top of the cross, pressed against it.

As a sub, I am flogged. I raise my thumb to indicate that I can take it harder. The mistress maintains contact, and communication, because this is my first submission. I am paddled and spanked. I am slowly stripped in the blackness under the blindfold. I am told that I'm grinning.

When I am Dom I tell her what I want to do, then do it. I make her come as I fill her with my hand. I make her choke. I don't have to hold her down because she fully submits to me. She takes what I have to give her, like a good little whore.

When I am Sub, I have been stripped almost naked,

taken from the cross to the couch, still in my own world of darkness. I'm fondled and fucked in the dark. My mistress lets me kiss her, and touch her, and I'm grateful, as cries of pain and pleasure continue from elsewhere in the room, in the world.

After I come, she removes the blindfold and my eyes take a while to adjust. My mistress is smiling at me, and the scene has ended. She comforts me with touch, and beckons me back to the real world. I experience the joy of aftercare for the first time. It's only when seeing the emptiness of the dungeon that I realize how much time has passed while I was in the darkness, while I was Sub, while she was in charge. I thank my mistress.

When I am Dom we lie in bed, recovering. The moments were rushed and frantic, the way they often are when months have passed with discussion of eventually being together, and distance is no longer an issue. We lie there thoroughly fucked, and take a few moments to reflect and breathe deep.

I realize that I am proto-dom. I am not as rough, or as tough, or as in control as she perhaps wanted in a dom, but not necessarily wanted from me. I feel she got what she wanted from me, as I from her. We just lay there, laughing a bit, turning back into people, friends, playmates. Perhaps this is what aftercare is...the transition, the interstitial between two worlds. I kiss her, and thank her.

When I was Dom I saw that giving and receiving pleasure often don't look as you expect, or as the world conditions you to expect.

When I was Sub I discovered a world where I could let go. By putting myself in that mindset, I learned why subs love being submissive. It's an amazing feeling to trust enough to give over to someone.

On my first night in San Francisco, I was both Dom and Sub in a single night.

Talk about a mind fuck.

2

IN THE BUBBLE

SEARCHING FOR
UNDERSTANDING / AFFECTION / SEX / CONNECTION
IN SAN FRANCISCO

T he weekend is now faded and hazy, as though it has been run through a gauzy filter, or was captured through a lens with Vaseline on it. How did I start to lose it so quickly, and why? Our flight home has been delayed, giving me an extra two hours to ponder, reflect, and look back. But already I wonder if it's possible that everything that I remember happening actually happened, in such a short time at such a short conference. Open SF really only ran two days, when all was said and done. As the clarity of experience is indeed quite brief, and the event so full of the amazing and the unusual, the surprising and the occasionally pedestrian, arguments about semantics and understanding squeezes on the shoulders of those welling up tears at the horrors inflicted upon them in a world full of straights that don't quite understand or care to take the time.

We came to the bubble, San Francisco, the lunatic fringe at the very edge of the United States. We came together to find, build, maintain, and understand our community; to see how we fit together, like the pieces of an unbelievably complex and abstract puzzle, neglected somewhere on the bottom shelf in the back of a Hallmark store.

In the city of broad shoulders on Lake Michigan, we can only catch the most fleeting of glimpses, always just slightly out of reach, of the way San Francisco shines as a beacon of hope that one day before too long we might all, the non-monogamous, the polyamorous, the swingers, the open, the queer, the gay, the lesbian, the transgender, all of us live as we truly are. That vision seems so impossibly far at times, but in a hotel in Nob Hill in San Francisco, I caught a very real glimpse of what that freedom might look like.

Conferences are heightened times when subsets of subsets come together in numbers, in compressed spaces. Emotions run high and strong. Relationships are developed and progress in the blink of an eye. You meet and are impressed by those who inspire you, and those inspirational people may be invited as speakers at the conference, but they're just as likely to be a random face in the crowd that you spend a moment with post-session. They may tell you something deep and meaningful and true, and in their story you can see not just the heartbreak and pain, but the hope and confidence, the festering rage that we have to feel this way at times.

Open SF represented two very important things for me on paper. First, it was an opportunity to finally sit down in really-for-real life with my fellow podcasters, something that had amazingly not yet happened after a year and a half together as a foursome. Second, it was a moment in time where we would put forth our ideas in person to see what people identify with, what speaks to them, and what they find to be tedious, trite, or tremendously off base.

Here it would be, *Life on the Swingset* on display, with its naughty bits right up front, unapologetic and unafraid to be who we are. When we were pondering early on what a presentation by the *Swingset* crew would be like, we touched on the idea of political correctness and inclusiveness. Political correctness in making sure that we always use open terms, and inclusiveness such as recognizing that maybe not everybody wants to be addressed by the greeting, "Hey, guys!" But we wouldn't do that, because it's so easy to find yourself in a pit of garbage language simply from the act of trying too hard. *The Swingset* is made up of individuals who are hell-bent, opinionated, head strong, not always right, and rarely apologetic for the things we feel. And we would all be in the same room at the same time, a thought that intoxicated me, knowing I'd finally be able to put a full corporeal form to Shira B. Katz, that I'd be able to sit across from her for meals, to talk, and whisper, and touch, and eye gaze with her.

Not to mention the shift in consciousness when I realize that this thing I started once upon a time to help those who are young and afraid, as I was, has grown to such a point where we are not only offering up the knowledge and advice we have, but are being asked to do so. This thing called Swingset that has, at one time or another, gotten me in trouble for posting too much, gotten me laid, helped me fall in love, forced me to fall in love, provided an outlet for pain, and a pulpit to brag about my pleasure. Never could I have peered down the timeline and foreseen myself at a conference with Tristan Taormino where she came to our presentation interested in what we had to say on the topic that she wrote the book on…my non-monogamy bible, *Opening Up*.

Nor could I have foreseen these friendships and connections I'd make. Dylan and I had known each other for over a year when *The Swingset* began, but both Ginger and Shira B. Katz came into my life from the outside, and I talk to the two of them more than I talk to my local friends, family—really anyone else in my life. In the lobby of that hotel on Van Ness in San Francisco, Shira B. waited patiently for me to finish talking with the clerk who was seeing if he could get our room ready early.

Ginger hadn't yet let go of Dylan, who she tackled hard upon seeing him in the lobby, while I got full on eye contact with Shira B. She laughed and I got that woozy feeling of disconnect. The laughing voice on the headphones to my ears in the basement recording studio of my house, almost two thousand miles away now, had form… and gorgeous form at that. We kissed hello, and hugged, and held it. So much passed in that hug, as she rested her head on my shoulder; almost two years of relationship and emotional catch up, applying the new information to the past. Later, I wished I'd said something wittier than "Wow." Perhaps that the infamous B stands for "beautiful."

When Ginger walked over to me, it was hard to believe that almost a year and a half had passed since I'd last looked into her eyes, held her hand, touched her. Her greetings melted me.

"What are you all here for?" The clerk asked.

"A non-monogamy conference."

"A monogamy conference?" He took a sideways glance at this small group of incredibly affectionate people in his lobby.

"No, no, *non*-monogamy."

His eyes widened and a grin spread across his face. "Oh! That makes a lot more sense."

I could see how it might and told him so. He told me he'd taken care of the room and handed me my key cards. Formalities finished, room gotten, a long day already behind us. A cramped plane ride here was followed by our introduction to San Francisco with an exceptionally long wait for my baggage at the airport, which made me think…no, made me certain…that someone had poked through my luggage and found fault with the sexual implements within. That I'd be rounded up as a pervert and taken down into the bowels of the airport to answer to pasty white men in black suits with thin ties and tell them of the perversions I get up to and how the nJoy Eleven could indeed kill someone but I instead intend to perhaps coax a gushing orgasm out of some special lady.

Realizing we'd misread the United baggage sign, which implied all United luggage from all planes was coming into the one carousel at which myself and the rest of my flight were waiting, we moved down to the other side of the baggage claim hidden from view by a wall and a flight of stairs. There my bag stood proudly, unmolested by the TSA, and full of the wanton delights of a hundred scattered thoughts and possibilities without a bit of expectation.

Now, we rode the elevator up in a comfortable silence, because at the moment really nothing needed to be said. We could feel each other's warmth and energy and let the fact that we were all actually together speak to the importance of where we were, and what we were here to do. Here to learn, to teach, to confess and be confessed to, to love and be loved. There would be sex, flogging, Domination, submission, snogging, nude photography, panic, pot brownies, dance clubs, kink clubs, hot tubs, constructive arguments, destructive arguments, fellow podcast geek Cunning Minx, heroes Tristan Taormino and Charlie Glickman, and heroes like Pepper Mint who brought it all together.

But not yet. Not quite.

3

THE BROWN-EYED GIRL

O h, the Brown-Eyed Girl; Van Morrison scored our meeting in my mind.

She had questions for me. How convenient. With a motive to meet, I didn't have to see her across the room and attempt to drum up the courage; though I surely would have made the attempt. After all, here I was in San Francisco, a city that I was sure may afford me some sort of plenary indulgence when it comes to confidence. Surely after presenting to a decent crowd at a non-monogamy conference, surely with half a bottle of wine in me, surely I would have. Though, perhaps not.

So convenient, to be sure, when she asked me her question and lingered even after I answered. We spoke of geeky things: of 90s television, of card games, of non-monogamy, confidence, and where to find people to fuck in a safe way. Again I marveled how once I maneuvered myself into a position of authority (however laughable I may find that idea) on a topic such as this, it helps to put all the dirty nasty secrets we don't talk about in polite society right on the table. Should be easier to get a girl's phone number once you've talked of sex clubs, and of floggings, and swinging websites, shouldn't it? Especially when you get a side of *Quantum Leap* geekery with it.

"I'd like your number," I said, as it became clear that there were others who'd attended our presentation who wanted my attention, as well as a significant need for mental unpacking and after care with my beloved co-hosts. I raised my phone. "Because I think you're interesting, and would love to talk to you more." It's entirely possible that this statement has been thoroughly processed through the ravages of short but significant time and filtered through the bottles of *Menage à Trois* that joined us at the presentation table. It's also entirely possible I used the cringe worthy term "digits" in an attempt to coax her to give me her number through a show of social awkwardness.

The Brown-Eyed Girl gave me her digits and I begged off to decompress for a while, hoping to reconnect later in the evening. There were promises of playing *Cards Against Humanity*, after all.

An hour and change later, with a mind altering substance in me that I had never had a direct encounter with in the past (due to Nancy Reagan's effectiveness when talking to Arnold Drummond), the *Swingset* crew rendezvoused in the lobby with some burners, some spouses and lovers to figure out where we should grab our celebratory dinner. There she was again, in the lobby. Feeling an intense need to follow up on this possibility that wasn't common in my experience, and not yet feeling the effects of said substance, I asked her to join us for dinner and we were off down the block before the screen on my phone became irregular.

I wish I could say that I held it together at dinner, but I didn't hold it together at dinner.

I came close, sure, and it's possible that my situation was far more dire to myself than those around me. But between Shira's constant staring and laughing at "the effects of its use on Cooper," a very quiet showing from Miko, the girl I'd dominated the night before, Ginger working hard to keep me grounded and also deal with a lot of *huge* emotions that were begging to be noticed post presentation, and The Professor, seated at the end, at the small table next to us, with The Brown-Eyed Girl I'd asked to dinner, being all charming. Because he's so damned charming.

Why must he be so *fucking* charming?

Dinner ended, and this was good because this feeling in my chest wasn't pleasant. But dammit, I could keep it together a bit longer. We were meeting up for the last few minutes of Tristan Taormino's time before her evening became packed and her keynote the next day. But in the meantime, there was the BevMo that this beautiful Brown-Eyed Girl wanted to show me, as a man who so very clearly enjoys imbibing. Only a few blocks down and back. My ability to focus was waning as we walked, and I'm sure I talked a lot of nothing before arriving in the Pinot Noir aisle and discovering a bottle of Hitching Post Pinot at the nexus point where the movie geek and the wine geek in me intersect.

The sudden inconsistency and irregularity of the text on my phone (for reasons I couldn't at the time understand) warned me via text (which likely came from Dylan, and not from the phone itself) not to drink under any circumstances tonight. I shrugged it off and paid the man whom I'm sure knew exactly why I would open my eyes wider after a blink. My extra wide eyes were simply, to my reasoning, to get more visual stuff. I was dutifully returned to the hotel, sure I'd missed my window, promising to text later in the evening when plans were made for really real. After a very short thank you and goodnight with Tristan in the lobby, I told Ginger at my door that I felt terrible and needed to lie down before Nina Hartley's reception for the Woodhull Sexual Freedom Alliance.

Three hours later I emerged from a sleep where my arms and legs had at various times melted together or disappeared entirely, to a text from The Brown-Eyed Girl that she'd been a bit overwhelmed by the conference that day and had decided to head back home for the evening to sort it out. There was promise that I'd see her the next morning at Tristan Taormino's Keynote Speech. But I'd certainly blown it.

The next day brought the wonderful keynote, then assorted other panels and discussions washed over us, flowed through us, and we became enriched and enraged and entertained and experienced ennui. Now the day was nearing the end, and those souls were gathering in the lobby as they do on graduation day, uncertain of how we become real again, after this weekend of unique. And there was The Brown-Eyed Girl, and she smiled at me, and told me she'd done well at Poly Speed Dating the night before as I had slumbered with my phantom limbs.

My quiet sub was by my side as we talked, making me worry for her feelings about my wandering attention. My attention that yearned to focus, if only for tonight, because there was only tonight, on this fascinating geeky girl in front of me with the wispy, blonde, lightly curled hair that men write sonnets about, and the brown eyes that only Van Morrison could properly explain. She knew I wanted to go to In-N-Out burger, because as a Midwesterner it's somewhat of an obsession of mine, and offered her car parked down the block.

Time was accelerating, and the lobby was filling. A number of folks I'd seen in passing throughout the weekend passed through and wanted to chat just one last time before the end and we said goodbye. Most of them returned to their corners of the bay, but many returned to their corners of the country to lament the fact that too little time had been spent together. Out of the corner of my eye, I saw The Brown-Eyed Girl flirting and laughing with a gentlemen who clearly might have the time to spend with her that she deserves.

"I don't think we're going to make it to dinner," I told her, with the sort of overwhelming sadness that is reserved for graduation day, the last day of vacation, the last day of camp.

She blinked at me. "Well, I just told him I'm going out to dinner with you, so I guess I'll tell him things changed."

I told The Brown-Eyed Girl it was really, really nice to meet her, resisting the urge to throw that third "really" on the fire. She hugged me and held it. And she did that thing midway through where it's about the time you would let go in a normal friendly hug, but instead you squeeze a little tighter.

I love that thing.

You're fucking this up so badly, Coop! She wants to spend time with you! She knows you're leaving tomorrow, and it doesn't matter. She wants to spend time with you! The voice in my head was screaming at me as the hug ended. I noticed Miko looking at the throng in the lobby with the same wistful sadness that was growing in me. I'd brought a posse with me to San Francisco, she didn't have the same luxury. Shira's voice rang in my head: *Don't Make Shit Weird.* The Brown-Eyed Girl didn't let go at first, looked into my eyes.

"Wait!" Came from my mouth without thought, no idea what I was asking her to wait for, or even if it was just wait a few more moments here with me before you go and join the handsome gentleman on the other side of the lobby to develop something interesting. Both The Brown-Eyed Girl and Miko looked at me, and waited.

So I scrambled. After all, this was the point of this trip, self-discovery and growth. *Time to grow a fucking pair and name that which you want, Cooper S. Beckett.* (In this instance, the S is for Spaz) Not having a plan, I just allowed what I wanted to spill out of my mouth. "I want to spend some time with you," I told the Brown-Eyed Girl, taking her hand. Then I turned to Miko. "And then I want to come back and spend time with you." Almost as an afterthought, I said, "and someone needs to go upstairs to the room and make sure that Dylan is still alive." Dylan had crashed after the keynote and not reemerged from room 815. I handed

Miko my key card and tried to ask her in the eye contact if everything was alright, if I'd made the right play. But my eye-speaking skills didn't fire up, and I got no real response.

"Let's walk," I suggested to The Brown-Eyed Girl. She nodded and reminded me that there would be hills. I felt I could handle them.

We talked about what made us who we are, why non-monogamy was important to us, what hurdles there were, what stumbles had come, and how we overcame those stumbles. We looped around and around, up and down the streets, stopping at a bakery just to smell the apple cinnamon donuts in the window. Texts from those I'd left behind periodically interrupted, asking where I was, when I'd be back. I pawned off with "busy" and "soon."

Time was short, and growing shorter. There were other plans for the evening, as there are always other plans, things we should be doing, people we should be seeing, talking to, bullshitting, and plotting with. After several passes by the hotel, I figured that it was unlikely we'd go past the door again.

Take a risk, Coop.

"So, with our hotel right around the corner, I've been trying to work up the nerve for the last several blocks to kiss you."

"That's a great line," The Brown-Eyed Girl told me with a wide smile, then leaned into my kiss. A kiss that lasted and continued, long enough that we had to move to get out of people's way, long enough that we briefly drew attention, long enough that I missed multiple texts. Forgetting about the logistics of it all, the 2,000 miles that separate us in "real" life, just two people making out in the sunlight on the streets of San Francisco.

I told her it wasn't a line, that I'm really rather shy, and had spent quite a large chunk of our walk debating whether or not to try for it. That led to a discussion on the difficulty of meeting people, approaching them, the conversion from talk to something more, like a kiss or a fuck. She thanked me for knowing how to kiss, and we kissed until it became apparent that we ought to get dinner at some point.

We rendezvoused with Miko as she was getting coffee, and sent her up to actually rouse Dylan for dinner, but really just so we could make out one more time in the hallway.

We ate at In-N-Out burger, we walked Fisherman's Wharf, we saw the sea lions, we squintily questioned whether the shadowy outline in the bay was Alcatraz or a ship. I was right, it was Alcatraz. Then we drove up and down the San Francisco hills until the car decided it had had enough, forcing us to back down.

When we returned to the hotel late that night, I said goodbye to my Brown-Eyed Girl, realizing that this was perhaps the elusive vacation crush that so many people I knew had talked about from their youth. Something special because it was never meant to be more, or could never be more due to necessity, proximity, and chronology…just an aberrant moment in time and space, its very own beautiful thing. The Brown-Eyed Girl who asked me a question, and geeked out about *Quantum Leap*, and showed me a tiny slice of San Francisco, and bought me a loaf of sour dough.

I don't labor under the delusion that we'll likely see each other again. But those moments with her will stay with me.

4

SWINGING IN THE NEW

The open relationship *slash* swinging *slash* polyamory folk are more alike than they've led me to believe. Each seems to have an attitude about why they shouldn't be considered the other, or why they're better. Because, after all, polyamory isn't about [*disdainful*] sex, it's about love. And an open relationship is just cheating with rules. And swingers are just old sex crazed perverts. And so on, and so forth.

Well, I may be sex crazed, and I may be a pervert, but I am *not* old. So that's settled.

Within our little niches we're awfully suspicious and distrusting of the others. We all sit on our lawn chairs or hippie blankets or swing sets on the side of the fence we supposedly share in the open relationship community, and snipe.

In my time as a swinger who tends towards both open relationships and polyamory, I've seen a shocking amount of closed-mindedness from a group paying lip-service to the idea of being open and free. I think it's precisely this bizarre internal warring that is keeping us super-glued onto the raggedy edge of normalcy instead of gradually evolving into a more and more accepted place within a society that is slowly opening up to differing ideals and perspectives.

Every time a poly person disparages a swinger or a swinger disparages an open relationship true believer, everybody loses because we feed the vanilla majority (like that? it's like the moral majority) more ammo than they deserve or otherwise would have.

Let me be clear. My assertion about this infighting is all about generalizations and the inherent desire to not only segregate ourselves but segregate those we don't quite understand. I submit to you, however, that these three subgroups are far more alike than different and would ultimately call them all iterations of the same subculture.

The believers in traditional open relationships who go on dates with others without their partners are but a stone's throw away from the swingers who sleep with others as a couple, who are only marginally different from the polyamorous, who just so happen to add the (forbidden in the first two iterations) element of love to the proceedings. Somewhere between the open-relationship folk and the swingers are those who seek out threesomes.

To put myself out as an example of my point: I identify as a swinger, yet I've gone on solo dates and developed relationships with people outside my primary relationship. At the same time I care deeply about the swingers I've grown close to. All three iterations, SOP, swing-open-poly. So, am I the aberration? The unique case that disproves the rule? Or, as I suspect, am I more along the lines of the truly-open-actually-more-flexible-than-we-usually-give-ourselves-credit-for?

Tristan Taormino, in her fantastic book *Opening Up*, discusses a fear that plagues most in the open relationship lifestyles. What happens if my wife / husband / girlfriend / boyfriend / lover / partner falls in love with someone else?

As questions go it's a big 'un, isn't it? For many swingers, it's the "WARNING: BRIDGE OUT!" sign in the road that causes them to go back to a life of (attempted) monogamy. Because it means your bond has failed, right?

I argue that it means no such thing.

Our critics ask how we can share intimacy with our partner as well as the hordes of others they're sure we're fucking at the same time without diminishing that intimacy. Our little dance is to remind them that the Starvation Economy Theory (one must lose for another to gain) doesn't apply to intimacy, because being intimate with two (or three, or twelve) people doesn't mean they have to split some quantifiable supply of intimacy.

Can I come over and borrow a cup of intimacy?

Nor does the Starvation Economy Theory apply to love. You don't love a first child any less when you have a second, after all.

You don't love them less, right? I just have dogs, by the way. Children confuse and frighten me.

Taormino's answer to the question is three options:

1. You immediately cut off contact with the one who the feelings have developed with and focus on "saving" your primary relationship (which may or may not be in danger).
2. You dissolve the relationship you're in because one person can't have this thing that they need.
3. You see the potential for evolution and discuss whether your relationship can sustain the evolution into a triad, foursome, or moresome, where love and sex is a shared commodity with an infinite supply.

I choose three.

"Get a job, you dirty hippy!"

Will someone please remove my father from the chamber?

It's true that what I've just suggested (with my words

and Tristan's) slides about as far into polyamory as you're liable to get, but my suggestion is sound.

After all, why are we swingers? Because the traditional monogamous relationship definitions that have been riding around the world for 2000 years have conditioned us in so many ways.

As swingers, don't we see that sex with others isn't part of the black-and-white storyline we've always been told it was? Bad! It's bad, we're bad, you're bad! Whores and sluts, all of us. Upon rejecting this tradition, why are we clinging to all these other beliefs and traditions that are really only there because they've been instilled in us?

Like monogamy.

Do we swingers *really* believe that there is one love for us? Do we really believe there's one cock or pussy to fuck for the rest of our lives? Hell no, we don't. So why the hell should we believe any of the other preconceptions we've been taught and programmed with?

Is it possible that every hiccup in this wacky road could instead lead to the evolution of our relationships? Maybe we ought to at least be open to the idea of going along for that ride?

And is it possible that maybe, just maybe, you should call all three of those iterations one thing? SOP, open relationships, ethical non-monogamy.

We are, at once, one…and legion.

5

TAKING YES FOR AN ANSWER

I have been in multiple relationships, as have friends of mine, where permission will be given to do a thing and we'll doubt that permission so much that we won't do it.

To clarify:

"Partner, I have been asked out by a sexy friend for Saturday night. Mind if I go?"

"That's fine."

Hmm, I think, *fine*. That's a weird word, isn't it? I wonder if Partner doesn't want me to go after all.

Later.

"Partner, you're sure you're okay with this Saturday night thing?"

"Yes, I'm fine."

There's that word again, fine. What the hell? Partner sometimes says fine when she doesn't mean fine. Could she just be going along to make me happy?

Saturday.

"Okay, I'm going to leave around six tonight."

"Okay, I'll just be hanging around here."

"Would you rather I not go?"

"No, it's fine!"

"I'll just stay home."

Ever been on either side of this conversation? It really is a textbook example of how communication can be miscon-strued and how Cooper Beckett doesn't know how to take yes for an answer.

Result? I don't get to enjoy my Saturday night plans, Partner gets a vaguely miffed version of me to hang out with, and most discouragingly, Partner realizes that some-times even though I'm given a yes, I won't do the thing I want to do.

This type of exchange isn't a big deal if it happens once or twice. But several times, over the course of budding non-monogamy? It can start to encourage bad behavior on both sides of the line. In the past I have engaged in a very bad practice called "really?" It manifests by continually retreading the path of a yes over time.

"Are you sure you're okay with this?"

"I don't have to do this."

"Really?"

I've found that "really?" has quite negative results, too. While the yes may keep happening despite my almost daring Partner to say no, it's implanting a new idea in Part-ner's head: "Maybe I shouldn't be giving the okay to this. If he's this concerned, maybe it's..." This practice is simul-taneously suggesting that Partner rethink her permission and giving her the illusion of sixteen safety nets on her Yes.

This encourages Partner to see a Yes as a Probably, one that can turn to a No at any time. I can't blame that train of thought. Simple repetition can cause us to adapt our thinking in a whole bunch of bad ways. If I doubt the Yes, I'm less likely to accept it and enjoy myself, which rein-forces the cycle.

If I wind up staying home instead of going on my date, it reinforces something else. That perhaps I'm going to stay home regardless of what go ahead is given. Why not give a Yes? I'm just gonna bail out anyway. The conflict that arises from this is that a Yes that's really a No can be very surprising if I do the thing.

Years of non-monogamy passed before I recognized this pattern. More years have passed as I've tried to rewrite my neural pathways so I don't continue to do it from *either* side.

I don't say Yes unless I mean it, and I question a Yes far less (though not never).

Taking Yes for an answer encourages my partners to fully think through their feelings so as to be responsible in their giving a Yes. This in turn allows me to trust them when they say Yes. This doesn't mean there'll never be "take back" moments when I say yes, or Partner says yes only to realize maybe we're not quite as comfortable as we thought.

But part of that clear and concise communication is giving it enough thought that this rarely happens, and keeping a stiff upper lip when it does. We can, of course, legitimately pull the plug if we feel exceedingly uncomfortable. That's built into our relationship agreement.

Knowing our partners will, to the best of their ability, give us an honest answer to those questions, and be supportive beyond that, makes everything better. Those times where I've wanted a "take back" have gotten less and less frequent because I've simply realized that what I was afraid of wasn't real; because most of those reactions are based on fear.

I'm trying really hard to refuse a life of fear.

And take Yes for an answer.

6

THE NEXT EVOLUTION

I don't believe that the polyamorous are simply swingers who've seen the light.

Nor do I believe that swingers are somehow smarter for realizing that sex is very often less complicated than love.

I am currently flirting with the edge of polyamory in my daily life. I call this The Next Evolution, but not because I believe I'm evolving towards some sort of non-monogamy nirvana that might be labeled with one of the three letters in SOP.

Instead, I go back to what I saw was the most important message in Tristan Taormino's *Opening Up*: be open to change in your relationship, be willing to adapt, be willing to evolve. Not all evolution is forward, some is backward, and most is tangential and sideways. Currently, I am sliding across the spectrum, dabbling here and there.

I'm building my future. I'm building my lifestyle. One that's firmly called Non-Monogamy, because it cannot be contained by any of the boxes anymore.

In the traditional paradigm, swingers don't love their playmates. Or at least they're not "in love" with them, hence we so often refer to them as "playmates." It's just playing, just funning, just fooling around with these awesome extra parts we were given that do such wonderful things when they interconnect. On the other end, the vast majority of polyamorists don't plan for their next orgy, house party, club visit. They don't make dates as couples. They don't go out for the fuck.

Am I generalizing? Of course I am. This is why I've always felt our labels are only good enough to point people in the vague direction of who and what we are, but are ultimately worthless when you get right down in the thick of things. I have always felt capacity to love many people. I have often felt strong love towards friends. I have felt that connection with people, despite being a 100% mono-gamous guy for a long, long time. Therefore, this has always felt like the next step for me.

When I first became open, sex was easy and love was hard. It was actually unbelievably easy to turn off that sex=love switch that society tries really hard to hardwire into us from the beginning. Love just seemed messy. Feel-ings could and would get hurt, most likely.

It took my partner falling in love to make me question the box I'd placed myself in. There are many in the swing community who would immediately say that is unaccept-able. That love, really for real love, only belongs within the confines of their relationship. Are they wrong? Absolutely not. For them, in their arrangement, that is their love. That's what it is and means to them, and more fucking power to them.

The Next Evolution for all of us has to be about deter-mining our spot in the world, in this life, in this lifestyle, in the non-monogamy and sexuality spectrums. We are all creating our little homestead out here in the raggedy open space beyond what our traditions, upbringing, and societal norms suggest is right and true. If we're rejecting those constructs of life and love and sexuality, why should we impose a new set of rules upon ourselves by determining that since we are now "A Swinger" we must behave as "A

Swinger" does? Or a poly person. Or a cuckold. Or a dom. All these are simply constructs of given communities in the same way that monogamy is.

Therefore, we can determine our own flavor. It doesn't have to be about black and white, it can be shades of gray (just not fifty). But now I've found the crayon box, and it's that spectacular 64 crayon collection with the sharpener built right into the box. I'll take a little magenta, and a little burnt umber, and when I'm done I'll find that which describes me, and I'll put it on the fridge with a little plastic S magnet. The ability to always be discovering new things about yourself could truly be the greatest gift of all. To never find yourself in anything approaching "routine" would be to sidestep one of the most significant sources of misery in this life.

I love that in my mid-thirties I'm discovering brand fucking new things about myself, the way I interact with friends and lovers, and the way I interact with the outside world.

I have come up against concerned friends in my explor-ation towards the poly side of the spectrum. I told them that there's no reward without risk. Opening up in the first place carries a spectacular amount of risk. The things I've learned about myself in this lifestyle since I began with that great risk have been spectacular. My trajectory isn't a steady flight-plan through Swingdom because I'm not interested in spending the rest of my life settling into a new kind of monotony that, instead of a standard of couple relationship, involves several relation-ships that never grow, or change, and are themselves just a larger web.

I'm willing to take that deep breath, and jump from the edge of the precipice because I know the potential for reward grows greater proportionately with the risk. Every action I take has consequences, which will be dealt with if they need to be. They'll be evaluated, and I'll determine the path to follow with my partners, playmates, and lovers.

Evolution is freedom: knowing that you are unbound, that you can and do change, that change shouldn't be a cause for alarm, but should be seen as an opportunity to learn more about yourself. To become more and more complete, while not feeling the need to ever achieve this artificial notion of actual completion.

Because maybe it'll be a never-ending evolution.

Wouldn't that be something?

7

COOPER'S FANTABULOUS
POLYAMOROUS
CONFIDENCE EXPERIMENT

I project well. By that I mean that I that I can appear to be something I'm not, to the vast majority of people who know the name Cooper Beckett, in fact. And what aren't I?

Confident.

Or grammatically sound.

I know, a total boner killer for all those ladies and men out there who look upon The Beckett and think: *Cooper's got it going on, he knows what he's doing, he's all over it. I wonder what makes him tick. I wonder if he'd be interested in learning what makes me tick.* Or something very much like that, I'm sure. Because not only do I lack confidence, but I'm then presented with this fact that what girls like most is confidence, which sends me into a death spiral that I may not recover from for days.

Or perhaps I'm exaggerating.

But this lack of confidence has its days fucking numbered, believe you me. Why for?

Polyamory.

Before I talk too much about that, though, I'll take you on a tour of a young Beckett's life (not Samuel...or Sam for that matter, both interesting gents to be sure [one a bit more real than the other, though {the other putting right what once went wrong}]). In junior high I formed a pretty strong opinion that children of junior high age were assholes, and really narcissistic assholes at that. So, you can imagine I did well with the ladies.

In high school I was the guy that all my female friends wanted to date someone like. They didn't want to date *me*, particularly; despite the fact that I was single, and at their beck and call, just someone *like* me. In the days before non-monogamy opened my eyes, I played the Facebook game with several of these girls. You know the Facebook game. It's the one where you say "You know, I had the biggest crush on you in high school!" and cross your fingers that they say the same thing. I wouldn't have known what to do with them if they had admitted to the same. I was, after all, in a committed long term monogamous relationship.

Two of the girls I'd been most into in my formative years asked me the exact same thing: "Why didn't you ask me out?"

To which I had no answer. "You were too perfect!" and "Why would you go out with me?" both seemed the rally cry of the loser so instead I just went with "Because I clearly was a fucking idiot" and left it at that.

Swinging has done wonders for my self-esteem, surely. But I was starting from a fairly subterranean baseline to begin with. I'm teetering around the level of a junior in high school with reasonable amounts of confidence. Once I know that someone is into me, I have no problem whatso-ever, it's just making it to that point that can be the scary road.

My *modus operandi* has always been throwing out little pings to see if there's some interest and, failing a massive ping back, calling it a day. This habit served my meager love-life very poorly, because my pings were barely audible in high school and college. It's a downright miracle I've ever asked anybody out! These days, there's a bit more flirtation, but it's still nowhere near where it needs to be to live a high quality and well-rounded life.

Which brings me to polyamory again.

I'm giving it a try. For me, this experiment is about exploring dating beyond my primary relationship and social circle, because I'm not currently in a swinging relationship with anyone that I feel could grow to be polyamorous in nature.

As I'm taking this deep breath and trying something that I was never good at the first time around, I begin to see this as an opportunity for self-betterment. Not just in learning more about myself, my relationships, and beyond, because it is all that; but in becoming a more well-rounded person.

So, dating. Now and in the glorious future. With the Internet and everything. Last time I was dating I was still on AOL, and what a treat that was. What I'm trying to do now is not pre-judge prospective matches the way I used to, in that "Well there's no way they'd be interested in me" way. It's not only counter-productive, but it's often downright incorrect, in that "Well why didn't you ask me out?" way. I will still pre-judge mates on political affiliation and religiosity - I reserve that right, and it saves us from long and unproductive arguments on the secondish dates.

This essay doesn't have a bang finish because it's just a realization I had. While I'm sitting at my computer. Late at night. After kinda sorta asking someone out online. Trying not to be that guy who stares at the little green ball indicating she's currently online, wondering why she hasn't responded yet, assuming what that may mean.

So this essay may be entirely just to distract the voices in my head.

But it's the journey, not the destination, right? Because we all know what the destination is. Everybody gets off at the same stop.

Before I go morbid, I'll just click refresh. She suggested we get pizza.

:: SWOON ::

8

SEXY SCHRÖDINGER

No one believes me when I tell them I'm shy. They protest. They point out the not-shy things I do. They occasionally suggest I'm pretending to be shy to score points with shy people. Do shy people even look up to other shy people?

These things aside, I am shy—because I'm insecure, because I don't really feel comfortable in my skin, in my job, in my life, save these pockets of confidence that show up here and there. In general, I don't take a lot of risks in fear of the blow-back that may result. Namely, rejection.

Because that's what we're all afraid of, isn't it? We the shy, nervous, awkward, dorky, unique. We're afraid of seeing something we want and being told it's not for us. Be that something a job, an expensive item, a kick-ass club, a pretty girl, hell, even the attention of our parents.

In high school, the question was "Would you like to go on a date?" As a swinger, the question morphs to a variation on "I'm attracted to you, are you attracted to me?" or even as simple as "Would you like to fuck?" As a polyamorous person, the question is more complex, but reduces down to a nice and simple "Would you like to go on a date?" reduction. I've come full circle.

Now I feel like I get a chance to put right what once went wrong. Like another Beckett I know. I have a dating do-over. I've been given legit access to "If I knew then what I know now."

Thus far I've blown a lot of that opportunity, because rejection sucks. But the idea of rejection sucks far more.

Looking back at my teenage years, I see that I really set the tone for what would become my interaction with those I'm attracted to. I'd see someone I'm interested in. I'd yearn to make my interest known. I'd be in their life. I'd listen to their stories and problems. I'd "be there" for them. The rare occasions that I made my interest known were when these girls were dating other people.

I set myself up for rejection that I knew was coming. At least then my expectations were met. When you know that the answer is no, there's no real risk, is there?

More often, I'd talk myself out of making any move or comment at all. I may not get the interaction I want, but at least I wouldn't get rejected, right?

Unfortunately, when I began swinging, more than a decade post high school, I continued down this path. I'd make my interest known to those who were not in a position to reciprocate (i.e. monogamous folk) or not say anything at all to the vast majority of those I'd like to talk to.

I'd hide behind the computer, instant messaging instead of meeting, vaguely pre-apologizing for the person (me) that they were going to meet. At parties, I'd wait for someone to introduce me and lead me to an opening. The most success I've had at swing parties with people I didn't already know usually came from following my partner around. Lead with the sexy girl. The worst experience of my swinging life was at a party where everybody was interested in her (and asked her to play - and she did) but nobody asked me. That's not me feeling sorry for myself, that's recognizing that I wasn't fulfilling my end of the bargain.

The risk-reward ratio is enormous here. Yes, it does take risk to put yourself out there. Yes, rejection is a possibility. But the reward that comes in the form of a "yes I'd like to play" is pretty damned spectacular.

"So, Schrödinger, Coop?" you ask. "Are you just trying to show off your cleverness or are you gonna take us there?"

Schrödinger, yes. Lemme explain a bit to the cheap seats quickly. There's the mental exercise of Schrödinger's Cat. A cat in a box and we can't see it or hear it. We have no way of knowing if the cat is alive or dead. At that moment it's both and neither. My thought is that the cat may as well be dead in that box, because you're getting nothing from it.

The risk of putting your feelings out there is the same thing. For so long I was so unbelievably scared of a "no" that I wouldn't ask. By not asking, I created the "no" that I expected. I wasn't getting to go out with (or kiss, or fuck) the girl either way.

And that's why the exercise is so important. We think of it as being a 50-50 shot, yes/no. But there are really three possible outcomes to the Schrödinger's cat conundrum.

1. I open the box, the cat's alive: I get to play with the cat!
2. I open the box, the cat's dead: I don't get to play with the cat.
3. I don't open the box: Guess what? I don't get to play with the cat!

Adapting this to (coarsely) "picking up chicks" gives us three possible results.

1. She says "yes" and you get to the next phase.

2. She says "no" and you don't get to the
   next phase.
3. You don't ask and you don't get to the
   next phase.

Two of these results are the same, but the crazy thing is, we the shy, we the un-confident, we the insecure *choose the third one all by ourselves*.

We're rejecting ourselves by fearing rejection. We're stamping "no-way" on that application.

And I'm fucking sick of it.

It's time to start asking. Time to start seeing if the cat is alive.

9

RAMBLING MY WAY TO DESIRE

I'm taking my leave. But don't worry, it's just for a bit.

I'm riding pretty high right now. We have around forty couples joining us in Cancún at Desire Resort & Spa for our little trip to paradise. Forty couples. It's humbling. It's insane, in fact. I first floated this idea to host a trip to my crew in May of 2011, when I was still riding the high of returning from my first trip to Desire, an oasis of clothing optional, endless drinks, great food, dancing, swinging. We thought that we'd maybe collect ten to fifteen couples, and I would've been thrilled with that.

Eighteen months later, I'm humbled beyond belief at the amazing collection of people we have joining us in Cancún.

And I'm reflective. Reflective, indeed.

It's not often, when you do work like this podcast and website, that you have really concrete evidence that you're doing anything at all. Don't get me wrong, we have a truly amazing group of listeners and readers, who tell us all the time that they appreciate what we're doing. But it comes down to things like our panel at Open SF to make things real.

There'll be no denying the reality of the situation, however, when eighty sexy *Swingset* fans descend on the Riviera Maya to celebrate sex positivity, openness, and I suppose there's no point in dancing around it, fuck each other's brains out.

And I'll be able to stand up on that bed on the beach, amid the billowing curtains, and say "I led you here, Sir. For I am Spartacus."

For the record, I'm quoting Skitch Patterson there (and those who know who that is should message me, because we'll get along FINE [and if anyone wants to start calling me Skitch...I'd also be cool with that]).

Ginger keeps telling me that I need to relax and enjoy the ride more. I keep reminding her that this is *me* we're talking about.

But I really should relax, shouldn't I?

After all, my proof of concept on the "disconnect sex from PIV sex" idea worked very well at the last swing party we had. This attempt to just enjoy moments rather than stampeding toward that ultimate sexual connection, when my penis goes inside someone's nether regions, it was rather amazing. Now I can go into this trip not feeling like every kiss needs to lead to a caress, to a blowjob, to eating pussy (or cock I suppose. Could happen) to fucking, to fucking, to fucking. Now it can all be sex. It can all be fucking.

I want to experience the spectrum of pleasure in Desire. To touch without needing the touch returned. To kiss and celebrate kissing. To perform oral and smile and thank the person who received my tongue. I can enjoy all of this and get off simply on enjoying it.

Of course much of this is still theory, and the party only somewhat proved the last part. But it's a goal.

The other reason I should relax is my whole neurosis is negated by the very fact that I led them here. The number one reason I don't visit clubs or meet and greets much is that I over-think the conversational portion of the evening.

Are they enjoying talking to me? Do they want to talk to me? Should I stop talking? Should I just walk away? Did she flinch when I touched her arm? This monologue that permeates my thinking as I engage in conversation with people is often distracting enough to cause me to wander off and find someone else. I don't read signals well. Or perhaps I just talk myself out of believing them.

But I know one thing to be true about this trip. Some of these people want to talk to me. Okay, perhaps even a majority. In the vicinity of most, I'd wager. I can start conversations and not think they're looking around the room for someone else to talk to—unless I'm boring, which I can be sometimes.

This little boost to my confidence, being able to shut off the faucet of drivel that floods my brain and takes me out of the moment, may indeed allow me to step the fuck up.

Perhaps I can continue this wave of (could it really be called) confidence that started back when I asked a beautiful brown eyed girl for her number in San Francisco. I've gotten little hints at it in my life since. Just asked out a girl at a Halloween party in fact. Told two girls of my interest in knowing them in the biblical sense before our last party as well. There will come a time when I'll simply have to recognize the fact that I've developed some simulacrum of confidence.

And that time very well may be on a beach in Mexico.

The path to self-actualization.

The path to paradise.

I wish you all could come with me. As I sign off here (for an extremely short run of radio silence before I start tweeting and Facebooking and posting from that beach in Mexico) I just marvel again at this thing called *Swingset*. A thing that is so much more impressive than the silly little swinger welcome wagon site it began as. And I marvel at all of you. And thank you. And hug you. And love you. And fuck you (with consent, of course).

You are why I'm here. Why I do this. Why I care. Why I try. Why I breathe. Why I cry. Why I love. Why I laugh. Why I come.

And most importantly, why I continue.

Thank you kindly.

10

WE BEGIN WITH TALK
OF DRINK AND DEBAUCHERY

B y the fifth melon ball I held onto the sides of the bar for dear life and wondered, perhaps to myself but likely aloud, if anyone could tell that I was really drunk. My eyes darted between my compatriots at the bar. Of course they could tell. Those around me have seen me for days here now, and never have I been known to swing my arms wildly through the air, cutting broad swaths with every ill-conceived point I felt I absolutely had to present to as many people as would listen at that moment. Still I felt for some absurd reason I could maintain, keep my cool. I raised my hand.

"Another melon ball, Alfredo." I made it a statement. Carlos, the bartender, was kind enough to not signify my drunkenness by mentioning that he was not, in fact, Alfredo. As my drink was being prepared, I found myself distracted by the *other* drink Carlos was preparing. "Alfredo," I asked, but he couldn't hear me over the sound of his blender, and because he didn't respond with his customary "*Sí*, Cooper" I began to wonder to myself if he wasn't Alfredo, who I'd ordered these very same melon balls from all evening.

In fact, looking closer, I was overtaken by the fear that I'd mistaken him for someone else. Was I some kind of racist? A man who would assign the same generic name to anyone under the employ of Desire Resort and Spa? Then the horror hit me deeper, was the earlier bartender named Alfredo at all? Had that name been conjured from the ether? I raised my hand, prepared to address this situation with the good man, eying his name tag with eyes that wouldn't focus.

"Melon ball, *Señor*." He set my pastel green drink in front of me and vanished down to the far end if the bar before I could explain myself about the incidental racism.

Another two melon balls had passed through my lips, and I was discussing horrible things: politics and religion. These are not topics one should attempt while a firm sight beyond drunk, naked and exposed, balls rubbing against the stools with imitation wicker seats at the bar. Before long the racism was forgotten, as were my companions, who'd moved on to wondering how our women were getting along on the couch behind us.

But this is the way one plays things, right? When you go to an "all-inclusive" the staff perhaps is disappointed if you are *not* drunk, aren't they? Or perhaps at this resort they're simply wondering why those who remain clothed choose to do so. After all, when given permission to let it all hang out, one really ought to throw caution to the wind and do just that. There are few things so free as a flaccid cock dangling between your legs and flopping against your thigh. Save perhaps an erection that occurs when a Brazilian with the tits and ass and eyes and mouth of, well, a Brazilian, looks at you and gives that little half smile to show her appre-ciation of your peacock*esque* display.

After all, I sat at the epicenter of the American dream on a small stretch of beach on a peninsula in Mexico. It's ironic that we in the states forgot to chase the dream when it went south of the border to a place where hedonism reigns; pursuit of pleasure over all else, debauchery and passion. A place where people do look twice at you, lying on a bed with a woman who's most definitely not your partner, who is straddling your face while you consume the juiciest portions of her beautiful anatomy. But instead of clucking their tongues, or drawing back with the shriek of a wealthy dowager, they nuzzle with one another and smile, watching what is often quite a sexy show. Then they look over and watch your partner on the next bed, performing fantastic acts of fellatio on a massive uncircumcised phallus.

There would be none of that tonight, however. Not if the melon balls kept arriving at my seat at the bar. The frequency has even been increasing, one arriving before 2/3rds of the previous is gone. Perhaps this is the *modus operandi*, chock me full of drink and point me in the way of the ocean to stumble into the surf and then on to commune with Bacchus in eternity. Dark thought out of nowhere. Though I wonder if any concept of Heaven throughout history has ever contained the things I've seen in just the last three days.

If not, I want this to be my Valhalla. I want to return here when I die.

I found my eyes blurred with tears as I tried to explain myself to a nude blonde next to me. The raving about the American dream and some concept of heaven must have moved her, because she leaned in and left a kiss on the corner of my lips, then leaned back and raised her eyebrows at me. She wrapped her crimson lips around her straw and I became vaguely aware that some would call these gestures signals. My descent has been all encompassing however, and I smiled, raised my glass to her and said something about the beauty of the ages.

"You're with the redhead, right?" she gestured with her drink to my partner and the collection of girls on the couch who'd moved beyond talking and onto the dance of tongues that has caused more than one guest to slow their gait as they made their way to dinner across the open-air lounge. Such a lovely pre-meal sight, three women enjoying the sapphic pleasures of one another's mouths.

The question struck me as odd, was I *with* the redhead? But before I could philosophize about the absurdity of being with someone, and mention that just now I was with the very woman who asked the question, something deep in my subconscious took over, bypassing my mouth, and threw my head forward with a nod.

"We've been watching you two." She again punctuated with a suck on the straw. Another kiss on the corner of my lips, her fingers find my hair, and this mystery woman stood from the bar and disappeared into the evening. I mourned not getting her number for a moment, then realized the absurdity of that urge. My phone has been in solitary confinement in the room safe since the moment we set foot inside, and there it would stay. But Desire is a village, a collective of like-minded sinners, and she'll find the hot tub soon enough. In a resort that only houses 200 people, we all see each other again. And those special few, again and again.

But what did that mean, that she'd been watching us? I began to reflect on the two kisses, the straw sucking, the hair tussle, and surely there were signs there, signs that anyone who hadn't sucked down (good god) twelve melon balls could've picked up on. All I could think of were The Police, and Sting being his best stalker self.

I stood before I realized that my brain wanted to stand, and perhaps it was due to this disconnect that I began to sway.

"How're you doing, Coop?" asked Violet, who'd also been watching me, when her extremely talented tongue wasn't in my partner's mouth.

"I don't wish to alarm anyone..." I proclaimed in such dramatic a fashion as surely frightened the other lovely hedonists at the bar, perhaps wondering if the man in a baseball cap and Chuck Taylor low top All Stars was going to announce he had a bomb. "...but I may in fact be drunk."

"Doesn't seem to be affecting you *too* negatively," Violet lobbed back, indicating my lap, in which I found a rather impressive erection, pointing out like the gnomon on a sundial. I felt if I were to lie down, we might find it to be playtime o'clock. I shared my joke that would've been funnier if Alan Alda had said it, and she agreed.

Thank Bacchus for the pharmacological assistance, with the finest bootleg erection drugs coursing through my veins, coming from miscellaneous red pills that almost surely are taking years off my life. But that's the time at the end, when I'm senile and can't get an erection anyway. I'll take the time just now, the time that included going back to my room with five other sexy people, throwing a Liberator Throe blanket down on the bed, providing at least one of the girls with a silicone cock and harness, and becoming a sea of bodies, just flesh writhing together, rising and falling like the tides and experiencing joys that many of even the most powerful people in the world never get around to.

Pure and unadulterated hedonism, beauteous sex triumphing over the forces of old, who would cast us out of the garden in a heartbeat, proclaiming our acts to be an affront to their god. Then in the dark, when perhaps that god can no longer see them, crying and masturbating and coming into the darkness, visions of debauchery in their heads that they can only imagine or catch on the Internet late at night after their frigid and pious spouses have retired to experience their own sobbing mediocre climaxes.

For us in that room, and those on the sacred acres around us, our acts were our own prayers, our worship at the temples of each other, each moan an Amen and each climax an Hallelujah. And in our afterglow we all drifted to the same thoughts of some sort of bargain with an underworld character (Hades perhaps) that would allow us to never leave this corner of the world.

This place and time of utter perfection.

This bliss.

11

NAKED POLITICS

I hadn't interacted with her much prior to mid-day on Tuesday. Tuesday the 6th. Tuesday, November 6th, 2012 to be exact. Election Day in America. And there I was in Mexico, at a lifestyle resort called Desire Resort & Spa. Theoretically, a great way to avoid the insanity of what was proving to be a squeaker of an election between Barack Obama and Mitt Romney. There are just better things to focus on. Lots of them, in fact. Sexy people, doing sexy things, everywhere! I make no secret about my liberal leanings, my positions on marriage equality, women's rights, things of that ilk. But I was trying to keep it in check in paradise.

I managed it just up until Tuesday.

You see, because I was foolhardy enough to donate to the Democrats a couple of times they had decided that I was their new best friend, and blitzed me with daily emails featuring wild mood swings. "The GOP are pissing in their pants!" then "We're all going to die!" No shortage of hyperbole coming from these guys.

On Monday night and Tuesday morning the last barrage of emails came in, lamenting "too close to call" polls, and what looked like sure losses of the house, the senate, and the presidency to what the good Dr. Thompson would've surely called the forces of old and evil.

That's where I started to panic.

I sat at the lobby bar and lamented what the above losses would mean for sex positivity, for this little thing we do, for our gay friends, for the women in our lives. And before you start telling me about fiscal policy, let me just stop you by saying I reject any argument that limits the basic human rights of being able to visit your loved one on their death bed. You want me to vote anything other than Democrat, the other parties best stop talking about foolish shit like that. My lamentations were heard and reciprocated by a few like-minded guests, though as our discussions progressed I was aware of a few down the bar who were listening without expression of agreement or disagreement.

I did feel bad.

When you read my ramblings that can barely be classified as essays, you expect snark and bitchiness and preaching. You should, anyway. It's what I'm known for. But you shouldn't have your vacation ruined because Cooper Fucking Beckett is weeping for the masses about an election that had barely begun at that point.

For the record, those down the bar later gave us a hug and celebratory toast when Obama scored his second term.

My plan had included ignoring politics that day. I'd asked a girlfriend at home if she'd text me if/when anything of note happened and put my iPad in the safe in the room. I tried *so fucking hard*.

A friend recommended I check 538, that it might make me feel better. It did. It did big time. Obama was projected to win with a 91% likelihood.

On a swinging bed by the lobby with other concerned souls, I put voice to the fact that while this was quite good news, there still was a very significant chance that it could swing the other way, that the world could be different when we returned to America. That Michelle Bachmann could still be running her foul and beastly mouth around the halls of the District.

And Elle, a girl on the bed next to me, whom I'd had very little interaction with, who was so very pretty, perked up at the statistics. She asked me if I'd seen The Big Board, and aimed her iPad screen at me. On it, NPR's election tracking board, all states represented, swing states up top, fifteen second refresh rate.

"You're watching this?" I asked, a smirk on my face.

"Non-stop," she responded, glancing at the refresh.

Still early, though. Nothing reporting yet. But we had a friendly oasis. Us two. In a world where everybody was focusing elsewhere (as we should've been, let's be honest) we two were free to gorge on stats and polls and obsess beyond any normal level of obsession on what we haughtily termed "the future of our country."

Simply having this kindred spirit made me feel as though things were going to be okay. Surrounded by people in sexy outfits doing sexy things that evening, Elle and I sat at the bar, making out to stop looking at my iPad sitting next to us. NPR's Big Board updating away. Results coming in. We tried so very hard to not pay attention to them.

It was impossible.

She and I saw when the Big Board crossed the threshold, and there was no longer a way for the election to go in any direction but ours. Gay marriage became a thing in two states. Pot got legalized (that one surprised us) in Colorado. And California continued along down the path with its schizo ways that have disappointed us too many times to count.

Would the world be different when we returned from Mexico? No, not really. Ultimately, very little changes from one presidency to another. And would "our guy" do any of the things he said he would do? Perhaps not. But the groundswell toward marriage equality and reproductive rights was happening. The dominoes were falling, and the opposing forces wouldn't be able to hold things back for much longer.

Today we're seeing the direct result of those first gay marriage votes. As GOP movers and shakers are "evolving" in their opinions on the topic. The groups banning birth control and fighting sex education are looking more and more fringe. And no, Barack still has not wowed us, and has done several things that make us question him, but the movement is happening. There may be no stopping it anymore.

Six months ago in Mexico, Elle and I asked for champagne and spread the good news amongst those we knew were likely to appreciate it. Then the iPad went away, and the stress was diminished, and it was back to the hedonism and debauchery that we'd traveled south for. For the rest of the trip, though, our bond was cemented.

We'd survived the election while away from our home shores.

12

IT WON'T STOP

THE EPIC PROSTATE ORGASM

I've been chasing the prostate orgasm for months, perhaps years now, the way many women chase that elusive first g-spot orgasm. While some assholes may still question the existence of a g-spot, there's no doubt that the prostate exists. The question is, rather: can it produce pleasure on its own?

I'd heard tell around the campfire, my friends, about the orgasm without ejaculation, conjured from prostate stimulation. I was told it could be long, multiple, and unlike anything I'd ever experienced (namely short and single). After all, our bodies are designed so once the come shoots out, the shop gets closed up, the lights get turned off, and our balls say, "you don't have to go home, but you can't stay here."

I think I'd once come close with a very special friend who was intent on focusing on me instead of her. She had me feeling all sorts of unique and new sensations before putting her mouth on me to finish the job. That orgasm had an ejaculation, indeed, but the erection didn't immediately subside. It looked like someone forgot to turn off the lights. The factory was still running.

This fascinated me because that never happens. I'm

one of those people who, once I've come, the chemicals produced change my point of view so dramatically that I feel like I never need to have sex again. Been there, done that, came on the t-shirt.

I'd never known anyone who'd actually managed a prostate orgasm. Compared to it, the g-spot orgasm may be elusive, but was fairly common amongst the open women in my social circle. Not only that, most of that circle seemed not to care that it might be a thing.

But I cared. I cared big time.

Much of my definition of sex has been caught up in that white, jizzy final expulsion. Since I know myself, and that I have that "closed for business entirely" sensibility after an orgasm, I tend to put my partner's pleasure first. Once she has had an orgasm, or many, only then do I allow myself to head in that direction. The idea of an orgasm that wouldn't end things for me is tremendously appealing.

The problems with chasing such an orgasm are myriad. It's a sensitive area indeed. The first prostate orgasm, much like a first g-spot orgasm, requires a lot of time, concentration, and effort to bring forth.

If they exist at all, that is. Tristan Taormino has assured me that they do, as not only has she seen one, but she's conjured one. Of course, if Tristan laid those beautiful hands on me, in me…I got lost in a thought.

Where was I?

All this talk about the possibility that they don't exist is silly, though, isn't it? Especially now that I've had one.

Oh, yes.

Yesterday, on a bed near the rooftop hot tub at Desire Resort and Spa in sunny Cancún, as I enjoyed demonstrating the nJoy Eleven on a very willing friend, I asked if someone might insert my favorite butt plug, handmade by the incredibly talented Boris.

A volunteer came forward, a beautiful woman with whom I'd shared a lot of eye contact and some kisses at

our speed dating event. I was assured she was a professional (though I wasn't certain what that meant at the time)
and that I shouldn't worry. I wasn't worried to begin with,
but I thanked her for volunteering, for her enthusiasm, and
returned my attention to the Eleven and my lovely
playmate.

My volunteer didn't step back after insertion. She
continued to manipulate, pressing the plug, moving it in
and out, circling it. Before long I was distracted. Then I
could no longer continue with the Eleven. Thankfully my
playmate had brought out her LELO Siri and whispered
that she might have had enough of the massive Eleven. I
continued to kneel above her as she played with herself,
responding compersively to my spasms that were growing
more frequent from the anal stimulation.

Before long I couldn't support myself on my hands and
knees. My lovely playmate below suggested that I lie next
to her and took my hand. My volunteer asked if I was
doing alright, if it was too much, touching my arm and
thigh as she asked. Tremendously comforting. "I'm very
comfortable saying 'Ouch, ouch, that hurts!'" I told her.

"Promise?"

I promised.

She became more aggressive, moving her whole body
in rhythm, gripping my thigh and my arm at times, putting
her hand on my chest to gain leverage, to hold me down,
to push the energy right into me.

Somewhere in there, it started.

I've always achieved small spasms during prostate play,
the kind of spasms you hit as your cock is being played
with, those early signposts that you're going in the right
direction. With prostate stimulation, these moments were
usually brief but very pleasurable. But on that bed, with
this expert, I found these spasms elongating and coming
closer together, becoming tremors and full-body shaking.
Bigger and bigger, closer and closer, until the gap between
them disappeared.

Here's where it all gets fuzzy and dreamlike. Once the gap vanished it was like a wave rushing toward shore that wasn't breaking, and the shore just moved back at the same speed as the wave. On and on the shakiness rolled, spasming, rocking my body. I couldn't breathe. I couldn't think.

"Shh, don't clench," she whispered to me, running her fingers along my very tense legs. My hands were indeed clenched into tight fists. I opened them and put my head back down.

"Just breathe."

This continued for the better part of an hour. At least I think so. I honestly have no idea because time had fractured and lost meaning. I may have been orgasming for decades or only a minute. I've since been assured it was almost fifty minutes from the beginning of the "clearly orgasmic" portion of my time on that bed to the end.

When I threw the flag down and tapped out.

I thanked her, words unable to accurately reflect my gratitude. She assured me that I had indeed progressed through many and varied orgasms if my face and body were any indication. As I lie there, basking for a while, a curious thing happened. An aftershock tremor hit, causing me to curl up my knees to my chest—an ecstatic moment of orgasmic delight.

This by itself was surprising enough, but when these tremors continued during the walk back to my room, during the shower before dinner, while getting food from the buffet, (I had to ask a friend to get me a deviled egg because I couldn't hold the tongs steady) and through on to dessert. Only after sitting at dinner for an hour or so did the tremors finally begin to subside.

A nearly endless orgasm with the vast capacity for more. Without the standard feelings of "Okay, I'm done." A whole new world. How thrilling that is. After all, I'm no longer chasing the possibly mythical prostate orgasm.

Now I'm just chasing the very real *next* prostate orgasm.

O, happy day!

13

THE SLIDING GLASS DOOR CONUNDRUM

I didn't realize the weight of the final day of a trip to paradise at Desire Resort and Spa until I felt the last day on our first trip. A pair of sliding glass doors await us all.

We spend so much time in the area just outside the lobby, getting drinks at the lobby bar, mingling around the fountains, relaxing or playing on the swinging beds, lounging on the couches and chairs, or just passing through on your way to or from the grill, the hot tub, the pool, or the restaurant, or shuffling off for a tryst in your room with sexy new friends. And in all this time, they loom.

The sliding glass doors.

We all pass through the sliding glass doors at the end. When the airport transport comes for us, and those sliding glass doors open, we pass through them for the last time.

When you arrive at Desire Resort & Spa after your first visit here, the first thing they say is "Welcome home." I've never in my life experienced a place that isn't home that felt so comfortable.

I'm the skeptic around these parts. The more woo-woo things get the more I slide on down the bar. But this resort. This place. There's got to be something more to it. Something special. Something other. A rift in space and time that came together to birth a new home for all who seek it.

Before this trip I was very skeptical when people talked about energy. The tides of the universe, ebbing and flowing, and changing and churning. This trip has opened me up a bit. I'm still not going to wander around talking about how we're all connected. But it's hard not to feel like we're connected to something bigger and more special down here than anything I've ever experienced.

One often hears the malarkey about places being imprinted by the bad things that have happened there. Bad vibes. I once believed that, and this place makes me believe that the opposite is true: that a place that is full of beauty, and warmth, and affection, and fucking, and community, and comfort, and all the joys of hedonistic delights, could be imprinted. Could feed on it. Could possibly be *why* this resort feels the way it does. All who come here call it home and immediately start planning their next trip.

We cannot stay away.

From the moment we pass back through those sliding glass doors, well, things start to evaporate.

We watch the sliding glass doors, warily, out of the corner of our eyes. Knowing that a day will come, a day not far off, that we will have to pass through them, dressed in travel clothes, and onto that transport, and back to the airport, and then back to the real world. This place, this resort, exists outside. In the margins. On the fringe.

A living, breathing creature of warmth, of beauty, of hope. A place where we can just be ourselves in a way we could never do at home. Even those of us lucky enough to be tolerated for our idiosyncratic lifestyles cannot *truly* be ourselves in front of those around us. But here, stepping out of our clothes and out of our door, we can.

Which is why as things begin to wind down, it gets hard. This morning I watched Ginger and the Professor pass through the doors. She was crying. I was too. Tomorrow more friends will pass through the doors.

Tomorrow I will pass through those sliding glass doors and back to reality.

It has been so wonderful to step outside of our reality if even for the briefest of moments in our lives. Fortunately for us, we know that when we pass through those sliding glass doors it's only a matter of time until we emerge back into the warm loving embrace of Desire Resort & Spa.

After all, reality is fleeting.

358 days until Desire.

14

TAKING THE POLY SHOW ON THE ROAD

I have a pretty active open lifestyle. Not as active as the peak activity time at the beginning, but quite active and satisfying. I have a few couples I play with regularly, some singles I play with independently, and now this poly experiment as I begin polyamorous dating.

It's going quite well, in fact. Due to an incredibly lackluster dating life in high school, I suppose I went into the new poly experiment (wherein I can and do date independently, and openly have "relationships") with that same feeling of apprehension with which I approached all of my high school dating. Not good, this I know. One ought not start a confidence building experience by putting into the universe a whole lot of inconfidence (word chosen [and I am well aware it's not a real word] because of the juvenile humor aspect that it sounds like incontinence. Teeheehee! Anyway…).

So, yes. Going well. I have asked out three women, and all three have said yes. Booyakasha, right? Hell yeah! I have people around me saying "Don't act so surprised" and "Maybe you should take that as a sign you actually have some value to offer people who might want to date you and stop being a mopey morose bastard." The people around me who said that second one were mainly me. And he's right. I am. I really should look at that and see the value. Should understand that despite all the high school shit (which we all have), I may actually be attractive to someone looking to date me. Physically, mentally, unique-situationally.

Two of the three women I've asked out consider themselves open. Neither of them have ever (knowingly) dated someone in another relationship, but both were, as they very quickly put it: game. The third is a friend from the lifestyle.

There's a novelty factor, I'm sure...a "This might be interesting" factor...which is totally cool, because I've got a "this might be interesting" factor going on with poly. I've made decisions lately purely on their potential to engage my fascination sector. As I've said, I never really got to explore that in high school, and pretty early into college I was dating long-term, so exploration stopped.

For one woman who's incredibly busy (like 5-6 nights a week busy) I offer a relationship that she won't have to coddle, one she can leave alone. A relationship in which she can get what she needs, be it affection, be it physical attention, be it companionship, and still have her "her time" to do the rest of her stuff. I won't get sad when I can't get her attention multiple nights per week, I won't put that "me or your passions" strain on her. I may not be what she wants in the long-term (in fact I'm pretty sure I'm not [and I'm okay with that]) but I can be a good option for her right now.

The one who has been open (swingers in fact) has to circle the wagons with her primary just now. I've told her I care too much about her (and her primary) to be a distraction. I want to help in whatever way I can. I want them both to be happy, with or without me, as a friend or as a lover. I suppose it's not really a breakup, because we only had one date, but it's a portent for my reaction to relationship flux now. Pretentious much, Cooper?

This was the big concern for me going in: relationships growing, changing, and ending. No matter how much I got from *Opening Up* there was still the very distinct possibility that when faced with the changing/evolving/ending relationship I would react poorly.

The second relationship went out with a bit of a whimper. Our priorities were too different. We kept trying to recalibrate but missed every time. At the end we all agreed that perhaps we were trying to force something that just wasn't going to happen. She's in a great relationship now, and that makes me very happy.

But those were still poly hybrids. Relationships with open people, people who swing, people who can separate sex and love. People who can combine those two things when necessary, desired, and longed for on all fronts. Now I move into uncharted territory.

The two women I have asked out are from outside anything they would term "the lifestyle," be it poly or swinging. Or even non-monogamy. Both are simply open to dating someone who is non-monogamous. This strikes me as having the possibility for great relationship flux. It introduces variables that I've never explored or considered, things that could crop up out of nowhere.

Yet I find myself incredibly optimistic. I feel like I'm an explorer, making my first tentative steps into fully uncharted territory.

Off the edge of the map. And here may be tygers.

Surprisingly, I feel ready.

15

POLYAMOROUS / SWINGER / NON-MONOGAMOUS / OPEN

I'm going through a rather unique period of self-discovery here. Swinging launched me through something similar, though not nearly as complex, in discovering a vast amount of new sexual ability and information. Now the ability and go-ahead to build relationships with other people is re-defining me for myself. I find it fascinating, terrifying, exciting—a host of adjectives that can be applied to the course I'm on in this polyamory thing.

Yes, that's right, I think it's time to retire the "experiment" and call it what it is. Though I think there would be many a polyamorous person who would have trouble with me, an avowed swinger who is planning a big spectacular orgy just next month, calling myself polyamorous. I perhaps have the same aversion to the term that many have for "swinger." The baggage.

Granted, the baggage is quite different for polyamory than it is for swinging. Where swinging calls to mind creepy gold-chain-wearing, leisure-suit-clad men named Larry, (hmmm...*Leisure Suit Larry* didn't get nearly the quantity of sex needed to define the term swinger) polyamory conjures pagans, hippies, tantra, and all sorts of other touchy-feely new age hoopla.

I'm rather loathe to define myself this time around. Whereas I've embraced the term "swinger" in an attempt to take it back (and because I think it's a funny fucking term, honestly), to slide into polyamory after just over three years of swinging feels a bit disingenuous. Especially since three years of swinging taught me nothing more fully than the fact that swinging is a loose collective of people with a few common points (namely fucking people who aren't in their relationship) and myriad different variations on that theme. My time spent with friends has shown me something very similar about polyamory.

More than ever I feel the need to identify as non-monogamous and let the dice fall as they will. Non-monogamy, or the vaguer but appropriate "open," is what holds us all together, what defines us versus them. Not that it is generally a case of us versus them, the open versus the closed, the mono versus non. It is, however, apparent that we need to all be in this together. My old saw of "our similarities are greater than our differences" is growing truer every day as our community expands. I won't bang that drum further here. Occasionally it seems to be all I talk about.

What I find truly wonderful about every bit of my opening up experience is that there is always more to learn about myself. I was at a very static point, treading water, convinced (as are the vast majority of the world) that once you find yourself in a family situation (marriage, children, etc.) there is little more growth for you independently, that it's all a reflection of those new people around you. When you get married, your growth is a reflection of your partner. When you have kids, it's in relation to them that you grow in the new role of parent. So we often don't even try to grow, change, learn. We accept the status quo. We accept that at a certain point we are all that we ever will be, and no more. Talk about a preamble to an identity crisis!

So to discover more about myself, to realize new and

interesting things, is huge! And now I build my confidence, something that I was pretty certain was a static and unmoving point, just something that would always define me. But now that's changing.

I had a first date with a girl that knocked me on my ass, a click that was immediately evident, a sense of self that was strong enough for me to stop and kiss her walking back from dinner instead of fretting about it until the end of the night. Something is new. Something is new within me, and it's a spark that feels as though it might catch.

Very internal, I know, but exciting on an entirely new level.

16

SHOW AND TELL

INFORMING POLYAMOROUS PARTNERS ABOUT OTHER PARTNERS

ow and when do you go about informing polyamorous partners about other partners? It's a dilemma I haven't really faced before. How upfront is upfront, and what is just rubbing it in people's faces?

As a swinger, the thing people most want to know is if you play safe. If you take precaution. If you get to know people first. Rarely does the subject of numbers come up. Rarely do you feel compelled to disclose when and how many people you've been with recently. Rarely does it come up that you're going to a sex club or sex party this weekend unless it's to ask the person you're talking with to join you. It's a sort of "We're all in this together" mentality, I suppose.

It's why when you find swingers who get jealous that you're going out with other friends, you want to explore that to discern if it's going to be a larger problem or not. Because the thought is: let's all be happy about all of our potential fun. There's plenty of sexy to go around.

As part of my moving into uncharted territory I find myself with a new anxiety, one I've never experienced before. Since I didn't date much in high school (don't worry, I shan't drone on about this again) I never experienced dating multiple people at once. I was pretty firmly serially monogamous for my entire life (with the odd blip here and there that we needn't get into). I'd find the girl I wanted to pursue. Then hem and haw and dawdle and find excuses not to ask. Then perhaps ask her out. Then go out with her. Then break up. Rinse and repeat. If you can believe it, it was even less appealing than it sounds.

For the first time, though, I find myself in multiple relationships, or at least having the potential of multiple relationships. A little while ago, when my primary partner and I were having a late night catchup talk about our respective polyamorous endeavors, she mentioned that she would be fine with me looking for other people beyond the girl I had, at that point, gone on a single date with. This surprised me, because I hadn't really been considering that yet.

I'd been on a date with a swinger friend, but didn't feel that would be a long-term thing for various reasons. After that I'd asked out R (in a stressful random late night ask-out message), a girl I knew a little bit from real life, and had taken her out for a single very long and not all together conclusive date. But beyond that, aside from looking around on some sites, I wasn't searching.

My partner's comment made me wonder why I really wasn't exploring, and wonder if my old habits of waiting for someone to metaphorically (or literally) land in my lap were rearing their ugly heads again. If there's one thing I won't do as a polyamorous person, it's fall back into my godawful high school dating routines.

After that came another far more successful date with R (and one that was far more conclusively a date), some comments from play friends, and a comment from a listener that really put me over the moon. I had confidence flowing for the first time, instead of just a tiny little trickle.

I surprised myself when I sent a message to S, a vanilla friend of a friend I'd met at a sci-fi convention party of all places. Yeah, I'm a geek, deal with it. I, a pretty damned experienced swinger, was impressed by all the shenanigans they get up to at those parties. She and I had been chatting a bit, but nothing substantial. All I really knew about her was she had very interesting hobbies (building puppets among other things) and seemed quite well put together.

Before I realized I'd typed it, I sent over the old: "So my wife and I are in an open relationship, and blah blah blah, would you be interested in going on a date sometime?"

And yes, typed it. I'm much better at dealing with the potential for rejection if I don't have to look people in the eye at the time.

After an agonizing number of minutes with no response, just the occasional "S is typing" message, she hit me back with, "I'd be into that."

Bam!

The unique position. The point of this essay after all.

Now there are two vanilla with sprinkles girls. Hitching themselves at least with a preliminary curiosity strap(-on?) to this wayward non-monogamist…this fellow who still attends orgies in the midst of courting beautiful women.

Both are well aware that my primary partner and I have been swinging for a while. Both are quite aware that now, for the first time, we're exploring dating separately. Is that enough? Do I have to get more specific? Do I have to explain myself when I have other dates?

Do I wait for them to ask me for more information, just make it clear that I am an open book for them?

So many questions, and I fear the answers are all, likely, "It depends."

17

TOO MANY HEARTS AT STAKE

A NEWLY POLY SEX EDUCATOR DOUBTS HIMSELF

I've asked myself this question several times this week. How can I educate? How can I educate when I've just experienced a week that made it rather abundantly clear that I don't know what the fuck I'm doing most of the time? Can I be allowed to just fall back upon that trope that says those who can't do teach? Is that really a saying, or just a Woody Allen joke?

This week, hard times hit the Beckett household. Storms have been brewing. We're still very new in the poly arena, and much has not been ironed out as of yet. Growing pains are rather substantial, far larger than they ever were with swinging.

I've had the conversation recently about why swinging is "easier" with my new girlfriend, the poly girlfriend. I maintain that it is. I told her that sex is, with all its pageantry and trappings, rather uncomplicated. Navigating the emotional minefield of additional people in your relationship, and the interconnected-ness that springs up all by itself (i.e. the connections between the supplementary players and significant others) can yield great rewards indeed, but also can blow up quicker than you would anticipate.

Or maybe quicker than *I* anticipated.

I thought I could do it. No problem. Swinging had its troubles, sure, but they were brief, fleeting. The yield was just so tremendous from that crop, as though we paid tribute to some Sun God on Summerisle. I naturally assumed that I could, without great fail, navigate the much murkier waters of polyamory.

This is not a giving up treatise. Far from it.

This week, my relationship with my wife was laid bare. Chest torn open. Vivisected. Exposed. All its horrible weaknesses and shortcomings on display to be picked over and examined. And when you're exposed like that, from either side, the goods, the positives, the awesome that make up the rest of your relationship, really easily roll off the table and behind a piano somewhere in the recesses and margins. Instead you dwell. You bathe in the horrors. Accusing. Snapping. Wringing hands, gnashing teeth.

NRE is still a bitch to watch. It loves to set up shop in your brain, handing out free boxes of doubt and jealousy, whispering in one ear those things that you're trying very hard not to think because you do trust your partner, you *do*, but these things it's saying are just so...plausible.

I was told very early on in my poly experience that I wouldn't be able to hold on as tightly as I did in swinging. I'd kept a pretty fair handle on all events and encounters, finding and maintaining the balances, making sure everything was kosher across the board. With poly, I was reminded, it's a completely different ballgame. Strict rules and boundaries tend to cause more problems than they prevent. I've encountered the most perplexing mystery of poly, the fact that combating a troublesome feeling, or a difficult moment, needs to be done by loosening the restrictions rather than tightening.

In swinging, when an issue was encountered, it was quite simple to close the relationship for a week, a month, two, work internally, get that engine running again and climb back onto the swingset.

In poly, though, there are too many hearts at stake. You're suddenly back on *The Gong Show* with plates on spindles and you're twirling them. If you focus on one, the rest will fall, and that aftershock, which could be big depending on the emotions involved, will likely upset the balance of that one plate you wanted to continue to spin in the first place.

I'm talking in metaphors and riddles, aren't I? The words of a man who wants to explain himself to you while not sure he should, he can, or even if words exist with which to do so.

There was certainly plenty of blame to go around, after all, along with plenty of compromise to be had. And a contract to be written. And interactions to be modified and redefined.

For now, though, dear friends, happily the Beckett plate is still spinning. Less wobbly than on Wednesday and Thursday. You've all been so good to me, coming to my aid and rescue without knowledge of what is actually happening, and I apologize for not sharing fully, but I feel it's still premature. After all, aren't the best lessons the ones you've lived through?

Perhaps that's where I get the balls to call myself an educator, or one whose advice is worth your time.

Trial by fire.

Because there's fire everywhere, isn't there?

18

CONTINUE?

THOUGHTS ON DIVORCE, NON- MONOGAMY, AND FRESH STARTS

T hings are different now, certainly. I'm not completely sure exactly how they are different yet.

A life reboot doesn't happen often. Things are new. Strange. There's excitement, yes, but also much trepidation and quite a bit of sadness and loss.

Divorce'll do that, I suppose.

And so we come to the end of the line for the Becketts. Over the last two years our interests were growing apart further and further. When it came right down to it, we stopped being friends. And we liked being friends. So after much discussion, planning, and exploring, we realized that we were better for each other out of the marriage than in.

Impermanence.

Things don't last forever. We like to pretend they do, don't we? There are cottage industries based on happily-ever-after. This is one of the single most pervasive concepts in all of media. That perfect fit.

But we, the non-monogamous, we know that isn't quite right already, don't we? If there was that perfect fit, that one person that we could live happily ever after with, we wouldn't really need anything (anyone) else, would we? Here's where some swingers will attack. They'll say that they don't *need* anyone else, they choose someone else. And sure, many of them could close up swing-shop at any time, for any reason, and live out their days with their partner in a return to monogamy. But I wager that's not true for most.

Or is it that we humans are just tremendously bad at picking our mates? The divorce rate is almost sickly high. Stage 3 at least. Is it because we feel pressure to lock in that perfect person early, before we're ready? We tick the boxes and say, "Welp, she got fourteen out of twenty, and the six she don't have ain't so important." Not sure why that was in a dialect just then. Could you hear it in your head? I could.

The bottom line is that most relationships end before death. Most. And not just the majority of marriages. All the attempts at relationships in our lives also end. The short term, the long term. The best one for us may simply be the most suitable at this time and in this place.

My relationship with Marilyn was like a great vacation. Most of it is awesome, you do fun things, you try new stuff. But there's vacation fatigue, and a little bickering, and ultimately, you go home. This doesn't make the vacation less great, though. I choose to remember my marriage fondly, like that great vacation that came to an end, as all vacations do.

So what of the non-monogamy?

Well, way back at the beginning of the podcast, we asked the boys and the girls a set of questions, one of which being "Could you ever stop being non-monogamous?" For me that answer has always been, and remains, no. Just because my primary relationship has ended doesn't mean I'm shopping for a primary mono. I firmly believe in the tenets of non-monogamy, namely that one person simply cannot fulfill all my needs. Many…most, perhaps… but not all. Emotional. Sexual. Most.

And the inevitable "did you break up because of non-monogamy" question? You saw it in the room, its trunk poking out from beneath the davenport. My answer is a no. But a little.

When a relationship is falling apart in the mono world, you often have nowhere else to turn. You feel a bit of "I'll never love again" or "if I still have emotional needs, I better try to keep those emotions flowing with my partner." Whereas in a non-monogamous relationship, you have other people to help shoulder the burden of these needs. Monogamy has an effect similar to kids on a relationship. One more reason to stick it out.

Boy, both the monos and non-monos may hate me for that one.

In truth, my marriage ended because of growing differences between us. Namely how we wanted to enjoy our lives. The non-mono thumb on the scale may have simply tipped it.

Four and a half years ago my marriage was ending, and non-monogamy gave us four and a half more years, arguably the best of our marriage.

I wouldn't trade my marriage for anything. Nor would I use a time turner to take back the non-monogamy. In my still-developing Zen mode, I see all of this as stepping stones. Without my marriage and how things unfolded, I would not be the person I am; and regardless of what the Internet may say about me, I'm a *damned* sight better than last year, five years ago, ten years ago, fifteen. I'm confident, I'm driven. I feel like I have purpose. That is thanks to Marilyn. That is thanks to where that decision four and a half years ago led.

Without that, I wouldn't have most of what is in my life currently.

Now, a reboot.

I've often thought, as many of us have, what would happen if I'd known "then" what I know now...if I had played things differently. Well, I get to experience a unique pleasure at the moment: that of knowing and starting fresh. The world is a scary place to suddenly change your life in a dramatic fashion, but Current Me is a hell of a lot better prepared than Past Me.

And I have such wonderful people to lean on, to love, and to look back on with fondness.

Thank you, Marilyn. Thank you for our time. You were fantastic, absolutely fantastic! And you know what? So was I.

I hope your reboot is spectacular!

I'm gonna do my damnedest to make sure mine is.

PART IV

EYES WIDE OPEN

1

FOLLOWING MY OPEN SEXUALITY
DOWN THE RABBIT HOLE

"I'm a little bit afraid of you," She told me, shyly hiding beneath a throw pillow.

"Afraid of me?" I was surprised. I felt like I'd restrained myself rather nicely. The day had been spent drinking wine at a massive outdoor wine tasting with a mixed group, so I hadn't been evangelical. Sure, my girlfriend and partner were with us, and they'd been introduced as such. Sure, I'd talked about doing the introduction for Tristan Taormino's podcast and possibly about sex toys at one point. The memory of the day does get hazy at times, perhaps due to the wine.

She nodded and ducked behind the throw pillow, hiding the grin on her face that worked in conflict with the blush crawling up her cheeks.

"Why are you afraid of me?" I asked.

"You're just...so...open."

So open.

I suppose to emphasize the intent, one could add a whole lotta Os on the end of that. Sooo open. I guess I am. I held hands with both women. I'd snuggled and kissed both of them, probably increasingly so once the wine really started to kick in. I highly recommend four hour wine tastings, by the way. I hadn't held back in answering the following questions: "Who is Tristan Taormino?" and the follow-up "What is a sex educator?"

Maybe I have reached that tipping point where being myself is simply being so open that, very occasionally, I may frighten someone who wasn't quite ready to hear all about it. I don't want to frighten people. But her grin beneath the pillow belied her fascination. It may not have translated into a desire to learn more that day, but I'm sure that's down the line. Discussion and interest begets more discussion and interest.

Jack and Anne, our friends, her neighbors, had prepped her a little bit, though the extent of this prep is uncertain because I was informed of it late in the evening (post four hour wine tasting. I did *not* use a spit bucket). I'm reasonably certain that they'd told her that I have an open relationship, and that I would be bringing multiple partners. You know, so as not to arouse that "what the hell is going on" thing that people do when they're not privy to the major info and a member of the group is snogging multiple people.

What I marvel about is the implication about me, about who I am now.

Not too long ago I discovered a journal from the summer after high school. By journal, I mean a book with about ten pages filled, and the rest scattered promises to write more in the journal spread out at ever-increasing intervals into the successive years. Most of the material is entirely inconsequential, but there was one interesting and very short passage in there: "Laura and I have decided to wait until marriage for sex."

There wasn't a lot of follow-up on this decision. As a future entry bore out, the decision itself didn't last very long. This was the girl I lost my virginity to. The girl I was certain was going to be my "forever after." At the ripe old age of 18 I'd had my entire life figured out. This planned life was very simple: marriage, kids, future.

That relationship lasted fourteen months. I believe we had sex a few months in, which also means we were discussing the future and marriage at that point. Fourteen years later, here I am. A non-monogamist, certainly. Flavors? Swinger, with a side of poly. Jeezly crow! How does one go from "waiting until marriage for sex" and, judging from the surrounding prose, believing that this was truly the *right* path, the *right* decision, all the way down the rabbit hole to "you're just...so...open."

Following the time line forward a bit, because I'm an archivist of my life, out of the ether arises a saved email exchange with Margot, the girl who came after and was two years younger than me. She was still in high school, still 17, but far more experienced and mature than I to be sure. Within a back and forth exchange that followed our first date, she asked what my stance on monogamy was.

With the benefit of hindsight, I realize that she was open. And that she was far too much for my 19-year-old boy brain to handle indeed. I told her that "I'm a firm believer in 'one man-one woman'" (something that makes me gag for entirely other reasons) "but wouldn't presume to tell you how to navigate our" (then days old) "relationship."

She assured me that she had no intention of looking elsewhere and the matter was closed. We dated for just around a month before she tired of me. I can't blame her. Knowing her now (what little I've gleaned through a passive Facebook friendship) I realize that she had opened the door a crack, only for me to quickly shut it again. I'm reminded of the Pink Floyd lines, catching a fleeting glimpse when he was a child, out of the corner of his eye.

Still today, I am so open that I frighten "the straights," so much so that this lovely girl was hiding behind a cushion on Jack and Anne's couch while I drunkenly tried to deconstruct why she might be afraid of my openness. Somewhere, at some point, things changed. Somewhere down the line, I changed.

Thank whatever imaginary god might want to take credit for that.

2

THE KEY TO A SUCCESSFUL REBOOT

I'm never swinging again.

I've said that. Yes, me. You know me. Swinging guy. My middle name is Swingin' for chrissakes. It's true! I mean, fictional, but true as far as that goes. I've said, multiple times over the course of my non-monogamous lifestyle, that I'm done with it all. Just like we've all had those moments where we're completely done with dating, or where we don't ever want to go back to that job. Or, where maybe we're just never getting out of bed at all again.

I'm someone who struggles with depression. For me, one of the defining features of depression is the complete lack of interest in so many things, often including sex. I've thought about a date I was supposed to go on, that most certainly would be involving sex, and just been uninterested in the whole thing. Be it because of my weight, or because of my exhaustion, or simply because of the nebulous fear/anger/sadness that accompanies depression. I'm done.

A close friend of mine recently experienced this first hand, agonizing on multiple occasions that she may never again be interested in swinging. She'd just gone through a major life shift. Depression and life changes are very similar. Both create valleys of emotion that are nearly impossible to see out of.

All we can see is what's directly in front of us, and the sometimes-crushing feeling that we're not good enough for it.

I had a major breakup early on in my poly explorations, and it made me seriously doubt I'd ever have any interest in doing that again. I've also experienced static in the swinging lifestyle that showed me the negative side of that, and again gave me that "pulling the lever and shutting it down" feeling.

These reasons can be small, like a single bad experience that just poisons the idea for you. They can also be big, like major life changes or depression, changing your whole perception of the world, of your choices, and of the lifestyle.

My friend's biggest concern was that she wanted to *want to* swing again. She wanted to want that physicality, because it had been such a huge part of her life, but she couldn't see outside the valley.

So I boiled it down for her. You may never swing again, and that's okay. But that isn't a decision that needs to be made. You don't have to say "Okay, swinging is over," or, "Swinging is still on," because life is fluid, evolving, changing. Sometimes it's the decision for or against that is the scary one.

So don't make that choice, especially from the depths of depression, especially from the valley. Instead look at yourself like a system that needs rebooting.

Like *Apollo 13*.

"...What?" you ask.

Okay, so remember that they shut down all the systems in the capsule and used the LEM as a lifeboat. But then they had to turn everything back on without ruining their vehicle to return to Earth.

First off, remember it's okay if you don't ever swing

again, or don't ever consider yourself poly again. This isn't a screed to convince you to "return to the fold."

But if you have those concerns, if you have those big feelings, turning things back on one switch at a time is a great way to go. When you turn on the lower impact switches (making out with someone new, going for coffee, trading dirty pics) it can tell you how well the system is functioning, and if you're ready to flip some of the upper switches yet.

Just like Gary Sinise learned time and time again as he was running through the simulated fix for Apollo 13 (and yes, folks, I know that it was Ken Mattingly who was actually doing the simulations, and that Gary Sinise is an actor and head of the *Lt. Dan Band*) if you flip the switches in the wrong order you overload the system and won't survive re-entry.

If you're in one of those valleys, and are trying to get back out, or simply to explore if you may ever come back out of it (you will), start slowly. Start methodically. If you overload the system, that's okay. You can start on the first switches again.

Or, again, you don't have to.

Being in the lifestyle is a choice that is no better or worse than not being in the lifestyle. It's all about how you feel, and what makes you happy.

3

SEX IS SEX IS SEX

WITH OR WITHOUT PENETRATION

S omehow, I managed to achieve that elusive disconnect between the traditional notion of sex (i.e. me putting my penis into things other than mouths) and the word "sex." Dan Savage recently said that if there was one thing the heterosexual world could learn from the homosexuals, it's that sex is any form of sexual congress. This concept ensures that we're not simply stampeding to the perceived goal line, and don't feel we haven't achieved something if there isn't penetrative penis-in-vagina sex.

I felt that way for a long time.

Recently I wrote about a party where I consciously tried to change this concept. I made myself aware of my pattern, which would be to try to blow my way through interactions to get to the sexual finale in order to be able to play with as many of my friends as possible in a short amount of time. It never had anything to do with not respecting the time I spent with each of them, I loved all of it. I care deeply about those women whom I manage to spend quality sexy time with at parties, and since many of them I only see at parties, it makes it all the more impor-tant that I find the time.

This line of thought was detrimental, however, because

it caused me to put a tremendous amount of pressure on myself, perform giving oral, perform receiving oral (but don't fucking come!), and then perform sexually all the way to the goal line. Often by the second tryst of the evening I was already beginning to struggle. Beyond that, all involved were lucky to get half-mast.

This, as an aside, is what caused me to go from pretty good at digital stimulation to exceptional. I know that sounds braggy, but there are few things I am good enough at to brag with such confidence, as fingering. And, I can provide references if needed.

So, why did I do this?

If I was shortchanging myself by not being able to relax and enjoy things, and if I was shortchanging my partners, what was it? It just made sense to me, because that's what you do as a full swap swinger, right? You swap and fuck. Rinse, repeat. Was that an ookier colloquialism than I intended? Hmm. It's because I'd convinced myself that this was what was expected of me. When I start something (say, putting my hand down there and feeling her response) I ought to see it through, right? *Right?*!

Then I began to recognize that these notions I had about swinging at the beginning (most told to me by my "swinging sire" about whom the less said, the better) were, perhaps, incorrect…or at least misleading.

Early on, I painstakingly shaved every inch of my genitals because I was told that this was how things were done. That no one would play with me if I wasn't immaculately groomed. That if I wanted it licked, it should be *bare*. I shaved daily, despite my skin clearly having a problem with this type of attention. It took my doctor asking me why on Earth I keep shaving when my body clearly doesn't want me to for me to wonder about the logic of what I was doing.

So I stopped shaving, and nobody cared. Nobody who mattered, anyway.

In my attempts to live up to the "swinger standard"

that was sent down from on high, I didn't see what was right in front of me. Rules only have value if you, and those around you, feel they have value.

It amuses me (and horrifies in equal part) that a group of people such as we swingers, so hell bent on ignoring that which we "should" be doing (i.e. being monogamous, sticking with one gender or another) could get so caught up in other "shoulds." You should always come, you should always get it up, you should always reciprocate, you should always fuck. Why the hell would these ideals always line up?

Well, the short answer is that they don't. And that we're often sheep. We reject one dogma to follow another and get swept away.

In the past, I've also felt somehow shortchanged if events didn't progress, if I "only" got a hand job. I stop and think about how amazing and disgraceful a thought that is, and how my 16 year old self would conspire to have me shot if he knew I'd even considered that thought. I was jaded, and had a bad case of "the shoulds."

But perhaps I've achieved enlightenment. Things certainly feel different.

I'm currently flying the final leg of my trip back to Chicago from a week in paradise at Desire Resort & Spa, the first *Life on the Swingset* trip to Desire. At the resort I decided to no longer focus on penetrative (penis-in-vagina) sex. It was like a weight had been lifted. The removal of expectations about what things would become allowed us to concentrate instead on what things are.

To live in the moment, for a change.

I focused on whether I was giving or receiving pleasure. I could make out for a while with someone. I could perform oral on others. I could allow an urge to simply do one single thing with someone be paramount.

And just as when I stopped shaving, nobody pitched a fit and banished me. In fact, everybody I was lucky enough to encounter seemed to be as excited about what was going on in the moment as I was. Never was there a "We're not going to fuck?" or "Why aren't you hard?"

I realized that I'm far more interested in the pleasure of others than myself. I spent the week giving pleasure to those open to receive it; orally, digitally, nJoy Elevenally.

"Cooper, you braggart," you say, "you think you're better than me?"

Not at all, random voice guy who interrupts my essays sometimes. I receive as well. I had some truly spectacular moments of orgasmic bliss. But because I was not focused on when we would complete the transaction and I would insert my penis into her (or his, I'm equal opportunity) nether regions, I was able to see every bit of sexual interaction as the glorious experience it truly is. Nothing makes people want to please you more than putting yourself out as a giver of pleasure.

And isn't that a wonderful way to live?

So, mark the date and time. My last party was not an isolated incident of emotional evolution on my part. That was just proof of concept. Desire represented physical, emotional, and (dare I say) spiritual growth within me.

My heart is full of joy.

4

FLIPPING THE SWITCH

P-SPOT AND G-SPOT ORGASMS

I continue to be impressed by the gushing orgasm, something that usually is connected to the g-spot orgasm, suddenly being achieved from clitoral stimulation, or even lighter, vaguer stimulation. In many ways it's like flipping a switch. Those women I know who have been able to transition from the gushing orgasm only being an occasional thing directly connected to intense g-spot stimulation (usually with a brute force g-spot stimulator like the nJoy Eleven or Pure Wand) to a more and more frequent occurrence that no longer requires direct g-spot stimulation, have told me that they just started doing it. I've had a few women lament that once the switch was flipped, there was no going back. I don't know why I didn't consider that the same might be true for the type of orgasms achieved from prostate stimulation.

I suppose it's partly because prostate orgasms are so rare in my experience, and in media, and conversation. They're also fairly hard to describe. And let's face it, we orgasming men are lucky enough to have very easy to describe orgasms. Hint: It usually involves ejaculation.

The disparity of descriptions of prostate orgasms, both from givers and receivers, is what partly caused me to still debate whether that was even what I had had last year in Desire, courtesy of an amazing blonde. But no, after talking to everybody (perhaps an exaggeration, but I talked to a lot of people) about it, the general consensus is that my tremor inducing, extended sequence was indeed that elusive prostate orgasm.

A funny thing happened since then. I think the switch was flipped. I've had a few minor prostate orgasms since then directly resulting from prostate stimulation, not including ejaculation. These definitely felt the same as that major orgasm last year, but were a bit shorter and lighter. Both resulted in the uncontrolled tremors that only seem to increase in sensation. Both caused me to draw my knees up to my chest. Both caused aftershocks.

Can I describe it? Not really. An ejaculation has always left me feeling drained. As though Brigadier General Jack D. Ripper's crazy notions about the depletion of Precious Bodily Fluids was actually true. This was, in fact, what caused me to really work to please my partner first as a policy, because once that orgasm comes, I occasionally even find it difficult to focus my eyes. But these prostate orgasms, I find myself laughing through most of the tremors. Fascinating. Exhilarating.

So the switch?

Well, the tremors started appearing during "traditional" orgasms that include ejaculation. Often just after an orgasm, I'd be able to ride the wave for a good thirty seconds to a minute. Whereas I'm sure many of my male bodied friends out there will agree most of them are a "shoot-sensation-done" affair.

Saturday night I experienced something new. After a particularly vigorous play session of mutual oral stimulation (am I the only one who finds those specific words *very* sexy?) I came, a big traditional orgasm, indeed. I laid down next to the amazing girl who brought me to climax and started to shake. The tremors that are occasionally that final wave just lapped and lapped, rising and falling, hitting alternately heavily and softly, on and on. Fifteen minutes perhaps.

I've wondered about these tremors in the past, because occasionally I feel like I jump start them mentally. By just going ahead and shaking on my own, I can kick one out. This has led me to wonder if these were a set of mental gymnastics I was doing in order to convince myself I was feeling something. But then I discarded that thought, because if I can mentally cause an orgasm, does that make it less real? And if I can mentally achieve the sensation of orgasm without the stimulation, is that somehow fake? No. They all come from my head anyway. They all come from all of our heads, don't they?

I'm unsure where this leads. Will the tremor orgasms be a part of all of my orgasms now? They don't seem to occur when I'm taking care of myself, which might suggest an openness to them in situations. I'm often just looking to shoot and go to bed when on my own. All I do know is that a switch has been flipped. I have one very important woman to thank for flipping it the first time, and then all who have flipped it since.

I can't wait to see how the orgasms continue to change.

5

I SUCK AT TIME MANAGEMENT

(AND TITLING, APPARENTLY)

My name is Cooper Beckett and I am terrible at time management.

As children, life seems so vast and open and full of empty spaces. As adults we take after Roger Waters and ask what we should use to fill those empty spaces. We don't even do it consciously, stuff just creeps.

I first started to notice it when I became non-monogamous. Where previously looking at a monthly calendar would yield a busy Friday here, Saturday there, one or two Sunday dinners or game nights with my family, post opening-up it's as though my social life decided to pursue aggressive expansion. Regular Monday night dates, Friday nights, Saturday parties, Sunday barbecues.

We became slaves to Google Calendar.

And, as an aside, if you come away from this essay with nothing enriching at all, at least understand that in non-monogamy, Google Calendar is a must.

Of course time and changes happened, and I became a podcast host, and webmaster, started producing other podcasts, plotting books with the byline *Swingset*, going to conventions, plotting epic trips to Desire Resort & Spa in Mexico. Becoming poly added another wrinkle. Where before playmates were pretty on and off throughout the month, more serious relationships begged for more regular seeing-each-other patterns, filling up most weeknights.

I learned something about myself in there. Every couple months I'd fall into a funk, a malaise accompanied by shortness of breath, headaches, and the occasional "I don't want to do this anymore," with "this" being so many things…swinging, podcasts, getting out of bed. Like a far less glamorous *Scarface*, first I got the headaches, then I got the panic, then I got the depression.

Ah, depression, my old friend. I can occasionally see it, waiting in the wings, ready to re-emerge; sometimes randomly, but usually with a bit of forewarning, and pretty definite inciting incidents.

A couple weeks back, Ophilia and I moved in with Miko and family. The move was stressful (aren't they all?) and left me with the horrified realization of just how much stuff I own even after trying to give much of it away before the move.

Running parallel to the move, two groups I'm actively involved in, *Sex-positive Chicago* and *Sex Geekdom Chicago*, were both throwing events. Prior to this, the groups were nearly dormant, with my monthly knitting circle at *The Pleasure Chest* being the only real recurring event.

I also thought it'd be a good time to launch two new podcasts, *Eat The Rudecast* (a podcast about NBC's *Hannibal* with Ophilia and Miko), and *Carnalcopia* (one I'm producing, hosted by Ashley Manta and Katie Mack) for what is rapidly becoming *Swingset.FM - The Swingset Network.*

There are all sorts of good here, truly. I went to a dungeon and participated for the first time since Mission Control in San Francisco. Ophilia and I demonstrated pegging techniques for a rapt audience. Well, really, Ophilia demonstrated techniques. I demonstrated what a jittery prostate orgasm looks like (for fourteenish minutes). Two episodes of *The Rudecast* recorded, two of *Carnalcopia*, and one of the most enjoyable mailbag double features in *Swingset* history.

But still, earlier this week, I looked at my schedule and felt the tickle. The shortness of breath, the headaches. These begat a lack of sleep, restless sleep, distressing dream filled sleep. My temper is short. Boxes around the house upset me. Even mine.

Too much.

This morning it came to a head and I experienced one of my "Just call in sick" mornings. I even debated what ailment I should use, as most US companies still don't recognize mental health days. I went to work like a zombie, snappy at most I spoke to, vacant from others. If this were five years ago, I would've been a perpetual orange "away" symbol.

I canceled multiple events I'd scheduled this weekend, then looked ahead and took a few random things off my calendar. I need a break. I need real time to just be here for me. And to get those things done that come up when I'm stressed. Like "Coop, you really should create awesome home pages for the different categories, especially since *Carnalcopia* is premiering next week," or, "Coop, why don't you finish that fucking freelance PowerPoint so you can get that extra money and we can finish paying for the flights to Mexico?"

Apparently my mind uses the royal "we."

I guess this isn't really about time management, nor is there much for you to "come away with" other than the fact that I, Cooper Beckett, the guy you listen to for advice on how to "do" non-monogamy, isn't very good at it. And that I regularly freak myself out by doing too much.

But *damn*, Google Calendar is helpful. You should use it. You should do all the things.

Unless they stress you out. Then take your time.

Maybe that's the moral.

If there is one.

6

CREATING A NEW FAMILY

I am a collector of people. I surround myself as much and often as possible with friends and loved ones. Solitude is an occasional need and I enjoy it thoroughly when I allow it for myself, but overall what I need, what I want, is family.

I'm quite close to my actual family. I see them regularly, we go out to eat, we watch movies together. But there are things you don't talk to your family about. Not because they wouldn't understand (though they may not) but more because they're just not things you talk with them about. I'm sure some do discuss sex with their parents or siblings. They talk about those dark and dirty secrets, joke about times they were drunk, times they were high, times they did things that they most definitely shouldn't be doing.

I am not one of those people.

I share things with my family that they need to know, that I think would be valuable for them to know, and that I think would benefit me to have them know. These are all good reasons to share. But for most of this we do need to draw our comfort elsewhere, from our other family.

For many this family is as small as "partner," and that may well fill their need fully. They may have that sole confidant role wrapped up and tell each other absolutely everything.

I am also not one of *those* people.

I've always had many confidants, ranging from long-time friends, to ex-girlfriends, to new friends who had the misfortune of asking. I'd listen to their problems and issues, I'd identify with what I could, I'd dispense the advice that's asked for (and often advice that wasn't asked for) and then hope for a return of the same from them. This was my proto-family.

Before swinging I threw countless parties, movie nights, dinners, gatherings, get-togethers. I didn't realize it then, but I now see that I was longing to extend the comfort of my small family with many more. Years later I'm doing the same kind of collecting that I did then, but now for very different reasons.

I believe that anyone embarking on a life of non-monogamy (be it swinging, polyamory, or really any form of alternative lifestyle that might shock/appall/offend the "straights") needs one thing above all others: community.

Community is how we learn that we are not alone. It reinforces that, despite the fact that all the network criminal investigation shows might portray your little niche of the sexuality spectrum as serial killers (or worse, jokes) there are, in fact, others like you.

Depending on what your own personal thing is, there are likely hundreds, thousands, millions like you. I think that discovering these people is the single most important thing that you can do when opening up. For obvious reasons, you can't swing or be poly alone. Beyond that, it's easy to get discouraged when you make a mistake. Or feel like it's not working. Or stumble. Or get that jealousy bug that websites like this one try so hard to tell you is bad. You need people you can talk to.

Personally, when I look at the swinging spectrum specifically, I see a disproportionate amount of people who swing as I do with friendship, with closeness, with community. I have a group of friends that I interact with, who know each other and like each other. I see many of my swinger friends in non-swinger environments, from barbecues, to even family birthday parties and graduations. In our group there isn't any of that concern about "What if someone who doesn't know met my friends...would they suspect?" I want to be surrounded by my open friends as much, if not more so, than others.

I've built a new family. A group of people whose lives are all very different, who if you saw them interacting at a party you'd be hard pressed to figure out what this group has in common, yet who all care about each other's lives and needs, and are willing to throw down and do anything they can to help. I treasure those I've met in the swinging lifestyle, and I look forward to the uniqueness of family that polyamory is sure to bring.

7

INTOLERANCE

With a title like *Intolerance*, you're likely expecting me to rant about the vanilla world and their intolerance for us over here on the open side. But this isn't about that, at least not directly. It's about me. Cooper's favorite subject is Cooper after all. How else can he pretentiously write about himself in the third person?

I preach tolerance. And as I do, I use the word preach in the most ironic fashion I possibly can. I'm all about getting along, and allowing for other people's opinions no matter how different from yours they might be. After all, isn't that what we're asking of the vanillas? Let us be? Don't get pissed at us because we've figured out something that goes against your ethos, or your morality, or your belief that jealousy is a healthy thing.

We want that, right? We want them to tolerate us if they can't get behind our lifestyles.

Because of this, I think a lot about how hypocritical it is that I am becoming less and less tolerant as I get older. I'm finding it harder and harder to smile and nod as friends and acquaintances and Facebookers talk about Christ's place in their lives. Even harder to listen to those and those with similar beliefs talk about how they don't hate gays; that they hate the sin, not the sinner. Harder and harder to even accept when people put forth the argument that the church does some good, that conservative organizations do some good, that *Susan G. Komen For The Cure* had some sort of right to sentence poor women to death from breast cancer when they *pulled funding for breast cancer screenings* because of the idiotic notion that life begins anywhere but birth.

See what happened there? I just sort of went off the rails. I started trying to be accepting and tolerant. But I couldn't do it.

And more and more I'm unfriending people on Facebook when they say things like "it's about babies!" when we discuss the contraception mandate, or who don't understand that more birth control equals fewer abortions.

Why is that such a difficult correlation to understand?

Or is Dan Savage right when he says they hate us because we're enjoying sex? Is that really it? That they feel guilty each and every time they have sex for fun, and each and every time they use a condom. And I believe that Rick Santorum asks for forgiveness from his incredibly petty and micromanaging God when he gets his little penis sucked on.

That was unfair. I don't actually know that Rick Santorum has a little penis. He may be massively well endowed.

Used to be, I could accept what the conservatives tell me: "Yes, that's part of our group, but a fringe part. You shouldn't judge us for the actions of our more extreme and hateful members." I'd nod and say, "Yes, that makes sense; no, you're not out proclaiming that I'm a sinner, or that anyone who explores themselves, their body, their sexuality, is somehow evil, or worthy of the furnace after-party."

But then I thought about the way they use that to get around the fact that they're still supporting The Church. I'm specifically talking about Catholicism and Pope Palpatine in Rome here - I feel I can speak to that mostly because that's the branch I escaped from. All money that goes to the church is tainted.

HYPOCRITE ALERT!! Am I really saying that they can't support part of an organization that they agree with while vocally distancing themselves from the portions they don't agree with, while I whine about Komen taking away funding for the part that they agree with because of the part they don't? I'm saying it's the same thing.

But here's where I consider my intolerance justified: the intolerance of reproductive rights for women puts the rights of *potential* humans above the rights of *actual living, breathing humans.*

If you care so much about the unborn baby in a teenage girl's belly that you won't help her not have that baby in the first place, because you teach abstinence only and that works *soooo* well, and you won't allow her school to give out the condoms or knowledge she needs, and you won't help her take care of herself if she can't afford it, and you won't help her raise the child after it's born, and you cut the amount of time she can be unemployed and still make money, you're basically saying "I don't give a fuck how you take care of that baby you don't want, or how you treat it after it's born, you must have it."

That's an unacceptable position.

And here's where my true intolerance comes in. I don't want to hear about it. Those stopping gays from being allowed to legally marry are *wrong.* The same way those defended slavery were *wrong.* The same way those who said women couldn't vote were *wrong.* The way impinging on basic human rights is *wrong, wrong, wrong.*

Freedom of religion is also freedom *from* religion. There isn't a war on religion, there's a war on those who feel that religion should govern everybody regardless of their beliefs.

See how intolerant I am?

8

ADVENTURES IN SUBSPACE

S ubspace.

Ginger assured me this was a thing.

At the time of our first discussion about it, the only association I had with the term was that weird little dark parallel world you could dip into with a potion to find the red mushrooms and avoid Shyguys and Snifits.

I may have said something eloquent and witty, like "Eyuh?" Non-committal by any stretch of human commun-ication, but simultaneously glossing over the facts that I both didn't know what she was talking about *and* was lost in reflection over whether I preferred the *Lost Levels* version of *Super Mario Bros 2* or the *Doki Doki Panic* fever dream version that the USA ultimately received after the original was deemed "too hard" for us.

(Hey, Coop here, I just wanted to mention that Subspace is a sort of "side quest level" in the American *Super Mario Bros 2* [and the aforementioned *Doki Doki Panic*]. I probably won't talk about it much more in this essay, but I make no guarantees.)

I don't remember what brought it up, probably one of my many "I just don't understand _____" conver-sations with Ginger back in the day, but it was then that she told me subspace was a state of mind you can get into as a submissive. This state of mind can result in many different experiences, but is often mentioned as being akin to an out of body experience.

Like that sidestep jaunt from Subcon to Subspace in *SMB2*. Sorry, sorry, I know, I know.

It's one of those abstract concepts that, unless you've experienced it, is really hard to wrap your mind around… like trying to get someone to explain their acid trip with any sort of lucidity.

Personally, I've only mildly skirted the edge of subspace. I've enjoyed being submissive, of course, but rarely is it *seriously* submissive. Maybe that's my personality, snarky to the absolute edge. My first submissive experience was three years ago, now. The experience followed much of my usual pattern. When I try something new, especially sexually, and have a guide, or someone far more experienced than I, I want to know as much as possible about it. I ask all sorts of questions and discuss the process. This feeds my sapiosexual side, and my fascination with processes, and begins to solidify into a sort of mental checklist on how I may eventually write about this or podcast about it. What it doesn't do is really allow for getting lost in an experience.

This isn't bitching, I assure you. I don't feel like I'm having less fun than someone who can fully lose themselves. I would even argue that at times I'm getting more out of an experience because of the different levels on which I'm actively engaging.

That's how I know I hit subspace that night. I wasn't drinking at all. I was asking all my questions. I am very aware of the sequence of events for about 45% of the experience. And then, I don't know…rushing through a dark version of reality in search of a mushroom, perhaps. When I reviewed the evening with my mistress and friends who were there, I remembered everything, but it all had this strange other-worldly haze accompanying it.

I mention this because, as a skeptical "that's not how brains work" guy, I feel it's an important point. I'm sure the arguments could be made about why the brain does this and why you can slide into this type of experience as a sub. I'm sure the same arguments can be made for many other types of experiences.

As a sub, though, you can let go of much of your cognitive function because you've discussed boundaries and rules and the scene beforehand. So you can, simply, let go.

I did that again this past Friday, stumbling into a sub position on a FMF date.

Yeah, like I tripped and fell into sub. Explanabrag.

I was my usual snarky and suggestion-filled self, sorta topping from the bottom, sorta guiding the scene. That is until they wondered about using a ball gag on me.

DING! New experience!

And then blindfolded me.

And then [REEL MISSING] fuck if I know, honestly. The snippets (not to be confused with Snifits) I remember are short and could be compounded into a five minute sequence, and I know we were at play far longer than that. There was flogging, there was paddling, there were eventually gloves slipped on my hands and then girls sitting on them. They came, I came.

I found it hard to stand afterward. I recognized the haze again…this overwhelmingly pleasant fog, knowing that I had such a wonderful time that the details were somehow inconsequential, knowing that perhaps next time I should shut up and roll with it sooner, 'cuz subspace is a thing. And while it's a similar thing to when I question whether I can psych myself up mentally to the prostate orgasm, again, it doesn't matter.

It's *all* in my mind.

And in *Super Mario Bros 2*. (Which all took place in Mario's mind. ['Cuz it was a dream. Really.])

9

THE PARADOX OF POLYAMORY

Nearly everybody I know who has experienced real problems in the polyamorous lifestyle (I'm including myself in this) has had the cornerstone of their issues be the Paradox of Polyamory, a cyclical problem that is incredibly difficult to work around. Those who manage to work around it are very successful at poly. Those who manage to avoid it entirely are gods amongst the rest of us and should be treated as such.

Because I really don't like using overly simplistic examples for my essays like A&B&C, I'm going to make it only vaguely less simplistic by introducing Adam & Beth & Connie.

Adam and Beth are a happy couple exploring polyamory. Who wouldn't be, after all? They've done some experi-menting, had some dates, had the high highs of open relationships, and aside from some bumps early on it's been pretty smooth sailing.

Doesn't that sound nice? Don't you want to know their *OKCupid* profile names?

Then Connie comes along.

Cue ominous music.

But Connie's not ominous in the least. She's an incredibly understanding and open person. When she meets Adam, they hit it off immediately.

Again let's sidestep that ominous cliché by telling you that Adam, Beth, and Connie get along just fine, but the connection is between Adam and Connie. So here's where the ball starts rolling, doesn't it? There's that little flaw. There's some unexpected jealousy.

Maybe you just have never seen your partner so happy with someone else before. "You," meaning Beth. Beth has never seen Adam so happy with someone other than herself before. She's seeing a mirror of the beginning of their relationship, back when it was all carefree and stolen kisses.

The compersion muscle kicks in, but the fact that we, in life, have very little reason to use this muscle regularly has left it…not great. Beth is happy for Adam and Connie, legitimately so, and she encourages the relationship. She really does mean it when she says that she just wants him to be happy.

The weak compersion muscle allows stray moments of jealousy to get through here and there. What if he'd rather spend time with her? We've been arguing about bills so much lately, he doesn't have to worry about that with her!

All of us, even those who've managed to achieve non-monogamy nirvana (non-mono-vana?) have experienced this feeling. I will call you a liar to your face if you tell me you haven't.

To. Your. Face.

And there's the turning point, after all, when it all goes pear-shaped. The wheel in the sky has begun to turn and many of us are helpless to do anything but watch it spin.

The pangs of jealousy that are coming through begin seep into Adam and Beth's day-to-day life. Conversations become a bit more unhinged. The stress has descended. That already overworked compersion muscle collapses from fatigue more and more often. Strain can cause even the happiest of relationships to slide into chaos.

While this is happening, though, Adam is experiencing a respite when he's with Connie. There's no stress, there're no bills to pay. He's still experiencing the glory of New Relationship Energy as he navigates through this relationship.

These secondary relationships can be a sort of "vacation home" to escape to, a place devoid of the problems of their day-to-day life. This vacation home can reinforce a sort of delusion that in this place there are no problems.

Adam and Beth argue more frequently as the heat gets turned up on the relationship. Beth zeroes in on Connie as the cause of the trouble as, after all, it hadn't been there before. With Connie to blame, the twisted logic goes to "cut out the cancer, save the host," which is a very dark way of looking at it indeed. I chose those words carefully, because of how deeply this cycle can shove you down the rabbit hole. You're desperate to save your relationship, and you can't understand why it has gone askew.

Adam isn't willing to cut the one sunshiney part out of his life, so he refuses to break up with her. He resents the request, assuming that Beth didn't want his happiness after all. The relationship with Connie looks absurdly simple in comparison to the growing resentment and anger that lives at home. He starts to, in his weaker moments, wonder if he wouldn't be happier breaking up with Beth and being with Connie full time.

Who hasn't seen this spiral in themselves or in their circle of poly friends?

The paradox for Adam is that he has changed since pre-Connie. We aren't static, after all. To go back would mean to change back, and he's likely to have changed for the better in a number of ways. Also, to break up with Connie would dramatically hurt the very real person he was dating all this time. To break up with Beth instead would be an admission of defeat, when the relationship is just strained now. There is no good solution to the problem, just different levels of shit.

The paradox for Connie is that she's getting fed a filtered version of what's going on, so she can either believe everything Adam (who is processing through hurt) is feeling, or she can look objectively and risk hurting everyone. To leave would be the humane way to "save the host" but would also hurt both her and Adam. There is no good solution to this problem.

The paradox for Beth is the worst because it is the one that ramps up quickest. By not being the "supportive partner" in the poly relationship, she is directly contributing to the resentment Adam is feeling for her not being the "supportive partner." She wants nothing more than for her compersion muscle to be strong, to endure this, to get back to the way things were. Asking Adam to leave Connie only reinforces her outsider status.

Being in this serious relationship means, perhaps, that their finances or living spaces are entwined to the point that she can't eliminate some potential major sources of stress on account of being a human couple that exists in the world. Completely full-throttling her support for Adam and Connie's relationship would mean driving down deep some of her most basic lizard brain reactions, potentially causing greater resentment if Adam doesn't seem to sufficiently recognize her sacrifice.

Once the wheel starts spinning, the reactions get less and less logical. It's like the carnival ride where you are stuck to the walls of the spinning wheel. You can move and lift your arms at the beginning, but the longer you are there the more difficult it becomes to execute any type of change without the potential for great pain. So, it's not a *perfect* metaphor. This is as dark as it gets for poly. Because the network of humans we bring into our lives add complexity, and complexity makes change more and more difficult.

"So, Coop, man, why'd…uh…why'd you have to go and bum us all out with this?"

Because you should be aware? I dunno. Because if you recognize these symptoms you can try to counteract them.

Because Adam could've tried not talking constantly about his new relationship. Because Beth could've relaxed a little and recognized how goofy new lovers make us feel. Because Connie, well, I didn't really flesh out her side of the story, so let's assume she was, in general, doing the best she could to make everybody happy without intruding into Beth's life too much.

Because the real paradox of polyamory is that it offers these connections. The reason we connect to all these people is because of the vast richness that each new person can bring to our lives, filling spaces that weren't filled before and helping to build the safety net beneath us, and the network of helping hands above us. That is the promise of poly, and what it can bring us. The paradox is what it can do to us, amplifying emotion when broadcast through the network.

It reminds us of the old adage that we all hate so very much: "If you love something, set it free." Freedom breeds gratitude, which breeds happiness, which tones that compersion muscle that we all usually allow to atrophy. And then we may not be so frightened all the time.

Let your partners be free to explore, and be gentle to them as well.

10

PODCASTING CAN BE LONELY

"Oh, poor Cooper," you say, immediately confron-tational for some reason.

I put up my hands. That means stop. Or sometimes it means "Look how clean my hands are."

Podcasting can be a lonely pursuit at times. You predominantly interact with people that don't have physi-cality in your world. They're avatars, they're ones and zeros. They exist for real somewhere, of course. Most of them, anyway…there are the bots after all. But few exist beyond text on a screen.

Writing for a website is the same way. It's a lot of work, and a tremendous output of self. We sex bloggers reveal so much to so many people (at least we hope for "so many") and can often get to wondering if we're just shouting into the void.

Over the last three months, as Swingset began its fifth year in existence, Miko and I have really pulled out all the stops building Swingset 3.0, after having been settled some-where around 2.5 for a couple years. We're re-launching the website and building our first real app.

I'm not complaining at all. I think I have had more fun working on the *Life on the Swingset* website this year than I have in the entirety of the two years before. Sure, much of my enthusiasm downturn was due to burnout and a general implosion of my personal life. But randomly, in mid-January, it became fun again.

So much fun, in fact, that I'd routinely leave my nine hour a day job (big shocker, *Swingset* doesn't actually pay me) and sit down for five to six hours of work on the website or the social networks. I rediscovered the love.

But no amount of that love for the work can compare to turning those avatars, those ones and zeroes, into actual flesh and blood people you can hug.

"Hello, I'm Cooper. I am a hugger."

I've only really had sporadic opportunities to do that, and I almost missed this one.

We realized late last year that *Swingset* couldn't afford another CatalystCon trip.

Want to sponsor us? Email me. "Hello, I'm Cooper. I am shameless."

Dylan and Miko were going to head to CatalystCon East to represent, regardless. With Swingset well represented, I could catch up on all the other work I'd been postponing.

But then Friday morning happened and I saw the tweets start rolling in from the Hilton in DC. And I realized that for me it ultimately wasn't about *Swingset* being represented, it was about connecting with the world. Seeing those people. Interacting. So I bought a ticket on a whim, something I'd never done before.

Within the first minute I was at the hotel I ran into Greg DeLong of nJoy and showed him my "I [nJoy] Anal" and "[buttplug] Inside" buttons.

There is definite value in as much *Swingset* presence at conventions as possible, and I'm tremendously proud of the factions that we have built over the last few cons who brand themselves as Swingsetters. They rock!

For the moment, though, what I see most is the value of me being present with people. To them, sure, in that weird braggy way, but the value of their being present to me. Refilling at a con is what allows me to keep plowing through. To recognize that we may be shouting into the void, but there are so many people out there who can hear us, and can interact with us. So many people shouting back toward us. So many wonderful people.

I plan to talk business this weekend, to talk pleasure, to talk *Doctor Who* (have already been shown TARDIS socks thanks to my NASA/TARDIS shirt) and remind myself what I've been working so hard for.

For, being The Narcissist at the center of *Life on the Swingset*, I often feel that we are still this tiny fish, that we don't make a big difference, that we're just talking the way we were 150 episodes ago (when our download numbers were ten).

The personal connections give me what I need: the recognition of reach.

11

THE BISEXUAL MALE APOCALYPSE

I'm doing the academic thing here. Perhaps the pedantic thing. Perhaps the persnickety-you-won't-want-to-hang-out-with-Coop-anymore thing. I'm using apocalypse's translation from the Greek. Oh yes, one of those. So while adding "pocalypse" as a suffix to indicate the literal end of the world is all *en vogue*, (my use of the word literal here is anything but, and all hyperbolic, 'cuz that's the way I troll, baby) it used to mean "lifting of the veil" or the giving of information, often life changing information.

And then religion happened. And the veil that was lifted was freaky.

'Cuz the *literal* end of days apocalypse would, of course, contain a lot of life changing information.

Anyway, what does it have to do with bisexual males, and am I going to use the term bipocalypse? Only that once, and doesn't it sound *awesome*?

There's a very real possibility that my perception of the swinger world that I inhabit is colored by the fact that I'm openly bi, and that I run a podcast that routinely reminds its listeners that we think bisexual males are the bee's knees. That said, since I decided to come out as bisexual way back on National Coming Out Day in October of 2010, I've noticed that attitudes about bisexuals have begun to shift.

Now, I'm not saying that I should get all the credit (just some of it. [Humor is fun. {Is this the literary equivalent of the ;) smiley that basically means "I meant it unless you're offended, then it was a joke."}]). I remember it being very hush-hush amongst the few bi males around back when I first began my exploration. You didn't talk about it on the websites. You certainly didn't do anything in public. But even then the facade was cracking, the veil was lifting, the apocalypse had begun.

In the scant intervening years since that podcast was released, I have met more and more bisexual males, seen more and more openly identifying as bi on the websites, seen and participated in bi male activity at Desire Resort and Spa. I've seen bi activity at parties, clubs, even heard about it on other podcasts, where once we were the lone island in a sea of hetero.

But this is what causes me to wonder: is there actually an increase in openly bisexual males? Is it an increase in visibility? Or is it just me sliding into a bubble, the sex-positive bubble, the podcaster bubble, the bisexual podcast host bubble (that's not a big one)? The numbers are still woefully low, especially compared to the disproportionately high numbers of bisexual females in the swinging lifestyle.

But there has been a distinct change, and I hope it's in the world at large.

I hope it's not just me.

I'd been debating whether or not the word "queer" suited me, because I'd always felt that queer was a term that had been rallied behind, that it was somehow political. It suits me in actual interest, much the way pansexual does, or omnisexual, as I'm sexually attracted to attractive people, regardless of gender. But when trying to increase visibility and show an alternative to hetero/homo, bisexual is the term I need, if not the one I deserve, because being openly bisexual is a statement too…a statement of alternative, a statement that doesn't need a paragraph of explanation behind it, a statement that can be made, and can allow others to make the same.

If you identify "queer," you should identify "queer" … same with "omni" and "pan." This isn't about how anyone else in the communities I run in or outside should identify. Someday I may identify as queer. For now, I'm a bisexual male, which is a concept that those on the swinger websites can understand. A concept that has, on numerous occasions, lifted the veil, and caused someone labeled hetero to ask a probing question, admit some curiosity, and give things a go.

Baby steps. Boot strapping. Other terms. Just words.

Apocalypse.

12

FLEXIBLE SEXUAL KINKERY

LOVER AS CHAMELEON

Non-monogamy and swinging have allowed me to be exposed to a wide variety of sexual interaction that, had I continued upon my plain ole monogamous ways, I might never have seen. Among these things are the vast spectrum that is BDSM, anal play, bisexuality, and other wonders of the sexual experience.

Have I liked everything I've been exposed to? No. Have I come out more complete for having seen these things? Absolutely.

I have always known I'm a pleaser. Much of my play time revolves around pleasuring my partners. What I've come to realize more recently is how much my sexual interests are informed by the partner I am with at any given time.

I am a chameleon. As I discuss sexual interests with a potential partner, I can feel myself attuning to what they're looking for and hoping to get from me. This begins almost immediately. I used to wonder if it made me disingenuous, but I realize I've never claimed to be something I'm not with a playmate. It's not like I run around professing myself to be a dominant, but when my playmate wants to be dominated, sure I can do that.

This portion of it, specifically, used to be a source of conflict for me. When my partner first wanted to be dominated and abused and spanked and called names, I had a hard time with it. The residual "You never treat someone you love like that" overpowered the decidedly non-vanilla "unless she asks you to" caveat. Knowing she wanted me to yank her hair and make her gag on my cock while calling her a cunt and a whore was so antithetical to what I'd learned in my life thus far.

At some point I must have become more open to pushing my conceptual boundaries, and when that happened my playmates must have sensed it, because some time around last November seemingly everybody started wanting it rougher. It was so common suddenly that I noted the change to myself. At once I was being asked to pull hair and spank and grab throats and toss around. This was with many of the playmates who had not asked for this in the past, so either they all spontaneously changed, or I did and they caught wind of it.

Committed to understanding the value of providing something for my partner and playmates that they seem to crave, I began playacting at first. I pulled every proverbial punch, and they could smell it. The feigned tug on the hair gets a half-hearted smile in return, the first time I grabbed a handful and *yanked*, lips parted, and ecstasy was exhaled. I took a moment and reflected.

When we are at our best sexually, we are doing something that pleases our partners. All of us have every right to be selfish lovers occasionally within our various relationships, but when we are being "givers" we are also being "receivers." For me, the most satisfaction comes out of watching that enjoyment in my playmate. Seeing that she (or he) is getting off makes me get off. So when I saw how much these girls were *loving* having their hair pulled, being treated roughly, being called those things that I would never call them unless asked (cunt, slut, whore, spunk dumpster) I got off on their enjoyment.

Which made me, of course, wonder about my "com-mit-ment to the domination or humiliation." Did it really matter if the act, the play, the domination, wasn't what spun my wheels? To those who take some of these kinks very seriously, I've been told that if they don't really feel it from their partner, it doesn't do as much for them. And perhaps I'm not going the full Monty all the way to the point that some might want.

But when a chameleon sits on a brown log, he doesn't turn into a log, he just begins to resemble it.

So to begin to resemble what our lovers desire in the deepest recesses of their kinky minds, and to get off on their enjoyment of those kinks, well, I think that makes me pretty flexible!

13

THE FIRST PLAY DATE STILL SCARES ME

I n the early part of my swinger origin story, my partner and I would go on a date with a couple, things would go well, and we'd wind up back at our place, or theirs, with drinks, to probably end up fucking.

The above was not an explanabrag. Just an attempt to throw into relief what swinging is like for me now.

The major change with swinging these days is that usually I know the people before a play date. We've met through friends. We've interacted. We've watched *Doctor Who* together, board-gamed together, knitted together. So there's a baseline for our interaction, our friendship. I don't have to worry about that whole, "God, what if I don't like this other person at all?" anymore.

I mean, sure, there's still the possibility that we won't like each other's play style or habits. But in general I find that as long as you're enthusiastic (don't have to be "fuck yeah, let's *do this thing!*" enthusiastic) and present in the playtime, usually there's fun to be had.

So what is it, then, that still makes me nervous? I guess it's the transition. I mean sure, we've hung out, maybe flirted, maybe even gone through the extensive elevator speech I like to drop on people that got me a, "Wow, that's a lot of information," recently. "No, it's good, just need to process it all," was the follow-up.

Maybe I'm nervous about altering the friendship too dramatically, or making it so it's never again about being friends…where it's assumed or presumed or some other -sumed that we're going to fuck every time we get together. That used to be my MO. Because my swing friends, while they'd come to other events, would rarely just come over to hang out. But now, I'm friendlier with playmates. I've always felt close to them, just not "down time" close.

Many times in the past, before a first date, I'd get that creeping feeling in my chest. That "almost to the 'bridge out' sign and I ain't got no hoverboard" feeling. So now it's happening with friends, and perhaps that's adding to the cycling feeling of concern, that "what if I cancel and it's never the same" feeling. But at the same time, I can't cancel because who wants to be that same old flake?

'Cuz they're everywhere, aren't they?

Mostly, though, I think it's because I'm a planner. Despite all the discussion of interests online, and even the planning that may go into the date, I know dates rarely bear much similarity to the prep-work. That doesn't stop me from, in my head, wondering if I'll make the first move or they will, or what if we both wait for the first move and no one makes it and suddenly they yawn and say "well, it's about that time" and go to get up? Will I be able to salvage it then?

Or should I take that Cockstar pill? Or just recognize that my erection, while welcome at the party, isn't responsible for the party?

Or if I put out the toys I feel might get used, do I look presumptuous?

And what if, what if, what if, what if…?

So I wait for the play date to begin, knowing that it's on the path, they're on their way, in their car, be here soon and it's too late to back out now and I may as well just write for a while so I don't think too hard about it but instead I go for a Charlie Kaufman level of meta.

Hmm.

Perhaps I should just relax.

14

FORGIVING EACH OTHER

THE FORGOTTEN FUN IN SEX EDUCATION AND ADVOCACY

I'm reminded of the prophet Hedwig, who implored us to remember all those we've come upon in our travels and all of those who've come upon us. That amazing creature, that Hedwig, also used what she had to work with, and so should we.

With that in mind, my friends and lovers, my glorious few, I have indeed sucked the marrow from life. I have *carpe*'d the fuck out of that *diem*. I've ridden the American Dream hard and put it away wet.

What of this, this strangely confident Cooper? What has become of the paradoxically shy and occasional grump? Who is this here?

CatalystCon remains an oasis to me. Much has been written about the chaos, the sound and fury that hovered in the air for months after last March's CatalystCon, hanging like a pendulous storm cloud, always waiting, always threatening to unleash its ferocious fervor once more.

For myself, though, this place, this conference remains an opportunity to connect with so very many people. Fans of *The Swingset*, old friends, new friends, peers, idols, they're all around. They're within touching distance, the kind of closeness that allows you to latch on with both arms and really express true feelings to another human being without fear and loathing.

As activists, as the bloggerati, we forget sometimes (and that sometimes is unfortunately often) that we are all we have. We are the voices shouting into the void. Like Hedwig screaming and singing into a sea of unmoved, uninterested, and unsympathetic beings. Occasionally those in the world catch a glimpse of the truth we're so vainly shouting. It's in vain because they so often don't listen.

In his song *Vincent (Starry Starry Night)* Don McLean, the poet renowned for *American Pie*, lamented the fact that the world wasn't listening when Vincent was painting, and that they're still not listening. He finished the song with the downer that perhaps they (the world, us) never would listen.

I don't think things are as hopeless as McLean felt they were back in 1971. Vincent was also speaking to a world that didn't understand or support him. The people are starting to listen now. They're at the very least beginning to pick up the beat that we're putting down, even if they don't quite understand the melody yet.

Meanwhile, McLean's world was crumbling, music was changing, identities and ideals were collapsing, and we were on our way to incredibly dark days, well beyond the hopeful wave that had already ended when Duke and Dr. Gonzo took their hopeless and horrific trip to the rotten heart of the American Dream.

So what am I saying?

I don't really know. What I can tell you is that it's just after four in the morning on Sunday, September 14. I have just left *Life on the Swingset* and *Carnalcopia*'s Saturday evening CatalystCon play party.

I've spent the better part of six hours watching all manner of debauchery and my heart has overflowed with joy. I've seen a mixture of people, genders, races, identities, politics, play levels, play styles, monogamous, non-monogamous, curious, confident, shy, D/s, everything. Every-fucking-thing.

It's hard to even describe the environment. After two podcasts today (or is it two panels, is there even a difference between our podcasts and panels for *The Swingset* anymore?) discussing play parties and group sex, we were still left with the "I'm not sure I understand the appeal" question.

And that I get.

If the idea of naked bodies here and naked bodies there, interspersed with conversation from daring and sexy negotiation to *Firefly* and *Game of Thrones* and *Doctor Who* (Ain't No Party Like A *Swingset* Party 'Cuz Our Geekdom is Paramount), on to navigating open relationships, discussing non-monogamy with a partner who may not be entirely on board, reconnecting and missed connections, if that doesn't make you immediately say, "Sign me up, Coop. And while you're at it, please put me on the mailing list for your newsletter," well then I may never be able to adequately explain myself.

But here we are.

Just another ramble from the edge of that precipice of sleep. Trying so very hard to eke out something of meaning and value. Trying so very hard to matter. To matter to those on the outside looking in. Because we must never forget that they're the ones we're after.

They.

Them.

The others.

We can tell each other these things all we want. We can proclaim ourselves bastions of consent and communication. That we are all very well aware of our privilege and do everything we can to promote those less advantaged. That we understand rape culture, and how it is perpetuated. That sex positivity is not yucking someone else's yum. Not pissing in the Cheerios.

We believe it all. We are so convinced of our own Kool-Aid that we willingly pour sucrose-filled glasses of it for each other to shotgun while patting ourselves on the back. The snake eats its tail. We feed and feed and circle jerk ourselves to a wonder of enjoyment and fulfillment.

Because the refill is tremendously important, after all. And we are refilling ourselves from the font of each other. While the words that are spooling from my fingers may sound tremendously negative, they aren't. They're the late night ramblings of someone who feels we can do better. Because we're doing so very well. At least until that last raggedy moment. When things start to unravel. As they do every year.

We can sit and stroke and drink and admire and love and fuck and support and engage for a weekend. We can rock it. We can love it. But then we forget. And then we're compelled to throw the others under the bus.

And that's when we *must* do better.

We don't have to accept everything that each other does. That would be a fool's errand, and we'd quickly collapse in on ourselves like a dying star. It's not about that.

We need to give ourselves permission to fuck up.

Let me say that once more with feeling. *The sex-positive community needs to be allowed to fuck up. Period. Exclamation point.*

Because we really don't allow that of each other, do we? When you dive right in and look around sometimes we are petty motherfuckers, writing in our own worlds of text on a screen, where almost nothing matters except for our causes. We scream using reverse osmosis, because our bubble is only permeable in one direction, and only when we can fight or preach.

But as they once said, "The Internet isn't written in pencil, it's written in ink," and isn't likely to sponge off when we've decided that someone is "cool" again. A fire bombing of a website or social media profile, when we put together our lynch mob because of something one of us once did, or accidentally did, or at worst didn't do but was misunder-stood.

Am I calling anyone out? Hell no. We're all guilty, our entire fucking subculture, which is perhaps why it's so frustrating. We are Brutus, thinking nothing of plunging that dagger into the backs of our friends, our lovers, our fellow educators and writers. Pointing out that, by the way, you aren't *really* an educator if you didn't train. That you aren't *really* a professional if a certain percentage of your income doesn't come from blogging. Paradoxically, the opposite crime is also pointed at with an anger shaking finger, that you've sold out and are untrustworthy if your writing or work is bringing in enough money that you can splurge on yourselves sometimes.

It's so difficult. We've been hurt for so long. Flogged by corporations and media and loved ones and the world. Told that we were sluts and whores and worthless and evil. We've all felt it. Long enough that when it lessened we felt the phantom pains of the flogging, and even began to beat ourselves and each other well beyond the point of re-opening the scars given to us.

Whether we began to write to process a cancer in the world, to expound wonderment at something new and different, if we teach to share of ourselves, to help others sidestep our errors, or to showcase the hypocrisy inherent in the nebulous system, we cannot forget that we are ultimately looking to elevate the world.

Aren't we? Can't we admit that?

Or have we crawled so far down the rabbit hole that we can no longer see beyond the thousands of clocks counting out the length of time we've been oppressed, wearing that oppression like a badge of honor because those who haven't been oppressed could never understand those who have.

Right?

Anyone?

"We are the music makers, and we are the dreamers of dreams."

   - Willy Wonka (Gene Wilder)

When we are dark and negative, we all suffer. When we improve lives, even just one, we add a little more light to the depths. We shine it down deep, even if it's just a penlight, because if I have a penlight, and you have a penlight, and she has a penlight, and they has a penlight (apparent grammatical error intentional due to pronoun choice) we can begin to shine.

We can be beacons.

We focus too much on preventing the horror, and railing against the machines. We forget to promote the joy.

Which is why I throw play parties.

And why I talk of foolishness.

While so many of my colleagues would tell me that the time has come to put away childish things (and then would quickly point out that paraphrasing Paul doesn't mean believing in the man or the Saint) I argue that we need them more than we ever have.

The negativity haunts us, like a veil across our eyes, so thick in places that we can't see anything beyond it. So dense that the world outside has neither sound nor smell. All we hear is the anguish; all we feel, the agony.

This is a disservice. To all of us. To the world.

For there is so very much joy. Seeing a newly trans identified man rock the space between genders. Holding someone's hand as they experience their first orgasm.

We are *sex educators*, people. How the *fuck* did we forget the fun?

Those that oppose us haven't forgotten the fun. It's what they throw in our faces time after time. We sluts. We filthy heathens. Look at us enjoying our selfish sex while the world burns. God didn't intend for us to use our bodies like amusement parks after all. (Thanks, Mrs. Costanza) Because that side of the argument would also like the world to forget that sex is fun. Whereas most in the world might even say that the entire goddamned point is to have fun unless we're doing it only for procreation. And those who wouldn't say that may need a good talking to.

You know, by an educator.

Who remembers the fun. Who can deliciously embody joyful sexual expression.

Both sides can't be downplaying the fun in favor of the negative. Those things that we feel and see and fear. The oppression. The abuse. The discrimination. They're very real.

They're *very* real.

But they can't be all we talk about.

We need the play party. We need the orgasm. We need the hug and kiss and fuck and finger and grope and lick. Because it hits us right in the fucking feels. And we know what lives in the feels.

Compassion. Empathy. Understanding. Love. Devotion.

We need it.

THE HARD TRUTH

IN DEFENSE OF DICK PICS AND COCK SHOTS

I have a collection of pictures featuring my cock, with me at this very moment.

Not Polaroids or anything, what is this, 1996?

I have a collection of the hated, reviled, cock shots. You know the ones. Big dick in frame (not an explanabrag), occasionally a hand, not much else. Seriously.

Why?

Reading the multitude of comments on twitter and Facebook and in the blogosphere presents a unified front that no one would ever want to see these. There is never a reason anyone wants to see a picture of just a cock, right? Never. Not no one, not no how.

Aesthetically it's like a picture of a bratwurst. Who wants a fucking picture of a fucking bratwurst? You want to eat a bratwurst, sure, especially if you're on the shores of Lake Michigan with a beer during the beautiful city of Milwaukee's epic Summerfest, but you don't want a picture of it.

Except you do want a picture of it. Not a picture of a bratwurst, a picture of a cock. (Not necessarily *my* cock, though a lot of you want that too. [*There's* that explanabrag! {And I don't want you to feel shame if you happen to want a picture of a bratwurst.}]) How do I know this? Because I know a lot of women and a lot of men. My community is vast. I know that a lot of cock pics were sent via 3G and 4G. And I know *many* of them were solicited.

Is that the thing? The solicitation part? Have guys sent so unbelievably many unsolicited cock pictures to people that they've turned everyone (outwardly) against the very idea of cock pics? That's shitty. Really, really shitty.

I'm serious. To anyone who's ever received an unsolicited cock pic, I apologize. That sucks. Especially when it's from someone so incredibly dense or socially awkward that they truly believe that's the way to get anywhere with you.

But on behalf of all the penis-havers who would only send a picture of their member when it's asked for, and then would jump at the opportunity to send one, I ask that you not make broad sweeping statements about #1, the attractiveness of penises, and #2 the fact that you'd never ever for any reason want to see that.

As a person who likes both penises and vulvas and who thinks that human genitals are amazingly diverse and beautiful things that I could look at for hours...aroused, flaccid, doing things...sorry, got distracted there.

I am taking a stand.

Let me be perfectly clear. No one should ever send a picture of their genitals without at least asking if the recipient wants to see them. I'd be shocked, *shocked*, to open a text on my phone and be staring directly into that.

But I firmly believe that all the venom spewed toward pictures of dicks has a large bearing on the lack of pictures of men on swing dating sites, as well as size concerns, and other body issues.

Yeah, I'm blaming you (the metaphorical you) for the very thing that is one of the biggest complaints about swinger dating site profiles. The lack of pictures of men. The overwhelming perceived hatred of pictures of our cocks makes us far less likely to put any picture of our bodies on there.

"Listen Cooper, you jerk," you say, perhaps remembering how much I irritate you, "I'm not saying that penises aren't attractive, I'm just saying I want more to a picture than a close-up."

Fair enough. And I agree. Most pictures should be more than just that close-up of a cock that I have several of my own in my phone on the table next to the iPad where I'm typing this incredible run-on sentence that I don't really want to end because I'm curious how far I can take it. Oh.

But let's talk seriously here for a sec. It's just you and I. Cock pics can be pretty cool sometimes, can't they? And I can make a sweeping generalization (because that's how I roll) about them due to the fact that I'd say 80% (that's *most* to those of you playing the home game) of the people I've ever played with have requested, at some point, a picture of my cock. Some out of the blue, some before we've played, most after, some in a photo exchange, some by sending a picture of their own. Tit for tat. *Quid pro quo.*

Hence, they're on my phone. 'Cuz then if I'm in, say Barnes & Noble, I have something to send.

And while you should never come to definitive statistical conclusions based solely on personal observations...I choose to do so anyway.

So, let's not hate on the cock pics. Let's hate on the *unsolicited* cock pics. Let's also not hate on the lack of creativity. You want to see something new and different and sexy and fun, make a request. Requests are sexy.

Meanwhile, I'll continue to enjoy the bounty of genitals that the human race has to offer.

16

THE SENSE OF SELF

W hen you first decide to step over the threshold into swinging, the bounty of sexuality that opens up for you can be, at the same time, wonderful and overwhelming. If you have been monogamous for your entire life thus far, even if you've had a lot of sex, it's unlikely that you've been a party to the myriad permutations of orgy. Three, four, five, six, BINGO!

If, thus far, you've been heterosexual-leaning, but see the world through your new eyes and realize that maybe you don't have to consider yourself a zero anymore, (a zero on The Kinsey Scale. Not making fun of hetero people, I assure you) that first breath of new and different air can cause a panic. Where options were once far simpler, now the choice can be frightening.

This is especially true of uneven coupling where one of the partners has experience and the other doesn't. Regardless of what that experience is or looks like, it is quite natural to look at the possibilities opening up and be a little nervous.

"What if I don't like _____ ?"

Fill in the blank with anything on the spectrum. That sexual thing that scared you before you did it, but you loved afterward. Also remember that sexual thing that scared you, that you did and didn't like. What if I don't like BDSM, watching her fuck another guy, letting another guy fuck me, taking naked pictures, oral sex with barriers?

What if you don't?

Our lives are littered with things that we tried and didn't like. Like olives. Some of these things we regret trying, in fact. These are the moments that make us not want to try anything new. Because what if it's bad? Because what if my playmate sucks? Because what if I do? Because what if I don't like it and I have to tell someone I didn't like it?

But we're usually not so nervous about not liking something for someone else's benefit. Instead, those nerves are mostly just about us. What if I don't like it? This suggests that our desire to like something we try is motivated by a sense of failure if we don't. Which makes it scary. Which makes us less likely to try.

I would suggest, though, when seeing the breadth of options suddenly available to you, the vast spectrum of human sexuality, you recognize that you just won't like everything. I mean, that's really a given. Do you like all the movies you've ever seen? All the books you've ever read? Aside from a snarky, "Well that's two hours of my life I'll never get back," does it have any lasting effect on you when you don't like a movie?

No, because it doesn't affect your sense of self.

Someone who is confident that they are heterosexual can have an encounter with someone of the same sex, enjoy it or not, and still be heterosexual on the other end. This is why I always tell people that if they try swinging and it's not for them, that's okay. It's a big 'un, because they'd be seeing something they can't unsee. But it's *okay* if they ultimately don't find it works.

The same with bondage, anal play, and then let's just slide right up that kink-o-rama spectrum.

If you know who you are, even if you don't know what

you want, you'll still be the same person on the other side. The difference is now you'll know more about your likes and dislikes. The more we can learn about ourselves in that department, the better we can shape the future of what our non-monogamy looks like.

17

FEAR AND SELF LOATHING
ON THE WAY TO SAN FRANCISCO

L ying in bed, the night before this big trip to San Francisco, I came to what I perceive as an important and rather surprising revelation about myself. Many of my big concerns in life are fictions. There are people in my life who would assure me that this is true of most people and most worries, concerns, etcetera. The concept of invented worries isn't new to me. Many of my big worries in life are baseless, or at the very least premature.

But lying in bed before this flight, the worry that kept coming back to me was my fear of flying.

This is a huge common fear, I know. It can be crippling in many people, forcing them to either confine themselves to their general area or take long road trips.

"Cooper," you ask, "are we really talking about fear of flying? This is a fucking book of essays about non-monogamy!"

Oh, my friend, haven't you learned that I like to meander before getting to a point (if I even arrive there at all) and almost everything I talk about eventually circles around to sex. This one will, I promise. And kudos if you recognized that the quote attributed to you was adapted for this book from the previous version referencing the website where this article originally appeared. You win all of the things.

My fear of flying wasn't present when I was young. While my family preferred the great American road tripping tradition to flying, some of our vacation destinations required it. I enjoyed every bit about the experience, reading on the plane, watching the countryside pass below (as I am right now, in fact; I believe I see Iowa). If I had any distaste for flying back then it was only the fact that, as a voracious bookworm, I was unable to spend as much time reading as I could on family drives.

What happened?

Many years passed without the need to fly anywhere. As an adult, when I began to fly again, something imperceptible had changed. The words "I'm not a good flier" escaped my lips on my first trip as a grownup. I would ask to sit at the aisle both because I am a large person and airline seats were not made for people of actual size. This also prevented me from having to look out the window. I was abnormally concerned about being near the wing as well and they seemed to put me there on almost every flight.

This persisted for future flights: concerns, difficulties. "I'm not a good flier," I'd say to my neighbor on the plane. "Why don't you want to sit by the wing?" they'd ask me without actually using their mouths. "John Lithgow and William Shatner," I'd tell them without using my own vocal chords. "Too scary."

(If you don't know what wings of planes and Lithgow and Shatner have in common, Google that bitch and be amused and scared for a while. [The amused part would be from a *3rd Rock From The Sun* episode where the two actors referenced the role that they shared twenty years apart.])

"You've meandered enough, Cooper. Get to the fucking point, or at least mention anal fisting so we can feel more at home."

The point is, "I'm not good at flying" is a lie. Not an intentional lie, but a quirk I developed. A quirk I likely developed because it's a decent character trait. Writers look for these things that people can identify with for our characters. Fear of flying is a pretty universal one. It's a conversation starter for people at the airport (Flying, eh? Hate it!) and a way to get that "Aww, that sucks, anything I can do to help?" sympathetic nod from people.

I developed it. Hadn't been there before. Nothing traumatic had happened. Can't blame Lithgow, Shatner, or the '63 or '83 gremlins either, nothing permanently damaging there. Regardless, I was afraid.

Until last night, when I realized that I indeed had tension and nervousness, but all of that was about not being prepared for the trip. Nothing to do with the idea that I might somehow fall out of the sky. The fear of flying was manifesting itself. I resolved to try something different.

Walking into the airport this morning, I simply didn't think about it, any of it. The tension was gone during the wait to board, no gripping my armrest as we took off, even the creeping panic at the pressure changes. All gone. Fake. Completely inconsequential. I watched the American countryside roll by below. Farmland just now.

I'm sure you've realized by this point that this idea has broader implications. If something as simple (and statistically silly) as a fear of flying could be imaginary, what other of my various quirks, fears, neuroses or "character traits" might also be artificial?

Moving on. Since high school I've developed feelings of claustrophobia in large groups of people in small spaces. Also a common fear / concern / quirk, but not something I always had, or something I had any reason to have. This has caused trouble in party situations, most recently at Kendra Holliday's *Queen of Hearts Ball* in St Louis. Lots of people I don't know, small space, loud music. All results in Cooper standing outside on the sidewalk with the smokers just so he can breathe again. With as false as the fear of flying turned out to be, what are the odds such an obvious character affectation would be real?

Slim.

I find myself talking to people so often about these issues. Is it perhaps because, deep down, I feel they make me more interesting? Or a more believable character? And when one gets down to it, how obnoxious is it when a writer refers to themselves as a fiction? I think there's a lot of truth to that. These fears that I allow to define me are things that are universal in the world. The fears of rejection, fears of intimacy, fears of public speaking (something I actually don't have) they are part of our collective unconscious, like that dream about going to a class that you hadn't attended all semester and realizing all the work you didn't do or the test scheduled for today.

If they're simply collected fears, and so many people in my life have assured me that these fears can be mitigated in most cases and obliterated in many, wouldn't it follow that an obnoxious fellow like me might have developed neurosis simply to be cool?

Uh oh, the blog is spiraling out of control! Hope you have your seat belts on! The plane I'm in is experiencing turbulence, but certainly not out of control, and my pulse is still normal. Groovy. My biggest concern at the moment is my Coke Zero tipping over and spilling on my super awesome Bluetooth keyboard.

Okay, after a deep breath I've acknowledged that it wasn't to be cool that I developed them, *but* it's possible that I did so to be interesting.

Which stems from my fear of not being interesting / popular / choose your own adventure.

When I first started swinging, I had many fears about inadequacy, both in sexual prowess and in the body image department. Because of this, I wasn't as selective as I should've been back then. I had, as I'm sure many of us with body issues do, the feeling that I should be grateful for people having any interest in me, regardless of my interest in them. Luckily, there are only a few regrettable decisions in my past, and only a couple instances of "taking one for the team." As I've developed in non-monogamy, I've realized I can (and should) be more selective.

My fear becomes, "Should I approach that person?" Not because I'm necessarily afraid they won't want to fuck me, because I'm afraid of the part before all that. Will they want to talk to me? Will they be interested in what I have to say? Will they just be polite? Will they *not* be polite and tell me to fuck off?

I've never really needed to overcome this fear, because I never actually picked people up before I became a swinger. Most of my dating was either through referral (friend of a friend) or stumbling accidentally into a date-able situation. I never actually identified and approached. In swinging I had to pick people up, but the Internet, and swinger dating sites made that part easy-ish.

Parties presented their own challenge, the face to face pickup. So, I usually only went to parties where I knew most everyone. The fear of approach in these environments was mitigated by the friend of a friend referrals, and because I could throw my sexy partner at them. Boobs are an awesome attention getter that I just don't possess!

I coddled my fear, nurtured it, allowed entrenchment. This one has far more significance in my life than the Fear of Flying or enclosed spaces. It's been with me a lot longer, set up shop and hung its shingle in my cerebral cortex.

My question today is am I just playing a role? The role of wallflower. The role of the neurotic (and hopefully adorable) nebbish who saw one too many Woody Allen movies during his formative years. After all, Woody got Diane Keaton. Diane *Fucking* Keaton.

If it's a role, a character trait that I adopted, I can shed it, right? Redefine myself? Maybe all of our character traits really are fictions that we apply to ourselves from decades of watching characters on TV. Do we decide to be Chandler?

Now I sit on this plane to San Francisco for the weekend, where I'll need to actually step up and be a real person instead of a collection of character traits on a bio sheet. What if a weekend in a new city I've never visited before, amongst a throng of sex-positive people, is the game changer I need?

I'm Cooper S. Beckett, and I am jettisoning the portions of my personality that no longer serve the whole. Fear of flying? Check. Next up, claustrophobia and fear of the approach.

We're above the clouds now.

LEVELING UP

Before I became a swinger, I was under the impression that I'd done the vast majority of growing and changing I would do in this life. In the time since then, the emotional and spiritual (thought I still hate the S word) growth has been significant.

That first year after opening up was a time of tremendous growth and change. I explored, worked on, and partially defeated jealousy. I say "partially" because can you ever really defeat jealousy? It still rears its ugly green head on occasion. I gained the skill of compersion, something I'd never heard of before. Compersion is like pure empathy, the be-all/end-all of supporting people when awesome things happen to them and not necessarily to me. I learned about my body, my sexuality, my feelings, my ideas.

I started a podcast because I had some odd idea that people would want to listen to the rantings of a first-year swinger. For some reason they did, and never really asked "What makes you think you know what's up?"

After that I continued to explore, changing my perceptions of what non-monogamy had to offer as well as what I could handle, and what I craved in life. While swinging and poly may be very similar, the differences between them ask for the utilization of new skill sets, new applications for that compersion. It is a big change after all, moving from group sex to loving multiple people (and still having that occasional group sex). But I didn't really move from anything to anything, did I? I just added new things to my repertoire.

Now circling around to the geekery of the title, then. *Leveling up.* First, as I'm quite sure we have people in our audience (both listening and reading) who only tolerate our occasional dalliances with *Doctor Who*, our obsession with Captain Jack Harkness, quoting *Ghostbusters*, and other morsels of high potency geekery, I ought to explain. In role-playing games (board based, brain based, and screen based) you begin with a character that has some skills and weaponry, and you accumulate more and more as you continue to play, so after some time your character is far more powerful than when you began. You know, like Link starting every game sans sword, only able to pick up pots to look for Rupees. Yep, tolerate *that*!

Some will look at the above and say, "Why, that's like life! Building strength and skills." To which I reply, in my best Eddie Murphy plays an old white Jewish man voice: "Ah ha! Ah ha!"

We do level up in life. All the time, in fact. As we go through college we develop skills. If we work out we build strength. As we communicate and move through relationships we change emotionally. We all hope and strive to not level down, though we know it's inevitable. But perhaps, if we level up enough, if we learn and grow and change enough, we'll achieve something amazing. We'll...I dunno...win?

I feel like I'm leveling up. With all of the above changes, I still remained rather shy and reserved when it came to new people. When it came to saying "yes." When it came to taking a risk.

It's strange to feel like that's going away. In the past

month alone I've said yes to many things I wouldn't have previously. I've begun to make things happen in multiple arenas. I've allowed the worlds of Swingset and the dreaded "real world" to grow even closer. I've let go of a lot of the walls I used to build.

After building his wall so high that he could not escape it, Pink laments that there must have been a door in the wall, where he came in. I found the door. I stepped back through. I'm shedding the skin of neurosis and panic that used to surround me. No, not all at once, but it's surely happening.

I used to slide every potential relationship into a category. It's what caused me to feel that in order to focus on one poly relationship I had to end the other, way back after one month of being poly. Now a strange thing is happening. Relationships are simply becoming what they are. That's a lovely bunch of nonsense isn't it? They're filling the space they need. They're growing and changing on their own. Too often I tried to manipulate them to fit, to change, to cram them into boxes where they didn't belong.

When I was asked by a potential what I was looking for, I simply told her that we'll let things be what they are. If they're swing, we'll swing, if they're poly, we'll romance, if they're friendly, we'll hang out, and if they're incompatible there's no hard feelings and we'll shuffle off to Buffalo. I couldn't believe I'd said such things. I couldn't believe I was okay with such things. To not categorize, to not plan, to not fret, to not doubt, to not agonize over "What if she doesn't like me?" or "What if I'm not good enough?" or even ease on down the road to worrying about what'll happen when I introduce her to my other relationships, swing playmates, friends, family? Christ! My brain was a noisy place not so long ago. A place where I'd turn away from anything with potential because I was concerned with where it might lead and was writing the script for the end before it'd even begun.

On a first date, less than a month ago, the girl I was on

the date with gave me +50 Confidence Points. Then +50 Experience Points. There may have been some sexy points in there as well, but that's irrelevant to this discussion. The forces inside me are conspiring. Conspiring to birth a new version of Cooper Beckett. Cooper 2.0 was born into swinging. C2.5 introduced poly. Cooper 3.0? Man, it's hard to keep up!

Wait until you see the new skills and accessories!

BACKWORD

I know that it's traditional to call the post-script chapter of a non-fiction book the "Afterword" but I think the "Backword" is more appropriate. This book is a reflection, after all, rippling through time the way stars do across light-years. The first essays I wrote for *Life on the Swingset* have many elements that no longer represent the way I feel. These stars no longer look the same.

But this isn't melancholy. Far from it.

It's merely the realization that I have changed pretty significantly from then until now. Having recently completed the edit of all of the essays, I see the differences in sharp relief. I found it rather hard to digest some of my opinions from early on, and even some from not so early on.

We are a sum of our parts, after all. Our experiences shape us, piece by piece, brick by brick, as a man once said.

So what have I learned about myself on this reflection?

Mostly I've learned that no matter how much I thought I'd had it all figured out, I often wasn't even close. I write this Backword on the way home from my fourth trip to Desire Resort and Spa in Cancun.

This whole week I've been reflecting on something I wrote years ago entitled Zen and the Art of Swinging. The essay claimed that I had achieved Zen. That I'd figured out how not to have expectations. How easy things had gotten once I wasn't afraid to take risks. The echoes of that essay go both ways through timey-wimey space. I know, I know, echoes can't go back in time. (Or can they?)

The most obvious echo is the one involving Schrödinger's Cat, and my decision to start asking for what I want. If you'll go with me on the whole backward echoes idea, you'll find elements of wanting to achieve this from the very beginning, in my first essays, evident in my first tentative steps into swinging, then poly, now this nebulous form of non-monogamy.

It's actually rather distressing to see a huge chunk of your life stretched out in vaguely connected essays. My favorite scene in the wonderful *Shortbus* has the former Mayor of New York (probably Koch) lamenting about the time of the AIDS epidemic. "Everybody knew so little then," he says. "I know even less now." I feel the same way about myself.

So this amazing week in Mexico, a week of firsts, of relaxation for a person who doesn't usually relax, of hitting on people I'd put way out of my league, of taking risks, of asking for what I want. I have sort of become the man I'd thought I was way back at Zen and the Art of Swinging. I have sort of achieved the Zen I sought. The big difference between that Cooper and Now Cooper is that I realize that I still don't much know what I'm doing. That this thing called swing, the non-monogamy thing, it's constantly changing and evolving.

It's mostly evolving because what I put into it defines what this lifestyle is. I'm not taking credit for The Lifestyle. I'm taking credit for My Lifestyle. It will continue to change, and expand and contract; a living, breathing, organism. And that's what makes it so exciting. That's what makes me so thrilled to continue doing it. Six and a half years ago I was convinced that I'd sorted the whole life thing out, that future upgrades would be minimal, more of the same. Like *Home Alone 2: Lost in New York*. Comforting in its similarities, slightly irritating in its repetition, but featuring Tim Curry.

These days my life is closer to…oh sheesh…painted myself into a corner with the movie sequel analogy.

This isn't an ending, it's not an afterword, after all. It's the respite before the continuation. Things will go on. Things will change. I'll learn more, I'll fuck up, I'll re-organize and re-configure.

Then I'll make another run.

Because while so many see non-monogamy as just an opportunity for more sex, or another lover, or another person with whom to have dates or dinner or wine, it can show us the world within us.

It can make us whole.

Or, at least, more than half full.

"My journey is the same as yours, the same as anyone's. It's taken me so many years, so many lifetimes, but at last I know where I'm going. Where I've always been going. Home. The long way around."

- The Doctor

FIVE YEARS ON THE SWINGSET

A SEMIFESTO

*This essay is new to this edition of <u>My Life on the Swingset:</u>
<u>Adventures in Swinging & Polyamory</u>, and appeared on* Life on
the Swingset *on March 3, 2015.*

Quite a bit of time has passed since I last put
forth a manifesto, a why I do what I do statement. I thought, on the occasion of *Swingset*'s
fifth birthday and 200th episode, it'd be worth
some reflection. I know, I know, it sometimes seems that
"meandering reflection" could very well be the definition
of "what I do." It's rare, though, to get to a milestone like
this, with this type of project. So milestone reflection can
often seem as unnecessary or premature as celebrating
monthaversaries in high school.

To tell an old story, *Life on the Swingset: The Podcast*, was
birthed in 2010, after listening to hundreds of episodes of
Sex is Fun and *The Savage Lovecast*, and thinking *That might be*
fun to do. Then psyching Dylan up to a similar frothy level
of "we know what the hell we're doing in this whole
swinging scene, the people of the world should listen
to us."

I tend to jump into projects before I give them too

much thought. This is by design. Without this philosophy, I would've recognized that (like many abbreviated projects before it) Swingset would be an awful lot of work. Even back then when it was just a podcast and occasional toy review or blog post on the site.

Damn good thing I couldn't look down the timestream and see that first year (that we laughingly called a season, for reasons not even known to us anymore) and the work it would entail, for very little reward, a very small following, and almost constant upheaval of those making up Your Sexy Crew. But by the end of Season One, we'd cohesed, finding Ginger and Shira along the way, establishing a rhythm and routine along the way. We'd even done the podcast swap tango with *Sex is Fun*, our podcast sires.

When Season Two began with the one-two punch of having Christopher Ryan and Tristan Taormino as guests on the show, two people we'd deemed "way bigger than us," things started to change, and we found ourselves staring at something we hadn't really felt in Season One: Momentum. After that, there was ever only one White Whale Guest, but that comes later.

Swingset was about swinging, pretty hard core, too, until Shira B. joined our crew and we started examining our lives through her kaleidoscope. By Season Two we were already acknowledging the shift, the changed feel, the recognition that the idea of "lifestyle" seemed so much bigger than this artificial box labeled "swing."

It was there that we first caught a glimpse of the larger community that hasn't completely come together, what we termed SOP, Swinger-Open-Poly, or more recently, the ethical non-monogamy community. We noticed just how close to each other the swingers and polyamory folk were. Both sides still talk a big (obnoxious) talk about "not being like them," but we know better, don't we?

In five years, though, I've seen a community that has gone through similar curiosity and growth. When, early in my swinging career, I mentioned bi-curiosity, I was told to shove that deep down, to never show it, or risk being banished from the community, from the websites. Now, I know bisexual and bi-curious men in swinging. It's still not as common as bisexual women, but no one ever thought it would be. There was tremendous pushback and gnashing of teeth, as we called ourselves progressive swingers, and laid out our tenets within that. But the gnashing was short-lived. The wringing of hands limited to a small number.

I don't think we changed their minds, far from it. I think they were already what we termed progressive swingers. Already developing long term friendships with their playmates, coming out more and more as possible, building more and more meetups and groups, and recognizing the value of exploration, these "classic swingers" simply realized that we were right when we told them not to be afraid of or offended by the name progressive swingers because by and large, it referred to them as well. We've never disparaged those who don't subscribe to the tenets of progressive swinging, we've never thought of ourselves as better, we've espoused a number of ideas that we feel make the swinging lifestyle better, and suggested openness to trying new things.

My life is certainly different than it was when Life on the Swingset began. Now divorced (amicably) and exploring every facet of this strange and nebulous thing called sex educator, author, and coach, having had the opportunity to interact with nearly everybody we've ever desired. (But. seriously, if anyone knows the route I'd have to go to contact John Cameron Mitchell, please let me know…) If all goes well tomorrow (the timey wimey thing) the aforementioned white whale is currently on our 200th episode. If it didn't go to plan, he'll be on an upcoming episode. Not meaning to be coy, just writing this days before, don't want to jinx it.

But this isn't all a fifth-anniversary victory lap, even if I do think my wonderful podcast crew Dylan, Ginger, and Miko have more than earned a victory lap for their tireless work on this show. Hell, not only have they not gotten a week off in quite a long while, but we actually added a few episodes to make this bit of synchronicity (#ss5yrs200eps) happen as it has. (Don't tell anyone!) It's actually meaning to be a why I do what I do manifesto.

"Yeah, Cooper," you ask, coughing a bit as your voice is hoarse, "Why do you do what you do?" Then you grumble something about being a corporate shill and shuffle off into the night.

I still get "You saved my marriage!" emails. Seriously, with that subject line and everything.

I continue to "do" Swingset because even if it's just one person here and there, it's helping. And I know it's much more than one person, and you do too, so I doubt you'll let me get by with modesty. The Swingset, for whatever reason, touches people in just that right place. (And then rubs, and then lubes, and rubs some more…)

I'm convinced that the reason we're still doing this, and still getting the response we are, is because of something we decided very early on: "Be honest, have fun."

Be honest has definitely gotten some of us into more trouble than others. Sometimes I (especially) run my mouth like nobody's business on a few key subjects that make readers/listeners sit down and put pen to paper (um, finger to keyboard? Finger to tablet?) to decry my statements as broad generalizations, or just, like, my opinion, man. #NotAllCatholics. (And my response is, always: "I KNOW! Unfortunately the world doesn't, because the loudest people in your respective organizations are the nutjobs usually.") I don't have a solution, I truly don't. As Billy told us, the fish rots from the head, so you have to cut off the head. But he also acknowledged it wasn't a perfect metaphor.

But *be honest* has also given us some of the most vivid glimpses of real life that we've ever had on our podcast. From when Shira and I were both going through respective major relationships struggles, to Ginger's amazing control taking with her mastectomy. To almost every word Miko and Dylan speak: from the heart, real truths. We ain't just funnin' ya. We ain't doin' it for the moneys. (I assure you, we're not, 'cuz there ain't none.)

I feel like being honest is something that most bloggers and podcasters try at at the very least. They have every intention of honesty. Sure, some do it for the clicks, or the downloads, or the tweets, or the…grinds…is that a thing? But most of us think nothing of ripping our chests open and handing you our heart.

Point two is, I feel, why we still are doing it. Why people still are engaging. Because we're having fun. You know it. You hear it. Even our most ridiculous shenanigans, podcasting from our hotel room naked at Catalyst-Con, or on a beach…naked…at Desire. With Malort and absinthe and tequila and red wine fueling our ever more incoherent discussion of…something…we give you a one-two blow, of fun, and truth. Where many bloggers and podcasters find themselves mired in the negatives, "This is why these ways are bad ways to do things." "This is why you shouldn't do this." We strive to enjoy ourselves, even in the toughest discussions, even with the most serious of guests.

Because shouldn't we all strive for that?

It's no secret how I feel about life and beyond. We're all on the train, and somewhere up ahead is the final stop where everybody gets off. (Death. You got that, right?) And while some may argue that makes life meaningless, I argue that it makes life all that more meaningful! We only have the one. We should spend it doing things we like, things that make us happy, things that make other people happy.

We should stop being miserable bastards.

One of the most wonderful things in life is learning something new, especially when you're learning something new about yourself, or the people you're closest to. I don't think I've ever seen the amount of self-reflection, personal growth, and learning about oneself, that I do in this amazing ethical non-monogamy community that I am so very lucky to be a part of.

Why do I do what I do? Both the podcast and non-monogamy have their easy answers (sorta-fame for a sorta-narcissist and fucking people) which you know are a little true but not totally true. The other answers, the more nebulous ones, those are the ones with more value. Far more value. And really they're the same for all these silly things that I do. Podcaster, swinger, polyamorist (I apologize, Shira B.), author, promoter, play party facilitator.

All of these push out my edges. It reeks of philosophy to suggest that I'm clay, so I'll suggest instead I'm silly putty. "I knew it!" You say, as you rush back in, grab my pink gooeyness and slap me down on a Sunday Funnies comic.

So, it's a reach, perhaps, but when you're copying that comic image, all you have to do is push out the boundaries of that little pink blob and you find yourself moving into *Foxtrot*, or *Blondie* territory. It's the joy of discovery as you find the new. (I'm assuming, of course, that you're copying a panel of *Calvin and Hobbies*...because why wouldn't you be?)

I do these things to see if I can.

And when I can, I learn about who this guy named Cooper S. Beckett truly is, and what he has to offer the world.

I hope you'll let me continue to spray my goodness all over your faces for years to come.

Always good to end with a flagrantly single entendre. Huzzah.

ACKNOWLEDGMENTS

I would not be here without the many elements that have combined in this chemical reaction I call a life. I wouldn't be here without the myriad people that came before me and alongside me (and sometimes on me). You certainly wouldn't be reading this without them…and the elements, for that matter. 'Cuz science.

So, I give thanks.

To my love, my companion, my friend, my Domme, my sub, my top, my bottom, my dearest: Ophilia Tesla. Let us continue to live a life so unconventional.

To my dear and oldest friend Ri, who casually asked me if I was "lifestyle" as my marriage was falling apart. My "wha?" that followed, and her basic description, led me to this world, and this world is my everything.

To Marilyn, for without her none of this would've ever happened. I am forever grateful for the time we spent together, and for her continued support as I put together this book.

To *Sex is Fun* and Dan Savage, whose podcasts nurtured my budding sex-positivity, turning it into something that could start to accept non-monogamy beyond the abstract.

To Dylan, on *The Swingset* since day one, editor of

every episode, and quite possibly the voice that interrupts nearly 40% of my essays. We are a comedy duo to rival the best of them. If you have any doubts, just listen to him discuss trying to fuck "The Torso."

To Ginger, my Twinner. We share a brain in a bizarre form of quantum entanglement. We had thousands of pages of Google chat conversations that sprung up the day after she wrote me (and *Swingset*, I suppose) a fan letter, and they would make your eyes bleed from the constant and abrupt tonal shifts and topic leaps. She has been my closest ally, greatest supporter, and one of the best friends I've ever had.

To Shira, who completed the circle, who gave us not-so-subtle nudges at the beginning, and showed us the world outside the narrow vision of non-monogamy we were talking about. Arriving just before the end of our first year on *The Swingset*, she was a game changer. I miss her terribly.

To Sasha, Kylie, & Tyler, the early trio that helped birth the beast that is *Swingset*, who saw its first steps, words, and supported its growth. There'll always be a seat for you.

To Zoë, a great companion who ran a hell of a toy review department.

To Lyndzi, our pinch hitter.

To JV Altharas, who stepped up and said, "I am Spartacus." And I said, "I need an editor." And he said, "I am Editor."

To Damien, without whom the *Life on the Swingset* website would've died a fiery death in February of 2014.

To (In no particular order I can discern) Tristan Taormino, Sarah Sloane, Kendra Holliday, Carol Queen, Dr. Robert Morgan Lawrence, Reid Mihalko, Alex Morgan, Ashley Manta, Katie Mack, Charlie Glickman, Aislinn Emirzian, Cunning Minx, Kate McCombs, Christopher Ryan, Airial Clark, Dylan Ryan, Gay Rick, Lorax, Dr, Antionette Izzo, Rachel Kramer Bussel, Allison Moon, Jiz Lee, Betty Dodson, Nina Hartley, Sophie

Delancey, Pepper Mint, Susie Bright, Violet Blue, Ruby Rider, Clare Jacky, Jennifer Pritchett, Kidder Kaper, Dee Dennis, Dr. Darrel Ray, Sex Nerd Sandra, Dr. Ziggy, Maggie Mayhem, Shar Rednour, Dr. Dick, Shara Bono, Cat Maness, Elle Chase, Melissa White, Sunny Megatron, Ken Melvoin-Berg, Marcia Baczynski, Jackie Strano, Megan Andelloux, Monique Darling, Boris & Doris, The Swap Fus, John & Allie, Jean Franzblau, JoEllen Notte, Crista Anne, Lauren Darling, Corbett Vanoni, Polly Whittaker, and all the other amazing sex educators and sex positive people who have helped guide me on my journey.

To the person I've forgotten to list: You. Yes, you. You were the most important.

ABOUT THE AUTHOR

Cooper S. Beckett is the author of novels, A Life Less Monogamous and Approaching the Swingularity. He co-founded Life on the Swingset and hosts its swinging & polyamory podcast. He speaks and teaches classes on pegging, swinging, polyamory, play parties, and non-monogamy. He is a graphic & web designer, photographer, and voice over artist, has been a guest expert on Dan Savage's *Savage Lovecast*, & is the announcer for Tristan Taormino's radio show *Sex Out Loud*.

He lives in Chicago with his wife, constant, and binary star, Ophilia Tesla.

Want short stories, erotica, and essays in your email? Sign up for Cooper's email newsletter today!

Contact Cooper

coopersbeckett.com
me@coopersbeckett.com

PRAISE FOR MY LIFE ON THE SWINGSET

"Challenges the hard line between swinging and polyamory, tackles taboos with grace, and will make you rethink what you believe about relationships."

- Tristan Taormino
Author of Opening Up: A Guide to Creating & Sustaining Open Relationships PuckerUp.com

"It's not often that I'm seduced by an author. Expressive, honest, and often hilariously geeky, this collection of personal anecdotes on ethical non-monogamy is as enjoyable for the most jaded poly 'sexpert' as it is educational to the new swinger. My Life on the Swingset is the dirty cousin to The Ethical Slut. I can get with this."

- Jiz Lee
Genderqueer Porn Performer & Author of How to Come Out Like a Porn Star
JizLee.com

"A delightful and playful romp of a read. Fear & Loathing meets On The Road."

- Jackie Strano
Executive VP Good Vibrations and
Co-creator of *Bend Over Boyfriend*

"Combining compassion with pragmatism, Beckett shares his insights, his advice and his erotic experiences of progressive swinging in this compelling collection. A must-read!"

- Cunning Minx
Host of *Polyamory Weekly*
PolyWeekly.com

"Essential reading for anyone interested in all that is implied by the 'non' in 'non-monogamy.'"

- Nina Hartley, RN.
Author of Nina Hartley's Guide to Total Sex
Nina.com

"When you're standing on the precipice of exciting, yet unexplored territory, navigating the windy roads of ethical non-monogamy you want to have an expert Sherpa to guide you. Cooper Beckett is that Sherpa."

- Elle Chase
Director of Education at Los Angeles Academy of Sex Education, LAAcademyOfSex.com

"This is great advice for life wrapped up in poignant stories, all with a friendly approachable tone. It's progressive and heartfelt and it's what people exploring the lifestyle should be reading."

"Cooper Beckett's words inspire laughter as often as they impart wisdom and they leave one believing that when it comes to sex, it is indeed possible for the geeks to inherit the earth."

"Snarky, witty, vulnerable. Forget being a swinger—<u>My Life on the Swingset</u> is a page turner for any reader who loves a titillating tell-all. His genuine reflection and open-mindedness minus agenda was SUCH a relief and kept me reading. PS: His prostate multiple orgasm is worth the price of the whole book!"

"There are those who write about ethical non monogamy in theory, and then there is Cooper Beckett. His writing is ethical non monogamy in action. A warm, engaging, and relatable guide to the lifestyle."

"Cooper shows us by example how to break the mold, go against norms, and carve out a personalized lifestyle map that embraces authenticity, honesty, and happiness. Essential reading for anyone curious about or in a nontraditional relationship."

A LIFE LESS MONOGAMOUS

A NOVEL BY COOPER S. BECKETT

What follows are two chapters from A Life Less Monogamous, a novel about swinging by Cooper S. Beckett, and
the first book in his *Books of the Swingularity*.

1

Ryan found himself captivated by the small crack in the ceiling even as he knew he was supposed to be having sex with his wife. He stared at it, focused on it. Two and a half weeks since their last sexual encounter. That gap of time was a new record for them – at least when period, family, or occasional business trips didn't factor into things. He couldn't attribute the waning urge to age, either. As much as he felt old, past his prime, he knew he couldn't classify himself as "older" with a straight face. While thirty-two may once have been middle-aged, these days it still qualified as quite young. It meant figuring things out. Still unsettled.

Still unsettled, indeed.

Even if he could consider himself old, the fault didn't lie there. Things had always been like this. He and Jennifer had never been one of those couples that couldn't keep their hands off each other, not even in the beginning when they'd first started dating. Young when they got together, only eighteen and nineteen, with Ryan older by just a few months. They'd been good kids. They'd waited a couple months before the first fumblings, first blips of fluid, first trembling fingers down pants, perhaps stymied by the fear of pregnancy instilled in them from overzealous sex ed classes.

Jennifer had never seen a penis before she unzipped his jeans in the basement of her parent's house one warm summer night. She'd told him of her one and only prior sexual experience, which had taken place in total darkness with an excess of clothing. Her wide eyes and open mouth betrayed fear when she unsheathed Ryan. He knew his penis measured just on the happy side of average, so it couldn't have been fear of size. Instead, he read her surprise as dislike and didn't talk about it, beginning to wear that pattern of noncommunication into their relationship, setting back their progress around the proverbial bases by another four weeks.

Ryan had learned, through hand jobs from his previous girlfriend, how to keep things from exploding on contact and managed a respectable, though unremarkable, nine minute showing before the end of their first time. The tenor of their sexual encounters was set that day, respectable though unremarkable ever since.

We don't want to be one of those couples, Ryan's mind insisted, trying to rouse him from wondering how he had not noticed the crack before. Perhaps he rarely laid on his back, looking straight up. Only this position when cuddling with Jennifer, when cuddling before-well, before, before what? What were they doing here?

ROUGHLY FIFTEEN MINUTES BEFORE LAYING HER HEAD ON Ryan's chest while he stared at the ceiling, Jennifer had looked over at Ryan from the opposite side of their sectional couch. They didn't sit so far apart because they disliked being close; it was just for the simple convenience of each having an end table to themselves. She'd held the March issue of *Cosmo*, far out of date and vastly more insipid than the last issue she'd read almost a decade ago. The magazine had traveled home with her from Dr. Petrillo's office because she thought that, just maybe, one of the "How to Please Your Man" articles might be helpful.

Because helpful certainly didn't describe Dr. Petrillo.

The magazine's newest suggestion perplexed Jennifer, advising that while on a hike with her man, she find a small, flat stone and conceal it, so that later it might be pressed up against his anus. Her eyebrow cocked with skepticism, her hazel eyes narrowed. What on earth would Ryan do if she suddenly pressed a rock against his asshole? Flip out, surely, and not because of sexual prudishness, but because the whole idea was such an "out of left field" thing to do. Strange, unusual.

Though, if it might help...

No. She put down the *Cosmo*.

"Ryan," she said, more of an outward breath than an actual vocalization. *Again, girl, louder this time!* "Hey, um, Ryan."

He looked away from his game of *Super Mario World* and offered "Hmm?" with a smile. For a moment, the childlike innocence of the man she had married overwhelmed her, and all at once she felt a distinct discomfort about sexually ravishing him. Not that she had the energy to ravish anyway. Nor the inclination, really. Hell, they'd both be happy with a little missionary and then call it a night.

It's been too long. We're becoming one of those *couples*, she thought, biting her lip hard enough to surprise a yelp out of her.

Ryan hit pause and blinked at her.

"I was just wondering if you wanted to *go upstairs*."

"Oh," he said. "Yeah, hold on, I'll get to a save point."

He did, and they went.

But after undressing across the room from one another and climbing under their six hundred thread count Egyptian cotton sheets, Jennifer rested her head on Ryan's chest, and there they lay: naked, ready, willing, able, not having sex.

With her head high on his chest, every breath he took blew a small lock of her chestnut hair aloft, where it drifted for a moment, then settled back down.

RYAN'S EYES FELL TO THE TOP OF JENNIFER'S HEAD, THEN back to the ceiling where the crack watched them, wondering, he was certain, why the two of them didn't have more frequent sex.

He didn't have an answer for that, though when Dr. Petrillo had asked him alone, with Jennifer waiting in the vestibule for her turn to have one-on-one time, Ryan did admit to a wish she'd initiate more. Petrillo found that noteworthy, jotting a rare note onto his pad in a gesture that made Ryan feel a tiny bit validated. Petrillo never shared his own thoughts, just made that occasional small note and a request to "tell me more about that." Aside from the silly mantra worksheet he'd given them, Ryan had begun to think these sessions a superficial waste of one hundred and twenty-five dollars an hour. Petrillo had never even asked about his sex drive!

Once Ryan's youthful race to the top of Sex Hill had reached its zenith a decade and change before, his drive to climb the hill had become smaller every time, he knew. It wasn't for lack of interest, it was just sometimes easier to rub one out himself in front of the computer at three in the morning than wake Jennifer, she of the early work meetings. Also easier, certainly, than trying to coax an orgasm out of his wife.

Ryan frowned. Was that the crux? The orgasm thing? Jennifer had orgasms, they just weren't very...well, they were few and far between. When they *did* happen, they weren't so much fireworks, but more the kind of sparklers you find in the impulse buy section of 7-11 in early July. *That's not fair,* he thought. *Orgasms are harder for women.* Despite the fact that as a woman of thirty-one, Jennifer sat at her biological sexual peak, she also sat under a decade's worth of pressure to demonstrate her enjoyment.

Probably fakes it in case I can't stay hard.

His eyes widened. Now why had he gone and thrown that idea into the mix? Thoughts like that served no purpose. None at all! Except maybe to turn up the heat on his own performance anxiety. Of all the things that might need to be dialed up in the valley surrounding this fledgling marriage, he'd prefer his occasional inability to hold an erection didn't take priority.

WITH HER HEAD ON RYAN'S CHEST, JENNIFER COULD tell that he had some serious thinking going on, the kind with plot twists and mood swings. His breathing and heartbeat vacillated from calm, almost contemplative, to quick and wildly erratic. She wondered what he could be thinking about. Couldn't be that nervous about sex, could he? Was he worried that the performance anxiety thing would come back? How many times would she have to tell him that it was okay before he'd start believing?

She wasn't bothered by his perceived failings, and, unbeknownst to Ryan, about two years ago she'd discovered the healing power of the shower head massager. This discovery had led to finding an orgasm on her own. Unbeknownst to *both* of them, simultaneous orgasms had occurred on multiple separate occasions. A win, indeed, just perhaps not the win they'd reached for, as the orgasms had occurred in separate rooms.

Maybe she ought to tell him?

Maybe they could shower together.

FREDDIE MERCURY IMPLORED THEM NOT TO STOP HIM now, and insisted that because he was traveling at the speed of light, they call him Mr. Fahrenheit. Ryan's eyes blinked open. Blurry. He rubbed them. In the distance, he could hear the shower. He turned to his phone, which now wanted to make a supersonic woman of him, and tapped the triple zzzs to give himself nine more minutes of peace. His tap amounted to a shove, and the phone disappeared behind the nightstand.

We fell asleep, he realized. *Fuck.*

He ran a hand through his hair and counted the strands that came out with it. Twelve today. Seven of them still tan. Only seven. *Can't stop the march of time, bucko*, he told himself. *Got to get a handle on other things, though, they're all spiraling out of control.*

Feet on the floor, good start.

Ryan sat on the edge of the bed, elbows on his knees, hands propping his chin up. His morning wood asserted itself, but he regarded it as nothing more than a nuisance that would have to make itself scarce before he could use the toilet.

He lifted a sheet of yellow note paper off the night-stand, covered in several hand written lines of text. Their mantras. Lines that they'd worked out with Dr. Petrillo. A snake-oil lifeline out of the hole.

"So, we just say this stuff?" Jennifer had asked after they'd finished working it out with their doctor less than a month prior.

"When you both feel that the time is right, you'll decide to make the change." Petrillo had told them over tented fingers, a clichéd pose that made the quality of the content that much more dubious.

Jennifer had dismissed the mantras out of hand on the way home from his office. The paper had sat, folded, in the same spot on his nightstand for the ensuing weeks. Ryan didn't hold much hope either, but something had to change.

The shower stopped and Jennifer emerged. He watched her preen in the mirror.

"Today is the day we change our lives," Ryan read.

Jennifer poked her head out of the bathroom, electric toothbrush in her mouth, eyes wide, perplexed, a look on her face that silently asked "Really?"

"When we leave this bedroom today, nothing will ever be the same." He looked up again from the paper and shrugged.

Jennifer spat.

"We're moving forward," he said.

"Getting older, certainly," she added.

"I know, it's

"It's silly, Ryan."

"We fell asleep last night instead of having the sex we both claim to want." He threw his hands up and waved the paper at her. "I'm willing to give it a try. Are you?"

Her comically smug expression, accented by lips covered in toothpaste foam, hung and grew serious. She nodded.

"Then, today is the day we change our lives," he asserted.

"Nothing will ever be the same." She waved her hand in a circular motion. "Etcetera."

Ryan smiled at his wife, seeing the vaguest glimmer of hope in the smile she returned. "We change because we choose to do so. We change because we are no longer..."

"We're no longer content to be 'just okay.'" She sat on the bed next to him. The fresh, crisp scent of her shampoo wafted into his nostrils.

He'd always thought her the most beautiful woman, never once doubting his love for her. His commitment, though... There sat doubt. "For someone who doesn't hold much stock, you sure seem to know the text," he poked at her.

Jennifer stuck her lower lip out and cocked her jaw. In a flash of naked flesh, she grabbed the paper. "You don't?"

He knew the words too. That night in Petrillo's office had been a mild form of catharsis, the kind of night where you *realize* all the things you want to say and what you want to change, but can't quite make it happen. He'd read the mantras over and over again on the ride home, as Jennifer drove in silence. "Because 'just okay' is no way to live."

"It's not acceptable anymore."

"Because it's not what we want from our lives. Right?"

Jennifer nodded, sincerity in her eyes, but also a tinge of desperation. He knew the desperation well, because it had crept up on him, too. From the outside looking in, their marriage looked fine, healthy. At least, no more at-risk than anybody else's. They rarely fought, certainly not in public. They were nice to each other, affectionate. All outward appearances nominal. Internally, though, when the chips were down, they'd both felt an upsetting certainty: This is how friends feel toward each other, not lovers, not husband and wife. This is how roommates feel. Roommates that occasionally get around to sex when the urges reach critical mass.

"We can do this," said Ryan, though it sounded more like a question than a statement.

"We can do this." Jennifer sounded even less sure of herself, but they held eye contact a moment before she changed the subject. "Don't forget, the party at Barbara and Noah's is tonight."

The promise of the moment gone, Ryan flopped onto his back on the bed, sighing theatrically.

"You knew about this. I thought you wanted to

"It's been a long week," he griped

"I know," she said, moving her hands to her hips, a comical stance of nude defiance.

"Do we really need to go?"

Jennifer threw her hands up in the air. "I don't know, Ryan. Isn't this the day we, you know, live?"

Ryan scowled.

2

"We'll stay an hour, maybe two," said Ryan, fishing a grocery bag stuffed with chips and dip out of the back seat.

"I don't know, hon," Jennifer slung her purse over her shoulder and held a hand out for one of the bags, but Ryan shook his head. "It seems like we're always the first ones to head out at—"

"We work, they know that."

"They all work too."

She held her hands out again, this time with more insistence. He relented and slung one of the grocery bags around her right wrist. They both took a deep breath and turned towards Barbara and Noah Watkins' house, set far enough back on the lot to allow its upper middle class mini McMansion status to play its intimidation game with those who weren't able to park in the driveway.

Jennifer began to stride across the lawn, but Ryan didn't follow. After a moment she looked back at her husband, standing in the moonlight, two Jewel grocery bags at his side, shoulders slumped, hair falling in his face a bit, and there, for a fleeting second, she felt the stirring that has been so long slumbering, that bit of warmth, the tingle.

Let's just skip this party and go home and fuck...Stop this making love pressure and just go fuck for chrissakes!

But the words didn't leave her lips. Instead she half smiled at Ryan, and he half smiled back.

"Are you driving us home tonight?" she asked him as he joined her on the front porch.

"Do you want to drink?"

"I don't know."

Ryan's phone appeared, and he swiped through his calendar. "I need to be downtown by noon tomorrow."

"Maybe we just shouldn't drink." But oh, after the tingles, she felt that a drink might be essential.

"Yeah." Ryan rang the doorbell. "Just let me know when you're ready to bolt. They'll understand."

"I hate doing that," Jennifer sighed heavily. "Do I look okay?"

Ryan nodded.

"You've got something..." She pulled a fuzz off his lapel. "Got it."

The door swung open, revealing Barbara Watkins in all her hostessing glory. Tall and slender, clinging to the last scraps of her thirties, Barbara looked every inch the sort of woman who drove an impeccably clean white SUV, sunglasses on, black hair pulled into a ponytail. Her cocktail dress, midnight blue, was far showier than it needed to be, of course, but what should one do with money but spend it? "I'm so glad you guys could make it! Wouldn't be a Christmas party without the Lamberts! But what about that other thing you had?"

"Got canceled," said Jennifer, dismissing their excuse. She breezed into the house.

"Great! Well, not great, but, you know what I mean."

Ryan's smile appeared genuine when he told her they were glad they could be there. Jennifer marveled at his ability to do that. He was always able to seem at home, even when uncomfortable. Able to seem happy, even when—

"I'll take the food."

Jennifer snapped out of her momentary melancholy and realized what was missing. "Do you have the wine, honey?"

"Crap, it's in the trunk. I'll get it."

RYAN RELISHED THE MOMENTARY OPPORTUNITY TO vanish from the foyer and walk, all on his own, back across the massive front lawn. Moments alone weren't infrequent, but he hesitated to take them lest it be thought he didn't want to spend time with Jennifer. Rarely did he find himself able to stroll. Tonight he strolled, because Jennifer was with her friend, and while she might be thinking about how long his trek back for the wine was taking, she'd be at least partially distracted by some discussion of Christmas shopping or the Watkins' children. Surely something more interesting than Ryan Lambert.

"What's the plan?" The question drifted to Ryan's ears from a few feet distant, where a handsome man walked towards the house with his companion. Dark hair, very roguish, mid-forties, he had a woman of spectacular grace on his arm. Ryan had always felt that Barbara and Noah Watkins, while lovely people, were posers of class. Never sure quite how to do it right. But this couple, strolling up the walkway instead of cutting across the grass like a cad, exuded worldly class, and Ryan couldn't take his eyes off them.

He closed the trunk and hung back so he could observe, staying a moment behind in step.

The woman tightened her grip on the man's arm and rested her head on his shoulder, bunching her wavy cascade of strawberry-blond hair against him. "I don't think we need a plan, darling." Her voice was deep, velvety, almost having a weight of its own.

"Gotcha," said the man. "All vanilla tonight, right?"

The woman smiled, devilish, and bit her lip. "Unless someone surprises us, yeah."

The man laughed.

She swatted him. "Remember, I work with her! So—"

"I will be on my absolute *best* behavior."

She laughed hard at that. "Yeah, I know what that's like."

Re-entering the foyer, Ryan stood behind the man and woman as they removed their coats. Barbara returned with Jennifer.

"Oh!" said Barbara, a strange cautiousness in her words. "I didn't realize you knew each other."

It was only then that the classy man and woman turned and noticed him. Ryan Lambert lifted his hand in a weak wave. "I was just behind them."

"Were you?" the woman asked, making eye contact with him, as though she were asking a much more important question.

"I was getting the—" Ryan lost his train of thought in the woman's crystal blue eyes before his own fell just enough to begin to appreciate the expanse of bare skin below her neck, plunging downward into spectacular—

"Wine?"

He looked back up. Jennifer waved at him. Ryan swallowed hard.

"And now here it is, and here you are, and I'm Bruce Shepard." Bruce Shepard extended his hand, exuding the sort of confidence Ryan had only ever seen in men to be cautious of: sales folk, convention speakers. But somehow, as he took Bruce's warm hand to shake, he didn't feel the same concern. While holding Ryan's hand in his, Bruce made eye contact and smiled, dipping his head into a short nod, then relaxing his grip.

"Ryan Lambert," Ryan announced, and pointed with the bottle toward Jennifer, who took it from him. "My wife is—"

"Jennifer," she said, and gave them a wave Ryan felt

must have been eerily similar to the one he'd provided moments before. "Hi."

The woman turned back to Ryan. "I'm Paige, and she is gorgeous."

Jennifer coughed back a laugh.

"And lo, in my foyer came Shepards, keeping watch over my flock by night." Noah Watkins appeared, a touch wider than he'd been before Thanksgiving, neat Scotch in one hand, the other open for a high handshake that always became a half hug and a clap on the back. He delivered one of these to both Bruce and Ryan.

The women each received a kiss on the cheek, then Noah suggested that the four of them "join the festivities." He led the party as though out of Hamlin, with Ryan lingering behind, suddenly uncertain about whether or not they belonged here. Surely they did, their friends had invited them, but they didn't have the money, the class...

Bruce, at the end of the pack, looked back. "That man may have already had his limit."

Ryan laughed.

"Now that we're old friends, shall we?" Bruce raised his hand and led the way into the party.

ALSO BY COOPER S. BECKETT

Fiction

Approaching the Swingularity

Memoir

My Life on the Swingset: Adventures in Swinging & Polyamory

23579986R00236

Made in the USA
San Bernardino, CA
28 January 2019